# TIME
### ON THE
### OCEAN

*A Voyage from Cape Horn to Cape Town*

# THEO DORGAN

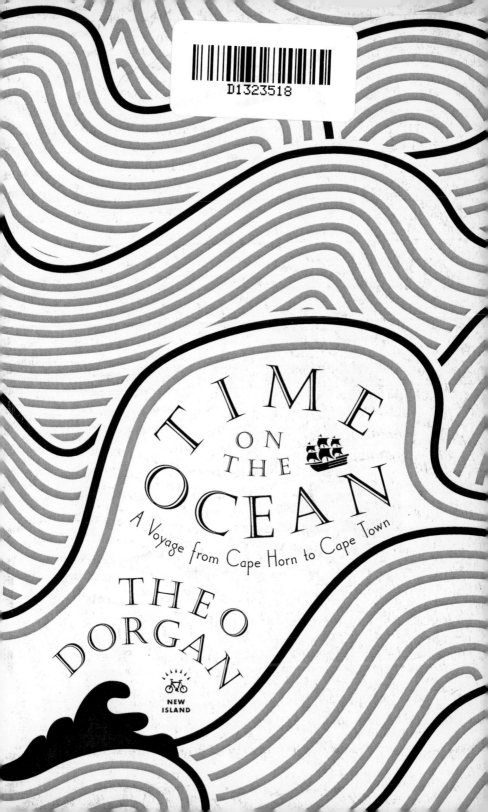

**NEW ISLAND**

TIME ON THE OCEAN
First published 2010
by New Island
2 Brookside
Dundrum Road
Dublin 14

www.newisland.ie

ISBN 978-1-84840-075-7

Book design by Someday

Printed by CPI Antony Rowe, Chippenham, Wiltshire

New Island received financial assistance from
The Arts Council (An Chomhairle Ealaíon), Dublin, Ireland

10 9 8 7 6 5 4 3 2 1

Time on the Ocean

# Also by Theo Dorgan

PROSE NON-FICTION

*Sailing for Home* (Penguin, 2004; Dedalus Press, 2010)

POETRY

*Greek* (Dedalus Press, 2010)
*What this Earth Cost Us* (Dedalus Press, 2008)
*Days Like These* (with Tony Curtis and Paula Meehan, Brooding Heron Press, 2007)
*Sappho's Daughter* (Wavetrain Press, 1998)
*Rosa Mundi* (Salmon, 1995)
*The Ordinary House of Love* (Salmon, 1990)

TRANSLATIONS

*Songs of Earth and Light* (translations of the Slovenian poet Barbara Korun, Southword Editions, 2005)

ANTHOLOGIES

*A Book of Uncommon Prayer* (editor and compiler, Penguin, 2007)
*Watching the River Flow* (co-editor, Poetry Ireland, 2000)
*An Leabhar Mór/The Great Book of Gaelic* (co-editor, Canongate, 2002; O'Brien Press, 2008)
*The Great Book of Ireland/Leabhar Mór na Gaeilge* (co-editor, Poetry Ireland/Clashganna Mills Trust, 1991)

ESSAYS

*John Shinnors* (Monograph and poems, Wexford Arts Centre, 2008)
*Irish Poetry Since Kavanagh* (co-editor, Irish Academic Press, 1995)
*Revising the Rising* (co-editor, Field Day Publications, 1991)

# Acknowledgements

I am grateful to Ita Kelly for her help in making this trip possible, to Steve Wilkins for his seamanship and his company, and to my comrades on this illuminating voyage: Debs; Diane; Federico; Justin; Kevin; Marko; Mike; Tony; and Simon. I am also grateful to Skip Novak for the opportunity to sail the high southern latitudes aboard the magnificent *Pelagic Australis*. Photos of the boat, and information on *Pelagic* expeditions, can be found at www.pelagic.co.uk.

In the course of this voyage I was asked to file a number of reports for *The Irish Times*, the response to which encouraged me to embark on this book. My thanks for that.

Máire Mhac an tSaoi has graciously granted permission to translate Pádraig de Brúns 'Valparaiso'.

My thanks to Edwin Higel for taking this book on, and to Deirdre O'Neill for her supportive and impeccable editing.

Finally, as ever and always, three bows to Paula Meehan for her love and support, and for quite the best advice anyone has ever given me about sailing: 'Stay in the boat.'

To my great-grandmother,
Annie Martin Dorgan,
and to all her descendants


'I had to have a change of air'
Bernard Moitessier

NORTH
PACIFIC
OCEAN

NORTH
ATLANTIC
OCEAN

Equator

SOUTH
ATLANTIC
OCEAN

SOUTH
PACIFIC
OCEAN

ARGENTINA

CHILE

Falkland
Islands

Stanley

Burdwood Bank

Cape Horn

120°W

60°W

0°

Tristan
Da Cunha

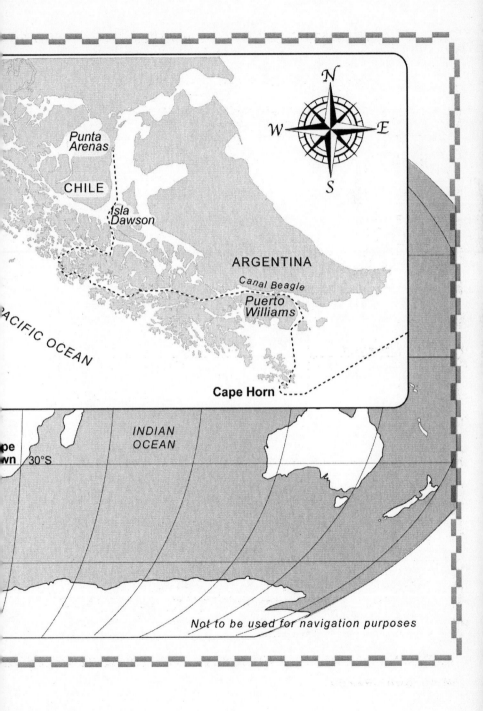

Not to be used for navigation purposes

# OVERTURE

The passions of our middle years can be as intense and mysterious as those of our youth. This thought comes to me on a bright morning in midair, far from home. We are 30,000 feet over the foothills of the Andes, flying south from Santiago to Punta Arenas, the long Pacific coast of Chile unrolling beneath us. The mountains are brown, featureless except where the sharp serrated ridges trail pennants of driving cloud into the bleached blue freezing air. I am on my way to join total strangers on a voyage that will take us down the Beagle Channel, around Cape Horn and out into the cold broad expanses of the South Atlantic, bound for Cape Town. Now, for perhaps the first time since I committed myself to this journey, I am asking myself: why?

I have no ready answer. The question shies away for a moment as I consider this land beneath me. Like most Irish schoolchildren of my time, I first heard of Chile when learning off by heart, as we did in the long ago, Monsignor Pádraig de Brún's luminous poem, 'Valparaiso'. I see the schoolroom now, the hard light breaking through the tall windows as that gentle man Dónal Hurley pulls down the spring-loaded map of the world to show us the long ribbon of a faraway country, tucked in against the edge of a great continent, squeezed in under the looming mass of an enormous mountain bulk. He points out Valparaiso, tells us it is a great port with a busy history of conquest and trade, he evokes for us Spanish galleons, treasure ships, great four-masters braving the Horn with their cargoes, back and forth to Old Europe from the New World through storm and tempest. He is, I see now, as carried away as I am by the poem, its hints and evocation of adventures beyond yearning, sights to gladden the most inquisitive and curious heart. Sometime last winter, forty years and more since that poem made me catch my breath, float out through the schoolroom window for the first time, I made a translation of it:

A Ship Came in from Valparaiso

A ship came in from Valparaiso,
Let go her anchor in the bay,
Her name in gold put me in mind
Of glorious kingdoms far away.

Come, she said, on the long journey
Far from fog and cloudy skies –
Under the Andes' blue-grey slopes
A jewel-bright dreadful city lies.

O I was young and would not go,
All in a dream and full of hope,
I still believed my future held
Plenty and promise, depth and scope.

That ship sailed off on boundless seas,
Long ago; her mast of gold
would write her story on the sky
where the clear stars are high and cold.

Someday, maybe, she'll return,
I'll see the white city on the slopes
Beside the shining sea of peace.
Dear God, I half-believe, still hope.

Now here I am, turning away from the first realistic chance I've had to see that city of dreams, turning south from Santiago, turning my back, so to speak, on Salvador Allende, Pablo Neruda, Victor Jara, barely touching down in Chile before setting out again. Under the rising sense of anxious anticipation there is a curious, detached sense of loss, of opportunity regretfully foregone. In another version of my life, I would have wanted to see La Moneda where Allende made his heroic last stand, I would have walked where Jara walked, and listened where he sang, journeyed to where Neruda stood to imbibe and then speak out the spirit of his country, of his people. I feel, very faintly, as if I am breaking faith with the young man I was, to whom these things would have meant so much. And as soon as I think this, feel this, I am swept away by the pulse of a lesser but more urgent passion: I want to be at sea now, immediately; I want a deck coming alive beneath my feet, the snap of cold wind in high sails, the deep roll coming in under us, carrying us on and out. Out and down to Cape Horn.

I have found in myself, over the past decade or so, with no forewarning, a commanding passion for the sea; more precisely, for long exacting voyages under sail. I have no real idea where this comes from. I know perfectly well, of course, how this journeying began. I remember the whim that saw me sign on for an undemanding week-long journey from Cork to Dublin in the schooner *Spirit of Oysterhaven*. I remember surprise at myself, raising sail on her for the first time, at the sense of ease I felt, the matter-of-factness of taking the wheel for the first time, of feeling the boat come alive beneath my feet. So, I can say how sailing started for me, but that doesn't explain anything – a cellist may remember handling the instrument for the first time, but that doesn't explain the grip that music will take on her soul.

No, this yearning for long voyages on deep waters has no obvious origin, puzzle the question though I may.

I cross to the other side of the plane, to an empty seat that allows me a view of the wide cold Pacific below. I am lost in reverie, sipping scalding-hot coffee when, with a quiet click, I find myself in my grandfather's house, in the tiny living room behind his shop in Cork. It's warm and snug in that room, the coal fire bright, the light of a winter afternoon through the small back window, through the frosted pane in the door out to the shop. He is showing me a black and white photograph of a great three-masted ship, a funnel incongruously set between the main and foremast. Some cursive hand has written her name in white across the bottom of the photo, *Rimutaka*. Grandda is not best pleased. Weeks before, he'd been telling me about this ship, how he was born on board her off Cape Horn, how his mother died giving birth to him. I remember that Sunday afternoon clearly, remember how pleased and mildly disturbed I was, aged twelve or so, that he was telling me this. I felt singled out, obscurely honoured, to have him telling me this; I remember my father sitting by the window, taking all this in, the gentle pleasure in his face; I remember realising he was pleased that in some mysterious way his father was *choosing* to tell me this story, that he was conferring something on me, his approval, it must be, of who and what I was. Running down Chile's littoral, high in the air, in a life neither they nor I could have pre-visioned, I am remembering all this.

Grandda had written to the White Star Line to tell them his story, and this, he shows me with some disgust, is their answer: a polite note, a 10 x 8 photograph of the ship. I know why he's disgusted, of course: he'd expected some kind of excitement, some engagement with his story, the offer of bounty, honours, a cruise! He was amused, I see now, to find me sharing his indignation; not half as amused, though, as my father was when, on our way home, I turned to him on the bus and said, so he told me years later, 'Ah well, Da, it was worth a try, eh?' I gather from his response that I'm not supposed to have spotted that, but he's not terribly surprised that I have. I know he wishes I were what he thinks of as a normal boy, sports mad as he was, and, young as I am, I sense his uneasiness at my remoteness, my constant withdrawal into books, day-dreaming; but sometimes I think he gets a glimmer of something inside me, as it were, that he might grow to like. As I myself, baffled and confused much of the time, get occasional glimpses of some creature who lives inside me, who, in some way I don't understand, *is* me but at home in the world as I am not.

The plane banks in a wide turn over Tierra del Fuego below, a crazed landscape of channels and islets, as if someone had taken a hammer to a sheet of rock, and water had flowed into the cracks. Is that what I'm doing down here, then, standing in for my grandfather? Did he *oblige* me in some mysterious way, that gruff old man, by planting his memory in me, by making me complicit in his story? Did he put me under bond to come down here some day, as I am coming down here now, to revisit the occasion of his birth, to pick up some rough patch in the fabric of family and smooth it out? Some years ago, sailing *Spirit* back from Antigua to Kinsale, I spent many solo watches wondering, as I am wondering now, what connection there might be between this late-flowering passion of mine and my grandfather's birth at sea. I could come to no conclusion then, and I cannot resolve the question now.

The seat belt warning sign is on. On my way back to my seat, I catch the eye of Simon, of Marko, two fellow-voyagers met in the transit lounge in Santiago. What brings them here, I wonder? What impulse has them, like me, travelling to this remote place we can see below us now as we circle, so that they, like me, can get on a boat with total strangers, risk their lives on a journey that has, let us face the fact, claimed the lives of so many? Steady, I tell myself then, steady. Let's not get carried away here. You get on a boat, hopefully a well-found boat, you sail the boat properly, with due regard for the forces in play, you make sure to stay in the boat and – nobody dies. People do this all the time. Almost always they get away with it.

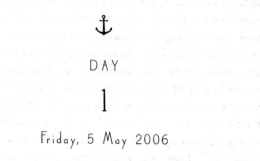

# DAY

# 1

## Friday, 5 May 2006

We are hanging off the jetty in Punta Arenas, buffeted by
the gusting wind, held off by enormous earth-mover tyres.
A Chilean naval patrol boat has just docked ahead of us,
there's a small Antarctic cruise ship astern of us. The wind
is in the west, 25 knots, and the forecast is for 70 knots later.

On the afterdeck of the patrol boat, the deck officer is
giving the ratings a hard time for a sloppy moor-up, but
the boy sailors are only half-listening, they're watching us
to see how we manage. There's a sudden gust, and now the

officer turns to watch us, too; the forklift drivers on the long jetty have stopped work for the moment, are lighting cigarettes, hunched over their wheels, watching us. Down at the gated entrance to the giant bare pier, one of the sentries is watching us through binoculars. We're about to head off into the southern ocean, down the Beagle Channel, around Cape Horn, and then 4,000 miles east to Cape Town. For the past three days, we've been provisioning the boat, carrying out engine, rig and hull checks, taking time off to wander around the ghostly back streets.

There's been a sense of time passing slowly, as if we're settling in here for the winter; it's got to the point where the naval guards at the gate are beginning to stir themselves to remember our names. Now, suddenly, I have the sense of a great void yawning open, a rising sense of panic, and at the same time a prosaic immediate concern: I'm on the bow line, and the skipper has made it plain that he wants a clean exit. I don't want to screw up this simplest of tasks. A last look-around: Tony Macken behind me, ready to coil the line as I haul it in, Justin on the helm, feet planted wide, head swivelling to check our clearance fore and aft, Federico and Mike on the stern line.

'OK, Justin. When we slip the lines let her slide sideways until I gun the throttle, then take her round to starboard, nice and steady.'

'Righto, Skip.'

'Let go for'ard, let go aft!'

And off she comes, the lines snaking and whipping clear, the boat tracking sideways as if on rails. Steve knocks us into forward gear, Justin begins to feed the helm over, and we curve out and away, turning for the south. I look over my shoulder at the patrol boat; an officer has come out on the flybridge. He throws us a casual salute, stands there looking down at us, impassive and thoughtful. He knows where we're going.

Macken nudges me in the ribs, 'That was ok, wasn't it? Nice and tidy?'

Behind us Steve is seeing to raising the mainsail as we come around to our bearing. 'Bring her head into the wind, Justin! All right everyone, let's get everything stowed.'

We coil the line, hand it down the forward hatch. Big Mike comes forward with the stern line, hands it below. Others come forward with the fenders, down they go. All neat and tidy. We're away.

She's a big boat, *Pelagic Australis*. Aluminium, 70 foot, a huge mast on her, three foresails on furlers. As with most aluminium boats, her hull is left bare, giving her a purposeful no-nonsense look. Designed for these waters, she has a roomy wheelhouse painted scarlet and grey, an outside steering position, twin drums of mooring line forward and aft, heavy-duty winches. As we gather way, I feel the weight of her in the water: we've all had a thorough look-through in the past few days, getting to know the boat intimately, and we all feel safe in her. She's built for heavy weather, built to get through whatever the sea might throw at her. We've all discussed this, in ones and twos, as we readied for sea. Now, looking around me at the others as they come and go, I see the same smile on one face and another, the same realisation dawning (and not without some relief) – she'll sail well, *Pelagic*; even now, only just getting underway, we can feel her grace beginning to come through, and we are all of us pleased by this.

It's a cold, crisp, bright winter morning, the water banded in grey and glinting silver, a chill blue sky overhead, small racing clouds. There's a 1-metre chop that the boat just shrugs aside; she heels over, then steadies into a long easy lope. We have the second reef in, but the mainsail still looks huge, leaning over towards Tierra del Fuego to port. In the cockpit, Simon and Debs are sweating over the huge winches, running out the high-footed Yankee, and then the staysail. The wake scribes out behind us towards the low-lying town that has been home for the past three days. The boat comes alive.

I wonder what I should be feeling. Months ago, snug to the stove at home in Dublin, laptop balanced on my knees, I wondered what I would be feeling at this precise moment. I couldn't guess then, and I don't know now, for sure, what I *am* feeling. Relief to be off, yes, a certain familiar anxiety, the flickerings of self-doubt, that too, and simple curiosity: how does she answer the helm, is she ungainly or sweet, how will she carry her sail? Practical questions come crowding to the fore, but under it all, I more than suspect, is the unease that haunts all of us from childhood: how will I measure up to this?

Steve, no doubt, is wondering how such a motley gang of people will shake down as a crew. Kevin and Debbie, his watch leaders, are old friends and sailing companions. They've done this run with him before. The rest of us are as mixed as our motives, and everyone, I know it, is wondering about everyone else. Big Mike, clawing his way back along the port rail, is American, over six feet tall, big-boned, and willing, somewhere in his late fifties. Federico, thirty-something, is quick, agile, sleek-headed and thrusting, a racer of small boats, Italian, competitive and lean. He's glued to Justin's shoulder, anxious to get at the wheel. Equally keen to get helming, laconic Simon behind him is a merchant banker, much the same age as Fed; chunky, also a racer, he has a cutting tongue on him that will bear watching. At the after rail, snatching photographs when the boat comes level, Diane is the baby sailor here, no more than 700 sea miles under her belt; a Brit like Simon and Justin. Marko beside her is busy photographing the Slovak pennant he's brought aboard as it snaps in the breeze. So far he's photographed it in the airport in Santiago, on the mast from the dockside, in the restaurant last night and dangling from the lee-cloth on his bunk. Macken looks over his shoulder at me as we make our way back from the mast, 'Where did you say Marko was from?'

A wintry smile from Justin, overhearing this as we go past. Tony is Irish, like myself, a retired greengrocer, in his early fifties but fit as a ferret behind those glasses, an imp of mischief when it suits him but clear-headed for all that, witty and shrewd.

The skipper stretches, has a good look around, ducks his head down to light a cigarette. 'OK, Justin, good job. Wanna take a break now?' Meaning, 'I want to see someone else on the helm.' The nod goes to Fed; Simon, thwarted, looks down and away. 'All right, Simon. Wanna get a brew on?' Diane offers to lend a hand and they go below. Steve watches all this, catches my eye when he sees me watching him, grins and winks.

A few minutes later, he swings into the wheelhouse where I'm poring over the chart with Justin. He leans in over us, points at Bahia Nevis on Dawson Island ahead of us.

'Can't go in there,' he says, 'not in any circumstances.'

'Why not?'

'Prison camp under whatshisname, Pinochet. Still won't allow anyone to land there. Here's where we're going.'

He traces his finger down the channel, points out a small bay on the north side.

'How far is that?' I reach for the dividers, set the distance between the points from the scale on the chart, step it out. 'About 60 miles?'

'Good enough, 'bout that. What's our speed? Nine knots? That'll be about right.'

There was a concentration camp on Dawson under Pinochet's junta, I know this. A number of Allende's ministers were held there, with up to 400 others. José Tohá Gonzalez, Minister for the Interior and Defence, was held here; he died, weighing 120 pounds, in Santiago, a victim of sustained and systematic torture. A prisoner known only as Fernando has written: 'I was tortured for singing a song by Victor Jara on Christmas Eve.' The island produced 'an enormous feeling of isolation, of intense cold, wind, few sunny days. It was a prison, surrounded by water, with absolutely no escape.' I have these things written down in my notebook, but I decide to keep this, as much else, to myself. I say nothing to Steve, or to the others, as we glide past that grim place. What do I know about these people? Very little, except that we are going to spend the next five weeks cooped up together in a very small, dangerous and threatened place. Best to keep certain baleful thoughts to myself.

Diane starts handing mugs of tea up from the galley beneath and behind us. Steve calls everyone into the wheelhouse, Fed and Kevin leaning in from outside. 'Right, watches. Debs' watch: Simon, Fed, Diane and Mike. Kevin's watch: Tony, Justin, Theo and Marko. Any questions? No? Good. Right then, Mike, Fed's on the wheel so it might as well be you guys on watch; here's where we're going, give him a course to steer. Watches'll normally be four hours on, four hours off, except when we're tied up of course. Questions? No? Good.'

Kevin looks pleased. I've taken an immediate liking to the tall tattooed Yank with the tiny gold shackle earrings. One of those slow-talking Southern boys with a SEAL look to him, always smiling, courteous, helpful – and with a liking for beer.

'OK, my watch, let's go.' He unfolds long bones, climbs out on deck. Well, I'm pleased, too. I get on with Tony already, and Marko's OK, we share a cabin, he has that Slav gloominess I find somehow easeful. Justin, I christened 'Admiral' on day one; something to do with that officer-class English accent, the solid imperturbability of him, the air of competence he exudes. Good man when the going gets tough, that sort of aura about him. And if he does think that Margaret Thatcher had one or two good points, and I think her funeral can't come soon enough, well, what of that? I already know that he's forgotten more about sailing than I've managed to learn yet, and that's good enough for the trip. I can trust him, he has good manners, he can tell a joke, what more could you ask for?

Kevin grins when he sees that Simon's managed to supplant Fed at the wheel, and we grin, too. OK, we see the same things, that's a good sign. Starting already, I notice, us and them. A small thing, trivial in itself, but a first sign of bonding. 'Hey, Marko, you want to put the camera away for a minute? Thank you. Gentlemen, we're going to go right up to the bow and work our way back, OK? I want you to know everything there is to know about this fine boat. Everything, OK? When we're out here in the dark changing sail, I want you to know where everything is. I want you to know where every shackle is; I want you to notice the slightest things wrong, wherever, whenever, OK?'

Justin looks at me, I look at Tony, we all nod. This is good, this is going to be good. Kevin is serious, and thorough, and we like that. Seventy feet of boat sounds like a lot, but, down where we're going, it needs to be seventy feet of tough boat, meticulously cared for. And we're the ones who will be doing the caring.

Back in the cockpit, Debs accosts Kevin. 'Eh, Kev, your boys all right then?'

Debbie is small, wide-shouldered and strong, favours yellow and black oilies while the rest of us are in uniform red and black. Sea-faded blue eyes, tow-yellow hair, merry, shrewd. Kevin cups a light for her, says, 'Well yes, yes, I think they'll do.'

'That's good, eh?' Meaning, 'OK, let's see who ends up with the better watch, eh?' Old friends, these two.

The water's turned steel-grey, little whitecaps flecking the air with spray. The wind is gusting 56 knots, Steve says, and we're a little surprised. Doesn't feel like that. In a small boat we'd be running for shelter by now, and making heavy weather of it. This big thing just ploughs on, the third reef in the main, Yankee and staysail pulling away, long-legged, unbothered.

There's land on all sides of us as we blow south, high ground, inhospitable, bitterly cold. We might be sailing on a great lake in winter. I get a real sense of what it must have been like for FitzRoy on *The Beagle*, pushing up through this tangle of runs and inlets, dead ends and shoaling channels. Looking for the way through, not knowing from one day to the next if there is, in fact, a way through. I'm making this sound like thought, but it really isn't like that. As usual at the start of a trip I'm in that fuzzy state of mind best described as 'here and not here'. I'm getting snatches of thought, like bursts of transmission on a dodgy radio, a phrase here, an image there. I'm a long way from home and the habitual, not just in terms of geography but in terms of time.

Like everybody else, I live for the most part in structured time; you wake in the morning and you're already having previsions, presentiments, of the day ahead broken into segments. The day is in some sense fore-ordained. Eating breakfast, you're already eating dinner; as soon as you wake you imagine yourself already climbing back into bed. Out there on the deep ocean, it will be different. Time will become as wide and untrammelled as the ocean itself. Here, now, forging down-channel, we are betwixt and between. Every evening we will moor up in sight of land, every morning we'll weigh anchor and turn out into a day's sailing that will see us fetch up, before the light fades, in a different anchorage, in the lee of a high slope, the smell of fresh and of rotting vegetation cut by the salt and spume of the sea. This isn't the ocean, not yet; this is the overture, and that means the ties aren't cut yet.

Put it another way, there is still time to get off, to decide that this was a really bad idea, to indulge the voyager's inevitable sense of doubt.

So, here and not here. On a boat with ten strangers, bound for... well, Cape Horn, of course.

'Penny for 'em?' Justin, come up behind me where I'm hanging off a starboard shroud, looking south and ahead.

'I was thinking about the Horn.'

'Ah, yes. The guys back in the club wanted to know if I was mad. It's something you talk about, isn't it? Read about? To be honest, I never thought I'd do it myself. Yet, here we are.'

I must have looked doubtful. I know Justin's a racing sailor, a serious racer, that he's a member, a committee member at that, of the RORC, the Royal Ocean Racing Club. 'What d'you mean, never thought you'd do it yourself?'

'Oh, well, it's a big chunk to bite off, isn't it? Serious stuff.' He's grinning now, gesturing to the mountains on either hand. 'But, I mean, we might as well be day sailing off Cornwall, eh, or southern Ireland?'

He's right, of course, we could be, except we're not.

'You know,' I say, 'I was just thinking that I'm not quite here yet? The long flight, Punta Arenas, getting to know all these strangers, and now... this.'

'Ah, I see what you mean. Me, too. I've just phoned home to say we're off, and it struck me that we aren't, really. The Horn's the thing, really, isn't it? It won't feel we've really started until we get there?'

Tony calls us back for soup and sandwiches, and as we go down I remember something, 'Hey, Steve, whatever happened to "never set sail on a Friday"?'

He grins, maybe pleased that someone remembers that old superstition. 'Right, right, talk about that later at the briefing, right? C'mon mate, soup's up.'

Early evening and Steve's at the helm, nosing us into a small cove on the north side of the channel. Home for the

night. The wind's been averaging a steady 40 knots all afternoon, but in here in the lee of a high slope it's dropped
away. Debs is forward with her watch, preparing to drop
the heavy anchor. Steve calls 'Righto Debs, lower away,'
and, with a thunder of chain, the anchor drops into the
brown-black water. Debs supervises the lowering of the RIB
(reinforced inflatable boat), drops from the rail, sets the outboard in the water, fires up the engine and she's off like a
Formula 1 driver, scouting the anchorage. She has to tilt the
engine from time to time, to clear massive floating rafts of
heavy kelp. Fed and myself are detailed to run the lines
ashore so we drop down to join Debs as she guns up alongside. There are four drums of strong line on the boat, two
forward of the wheelhouse, two on the boarding platform
right astern, under the polypropylene grid that makes up
most of the afterdeck.

Bow lines first. Fed and I each take a heavy line over the
shoulder and Debs drives us ashore. Fed scrambles onto a
small rocky beach, begins to haul in the line. Debs drives
me over to the other side of the cove so that the two lines
will make an angle between them of about 75 degrees.

'Right, then, get yourself ashore, see that big branch there
to your right, about 10 feet up? Make her fast to that, eh?'

Easier said than done, I think to myself, clambering awkwardly onto a wet rock, scrabbling for a grip as I dive
forward into the undergrowth. It's extraordinary stuff,
stunted, wind-blasted miniature beech, twisted and tangled
so that you can't tell root from branch half the time, loose
soil pungent with rotting leaf mould, sudden gaps underfoot, maybe 10 feet down to the underlying ground, or
maybe 10 inches, impossible to say. Ferns, what might be
dwarf rhododendrons, I can't tell whether I'm scrambling
on slippery branches or on soil-covered horizontal trunks.
Brute force and ignorance, I think to myself, and let my feet
and hands do the work all by themselves, a task made no

easier by having to drag the heavy line behind me, unsnagging it by feel as I go. I'm sweating by the time I make it to the trunk Deb had indicated, but I get a bowline on, and sprawl back to see how the others are doing. Big Mike and Diane are working the stern lines by now, Debs buzzing backwards and forwards between us all like a happy wasp.

'All right then, Theo, jump in then.' She catches me glancing over my shoulder and grins. 'Don't worry, mate, it'll hold. I had a good look, didn't I?'

Back on board, I hang up my oilies in the starboard passageway, go back, up into the wheelhouse, down into the galley. Justin is chopping beef, Tony and Marko are peeling and chopping vegetables, there's a pot boiling on the gimballed stove.

'That looked like fun,' says Macken, 'I thought we'd have Irish stew.'

Steve is explaining to Diane why we've got four lines ashore. 'They're called katabatics, see? Wind builds up behind those slopes, piles up in a great heap on top and then like a waterfall a great big lump of it comes rolling downhill. Maybe 70 miles an hour, you see? If we were on just an anchor, right, we'd be blowing all over the place, even if the anchor were to hold? So we always put lines ashore.'

The saloon stretches right across the stern of the boat, with two wings going forward, the galley to port and the comms suite, with all the radio and computer equipment, to starboard. Just by the galley, to the right looking forward, the steps up to the wheelhouse and through that to the deck. To the right of the steps, the diesel stove that keeps us all warm, and heats the radiators in the accommodation cabins forward on both sides. Behind the stove is the engine room. The engine's off now, of course, but there's a low background hum from the generator as we lay the table and all squeeze in around it. Kevin and Debs pass around the wine and beer, and Steve makes the toast.

'Well, here's to all of us. You're all very welcome, as I've said before; today was a good day, our first day out. I don't know about you but I'm glad to be sailing again. I know Debs and Kevin are. I hope you are too. In case anyone's thinking of coming back here sometime and didn't think to check our position, have a look at the log later. Never know when it might come in useful. [Anchorage tonight at 54° 09.909' S, 71° 01.279' W.] Now, the weather. I've been having a look at the GRIBs [gridded binaries], you'll all get a chance to have a look with me and get to know how to read 'em, and it looks like we're in for a bit of a nasty. Big dirty blow forecast for Monday, the 8th, when we're due at the Horn. Right? So I think, what we'll do, we'll ride this one out in Puerto Williams. Right then, I guess that's it, unless Kevin or Debs want to say something? No? Right, let's enjoy the grub.'

Everyone's relaxed, chatting back and forth, bits of information coming out here and there, eleven people, mostly strangers to each other, getting to know each other a little, sharing a meal at the end of a day's sail.

At the same time, you see it in those moments when someone drops out of the conversation for a moment or two, the inwardness as we each of us digest that little nugget of Steve's. 'Bit of a nasty. Big dirty blow.' This from a guy who calls 40 knots 'a bit breezy'. The shipping forecast calls 40 knots a gale. The shipping forecast calls 70 knots a storm.

After dinner, after the washing-up, after a cigarette on deck in the dark bowl of the anchorage, a fantail of bright stars overhead, I e-mail home from the laptop in the comms suite. 'Well we're off, in Beagle Channel now, tied up to the land for the night. More news tomorrow. Bit of a head cold, the usual after a plane journey. Miss you…'

Wriggling deep into the sleeping bag, photo of Paula taped to the cabin wall beside my pillow, I listen to Marko snoring overhead. Ah well, I snore too.

⚓

DAY

# 2

Saturday, 6 May 2006

Woke at 03.20, unable to get back off to sleep. Lay there with thoughts turning over each other in a slow scramble. Mostly to do with what's out ahead of us. I conjure storms, high howling winds, great waves for days on end, the edge of danger, the sniff of oncoming catastrophe. I wonder how the boat will stand up to the weather, I wonder how I'll stand up to it. I wonder what will happen if it all gets to be too much, if the boat should be overwhelmed.

There's no point to this kind of thinking, of course. My sense of it is that the mind calls these thoughts up at random, lets them fall and tumble over each other to no point, no purpose. The effect is a kind of despondency, and the solution is to get hold of the thoughts, line them up and beat them into some kind of order, preferably as a list of questions. The key elements are doubt and fear: I don't know how I'll stand up to really bad weather (so, wait until it comes, get used to the boat); I worry about letting people down (so, learn the boat, learn the duties, get tuned in, you're a competent sailor and you're ready to learn more); I'm afraid it will all go wrong, that I'll die out here (ah, that's the tricky one).

Earlier, on the edge of sleep, I had a thought that had never occurred to me before: what if you died to everything outside yourself, the world gone, your senses gone, perpetual darkness and silence, no other, nothing other – and your mind went on chattering and chattering to itself for all eternity?

Now I am wide awake and, to my own quiet amazement, laughing quietly to myself. Is that all that's bothering you? I ask myself. Would you ever just go back to sleep, would you?

And I do, snuggling down in the warm, contented to be here.

I wake refreshed, the tiredness of the long flights, the days provisioning and boat-keeping in Punta Arenas, all washed out and away. Breakfast noises from the galley, the smell of fresh coffee, toast. In the heads, washing, I look with disfavour at the scrubby five days of growth on my face. Makes me look thin, grey-faced. Ah feck it, never had a beard, persevere, see what it looks like on the other side of the ocean. Go on, you fool, can't make you look any worse.

'Was that you singing away down below?' Macken asks as I come up into the wheelhouse, 'I never figured you for a morning person.'

'Ah feck off,' I say, 'give us a kiss.'

He heads out on deck, shaking his head, grinning. I dive down below for a mug of coffee, then follow him out.

Bright fresh day, small eddies of wind catching us now and then, strong smell of humus from the hills around us; outside in the channel I can see waves being laid low by a strong, steady wind, a thin spray flying.

Steve follows my gaze. 'A bit breezy,' he says, 'nice day for sailing.'

Kevin is forward to starboard, supervising the lowering of the dinghy. Fed, Mike and Debs are ready to go down. 'All right, my man?' Kevin calls. I raise my mug to him. 'Better suit up, we're ready to go,' he says.

Marko is hopping from one foot to the other in the cabin, getting his boots on. I strip to dress again as he leaves. Thermal leggings for the first time, thermal under-shirt, fleece top and tracksuit bottoms. Thick socks and sea boots, then out into the passageway for the foulies hanging on their numbered hook. Chest-high trousers, adjust straps for snug fit, jacket on top of this. Back into the cabin to shove knife in outside pocket, cigarettes and lighter go in inside pocket, woolly cap, gloves – that's me ready for a day's work.

Debs is shuttling back and forth across the anchorage as, one by one, the lines are cast into the water, reeled home on the four big drums. All back aboard, the dinghy lashed on deck forward of the main mast, Justin and I are on anchor duty, Marko on the wheel as the big hook comes home to its rest on the bow roller. Steve engages gear and we turn out into the day.

Time to get the sails up. Backbreaking work, this. The winches are huge, bigger than anything I've worked before, and manually operated. Two to a handle as we sweat and curse, too early in the day for this, I think, and I wish to Christ I'd had the brains to spend a few months in a gym before coming out here. I'm grinding with Marko who is a strong lad, and I feel I'm not putting in the same effort he is. Even with two reefs in, which means the main won't be going all the way to the top, we're in a lather of sweat by the time we make the sheet fast. Steve, watching all this, has an enigmatic expression on his face. I know he's noticed how unfit I am. 'Jesus, Steve, a powered winch might be a good idea, you think?'

He shakes his head. 'Nah, keep it simple, that's the ticket. Manual winch, right? It goes wrong, you can fix it. Electric, they break down too easy, mate, and you can't always fix 'em.'

Yeah, right. Justin and Tony, standing back from making the genoa sheet fast, are gasping for breath. Kevin, who's been setting up the running backstay, has a smug grin on his face. 'Gentlemen, wasn't that good! Bet you feel all awake now? Next time, let's do it in half the time, ok?'

And then Steve chimes in, and he isn't smiling. 'Jesus, guys, that was shit. You're gonna have to put your backs into it, right? Right?' He stomps off, radiating bad temper.

We're not impressed. We look at each other – me, Tony, Justin – and we're not impressed. Marko is even less impressed, 'That's not right, you know? To talk to us like that. I paid big money to be on this trip, not to be treated like, I don't know, like bad.'

Well, he has a point. This is a delivery trip, the boat's on its way to Cape Town for a refit, and we've paid good money, near on €6,000 for the trip, and for the Yachtmaster theory qualification we'll earn along the way. It's a conundrum, and one we haven't really faced up to until now. On the one hand, we're paying passengers, and wouldn't mind not being treated like shit. On the other hand, this isn't a day out on the pond, we are the crew, Steve is the skipper and the only way we're getting to Cape Town in one piece is if we sail the boat to his instructions, and to his liking. So, OK, it rankles a bit, being shouted at, but we process the thought and look at each other again, shrug and decide it's best left alone. Simon and Diana are standing in the wheelhouse looking out at us, nobody saying a word, and Marko pushes in past them, muttering. Kevin, who's let this play itself out, gives Tony a gentle elbow. 'Never mind,' he says, 'that's just Steve, that's just his way. We need to be in good shape for the rough stuff, right? He knows that. Anyone for a coffee?'

By mid-afternoon we're bowling along east-south-east, the wind in the north-west pushing us. It's a good stiff breeze by now, 50 knots or more, but it feels a bit unreal. We're motor-sailing, making 9 to 10 knots, but it's really difficult to grasp how hard the wind is blowing, probably because we're in a channel no more than 2 or 3 miles across. I've had a nap below, my head is a bit clearer when I come up into this. Marko is engaged in a pilotage exercise, checking our course, setting the course for the next leg, listing lights, rocks, any obstructions or aids to navigation that we're likely to encounter over the next two hours. Steve is studying possible anchorages for the night, Justin peering over his shoulder. Diane, who seems to have acquired the nickname Floss while I was asleep, has on her hat with the furry earphones and is interviewing Fed for the radio documentary she hopes to make. Simon's on the wheel, constantly calling to Marko for directions.

We haven't seen any other boats all day but now there's a small fishing boat offering to sell us shellfish, the crew in diving suits asking for cigarettes. God, that's a hard way to make a living, diving for shellfish in these waters. Next, off to starboard, we spot three small boats nosed into the land, there for the night probably, an impromptu party. Then, a short while later, another small boat, terrier-like, pushing up channel towards the party. We have a look at the cove he's come out of, decide against it. A short while later, we point into a narrow inlet Steve hasn't tried before, but then there's a bump, and we're aground. Diane, not unreasonably, looks a bit anxious but says nothing. The thing is, there's a 3-metre swing keel under us, 9 tonnes of iron, and it isn't all the way down; there's a strut to keep it pressed down when fully extended, and, earlier today, Simon and Debs removed it. Now the keel does what it's supposed to do in the circumstances and bounces up into its housing. Debs goes below to put five turns on the electric winch, lift the thing higher, and we gently back out.

When we bumped, Steve just shrugged, said, 'Bah, it happens, not to worry' – and of course we took him at his word. Why not? Normally it's a cause for concern when a boat hits the ground, but this boat is designed to go exploring, and the design has factored in exactly this sort of occurrence.

We head back in the pitch dark to the bay we'd rejected earlier, nose in for maybe a mile, radar on. Same drill as last night: this time Justin and I drop the hook; Debs, Fed and Kevin are away in the RIB to set lines ashore.

Steve is at the chart table writing in a ledger. He's sketched in this long, deep cove, tending northwest, Puerto Abrigo marked with a cross in the southeast corner. He'd been scribbling away on a notepad as we nosed in here, and now I see what he was at, recording the depths as we came in. He's never been in here before, and he's making a rudimentary chart of the cove. He pushes the ledger over to me. 'See? Every time I come into somewhere I've never been before, if it's not on the chart or in the pilot book I make a plan.'

'You got many of these?'

'Oh yeah, lots. See, you have to remember this is home to me now, I've been down here for, what, three years? Living on the boat? I love it down here, and I'm always trying new places. Maybe I'll get a book together some day, all these little anchorages.'

I think of FitzRoy again, and all those before him and since, charting the channels, piece by tiny piece, and I am oddly comforted that it still goes on, this ancient practice opening down through time and out into some future where, who knows, some hard-pressed soul, battered by weather, a failing engine, an exhausted crew, will make in here for shelter and respite, his night's rest underwritten by Steve's attentive, meticulous notation.

First e-mail in from Paula, it lifts my heart. If my response seems stilted to her, laboured, uncertain, as I fear it will, it is because I am still in two worlds and this, for now, is the one I need to be in, whole and attentive.

Before turning in, we double the line off the starboard quarter. If we get weather, that's where it will come from during the night.

Position at anchor, 54° 38.8′ S, 71° 28.8′ W.

⚓

DAY

## 3

Sunday, 7 May 2006

Strong winds as we rise at 06.30. Heavy gusts from the north-west, tumbling over the saddle at the head of the cove, fanning out to either side of us as we lie back hard on our anchor. A forecast, I remind myself, is not a promise; these winds were meant to blow through during the night, that's why we're up so early.

We fooster about most of the morning, chatting, tidying this and that, still settling in, waiting for the wind to quieten down a bit. Finally, just before noon, we make away. The days are short here at this time of year, we aim to be settled in tonight's anchorage by 16.30, just before dark.

Steve started us in on the Yachtmaster syllabus yesterday – collision regulations (colregs). Some people know these backwards already, some of us have a working knowledge, some are seeing these rules of the marine road for the first time. Today, each watch as it comes on must face into intensive navigation exercises as well as sail the boat. We have the afternoon watch, and we have to work out the pilotage down to O'Brien Channel. It's narrow in there, with a small light at the entrance. As we approach, we spot a landing-craft-type ferry coming out towards us, and then a big container ship gaining on us from astern. Suddenly it seems very busy around here. The small ferry clears away to the north of us, keeping inshore to gain some shelter. The container ship hails us on VHF, signalling her intention to pass ahead of us on our port side. Steve on the radio acknowledges, adds, 'Confirm, please. You will pass us your green to our red.'

The voice that comes back to him is laconic, bordering on disdainful, 'Yes, *Pelagic Australis*, your red, our green.' Diane is confused, she knows her port from her starboard but wants to know why they're talking about red and green when it isn't dark yet and neither of us is showing lights. I'm more intrigued to know why the container is being so snotty; it seems to me reasonable that Steve wanted clear, unambiguous confirmation of their intent; what's with the attitude?

It's Diane's birthday today, and Marko has baked her a cake. Tony's up for cooking dinner but has to suffer Justin and myself butting in on him. Truth to tell, he seems pleased enough. We settle on a kind of sea-shepherd's pie: ratatouille and minced beef base, topped with mashed potato, dusted with parmesan. Not only has Marko baked a cake, he's somehow contrived to ice it as well, even to the lettering of 'Happy Birthday'.

I get talking to Debs about her life back in New Zealand: her garden, her dog, her nearly grown-up son. I get talking to Kevin about the two tattoo shops he owns in Baton Rouge, the Hummer he drives. Simon, overhearing this, weighs in, scornful of Hummers, the people who drive them, the damage they do to the planet. And so on. Kevin is amused, well perhaps not exactly amused but determined not to rise to this.

'Well, Simon buddy, when Katrina hit n'Orleans, that Hummer made a damn good job of towing me an' my boat down there to go help those good people, so I guess it's good for something.' Big smile. Nice one, Kev, I think but don't say; I'm not too keen on Hummers myself, to tell the truth, ridiculous things, but I'm not terribly keen on investment bankers either. I can't figure Simon out yet: he condescends to Kevin, blind to the man's courteousness, his helpful instincts, and yet he himself has shown kind instincts, even if he's inclined to mask the impulse behind a curled lip. Justin down the table is being very funny about Terry Wogan, Fed is scrolling through the day's photos on his camera with Diane, Marko and the ever-affable Big Mike are muttering together just beyond my hearing and Steve is telling Tony how he intends to leave the boat in Cape Town, head home to Australia to his sister's wedding and then maybe New Zealand, go skiing in South Island. 'After that, who knows?'

We're dancing about a bit in the anchorage, not much, just enough to let us know we're on a boat. It's been a full day – sailing, studying the weather, learning flags and lights, but nobody's ready quite yet to hit the bunks. We're sounding each other out, I realise; we're probing for facts, information, the kind of detail that makes some stranger's life feel real for a while. Underneath, though, we're all asking a different kind of question: What are you like? What will you be like, if push comes to shove? Will you carry your own weight or will you have to be carried? What do you bring to sailing this big boat? Can we rely on you? Are you really up for this?

I'm looking around at everyone, all absorbed in conversation, when Big Mike suddenly raises his head, stares straight ahead then turns to look at me. 'Yeah,' he says, 'yeah, I getcha.' I have to laugh, even while I'm trying to figure out how he did that.

'Hey, Steve,' I ask in a lull, 'what about "never set sail on a Friday"?'

'Oh yeah, didn't get back to that, did we? Well, the way I see it that only holds for setting out on, like, a trip, right? All we're doing at the moment, if you like, is day sailing, tying up every night. That's all right, isn't it?'

Fed wants to know what this is about. Old superstition, Justin explains. In the old days, nobody would ever set out on a long trip on a Friday. Fed's impatient, yes, yes, he's understood, what he wants to know is what does this mean, why Friday? Tony butts in, 'It probably goes back to Good Friday, you know? Inauspicious day to start anything.'

'An auspicious day,' Fed asks, 'why an auspicious day? I thought you said it was bad luck.'

'No, no, an in-auspicious day.'

Now Steve breaks in. 'Theo, I saw you pour a glass of wine in the water when we were leaving Punta?'

I nod: 'Yeah, and I saw you pour half a beer over, too.'

Now Diane is puzzled, what's that about?

'It's called a libation, goes back a long, long way, to the Greeks, maybe to the Phoenicians. You offer a drink to Poseidon for a safe trip, freedom from storms, isn't that it, Steve?'

'Yep, not sure where it comes from but it's always done.'

And that's it in a phrase, that's why superstitions endure; there's always someone to assure you that it's always done.

I'm willing to bet that after this trip, no one aboard will ever again set out on a long voyage without pouring a libation, explaining to any neophytes aboard that 'it's always done'.

Anchorage in Puerta Americana, 54° 52.95′ S, 70° 22.9′ W.

then the anchor, Fed and Marko to the stern lines. What next? Warm up the engine (make sure it's in neutral), Kevin to midships, ready to haul out the RIB when they're back. Anything else? Nothing I can think of. How are we doing? Lines are coming back, winding onto the drums. Good. Tony and Justin have their lines secured, 'OK, lads, on to the anchor.' Debs is back, Mike clambering stiffly aboard after Di. Debs comes up standing in the dinghy, Kevin winding slow and steady on the winch. Anchor, Jesus, anchor. 'How are you fixed, Justin?' Thumbs up. 'OK, raise 'er up.' Stern lines clear? Yep, on the drums, the lads are back up off the boarding platform, grid is back down. 'Ready, Simon?' 'Yeah, ready.' Anchor is straight up and down; a short burst of reverse, Justin yells back 'Clear', the windlass hauls it home. Bow beginning to drift off with the wind. Engage forward, 'OK, Simon, come around and head for that gap between the islands where we came in last night.' Anything I've forgotten? No? Quick glance at Steve, no signal there. 'Kev, dinghy lashed down OK?' 'Yessir, all secure.' A quick grin. Justin's back, 'Anchor secured and lashed down'. Thanks Justin, anything else? No? Well then, first relaxed breath in ten minutes, reach for a cigarette, Steve waits until I've taken that first deep drag and asks mildly, 'OK then, Theo mate, where are we going then?'

Oh dear. Stupid me. I thought all was required was to get us off the anchorage and moving. 'No, no, mate, what's our course, what are Simon's instructions, come on, he's waiting.' Cigarette goes overboard, jacket off, into wheelhouse. Chart, is our position last night marked? Yes, thank God, marked it myself. Start from where we are, yell out to Simon, 'Simon, could you throttle back a bit for a moment? Thanks.' Gains me some time. Plotter not switched on, switch it on, wait a mo, punch up larger scale. Right, here we are at top of cove. 'Right, Simon, see those two islands

I mentioned? Make course 135°, no, make that 140°, that'll keep us in deeper water, I'll be back to you in a second.'

Stop to think for a second. Right, we're going down channel, don't neglect the obvious. Bugger the plotter, more comfortable with paper chart. OK, we clear those islands, then what? Over there, deep water, where's the wind outside? Looks like west-north-west, so stay slightly to north side of main channel when we get there. Notebook, quick list of rough transits, lights or marks we can expect to see. Christ, rain coming in ahead, visibility closing in to, what, a quarter of a mile?

'Come on, Theo,' Steve by my elbow now, pressuring, 'give the helmsman some information, visibility's gone to shit, isn't it? What do you do about that? What about the radar for Christ's sake, come on, man, wake up.'

Oh this is all I need, I'm about to blow up and tell him to fuck off when I catch myself, catch on to what he's up to. I hate being tested, pressured, I'm a slow man to wake in the morning too, and this is all deliberate, he wants to see how I'll deal with this. Marko, yesterday, remember? All that pressure to come up with a pilotage? Bet the fucker will do something like this to everyone in turn, see what he has to work with. All this goes through in a few seconds but meanwhile I'm telling Simon there'll be a course change in about five minutes, the radar is warming up and I'm looking to see if there is an alternative course we could take after we enter the channel. Would it be shorter, trickier, easier? Which would be the best choice in diminished visibility? Get on with it; decide, decide. I sweep Steve away with a backhand, 'Sorry, Steve, I need to get at the chart.' Out of the corner of my eye I see the tiniest flicker of a smile. Over his shoulder, framed in the wheelhouse doorway, Kevin is grinning; a slow wink, a nod, go ahead, go ahead.

So out we go, bit by bit, Steve keeping the pressure on, Simon replaced on the wheel by Di, under the watchful eye of Debs, and after an hour or so the skipper says, 'OK, Theo, take a break, mate, grab a smoke, eh? How do you feel now, eh? All right?' What can I do but laugh?

Tony's brow is furrowed as he hands me yet another mug of tea; he's been keeping the tea coming. 'Jesus, boy, that was rough.'

Justin looks sombre, thinks that was a bit much to spring on someone. Kevin punches me in the upper arm, 'That's Steve for ya. You did good, kid.'

Kid? Interesting, I'm about ten years older than Kevin, but what I'm feeling, the colour of what I'm feeling if I can put it like that, is how I used to feel after a rough unexpected exam when I was twelve years old. It must show on my face. What doesn't show, I hope, is the sense of accomplishment I feel, that and the not-quite-extinguished belligerence, the childish resentment at being put under pressure like that. Marko wants to take a group photograph.

The early-morning fog has burned off by now, wind is around 40 knots and we're bowling along, it looks like, between Kerry to starboard and Switzerland to port. To the south of us, low, rounded hills, green and brown, water-saturated, stunted heathers and dwarf beeches, isolated boulders grey in the harsh light. To the north of us, a succession of *ventisqueros*, glaciers. The glaciers are like embalmed or frozen katabatics, piling up in the saddles between high ridges, then falling away downhill in broad fans, pinched here and there by spurs of bare rock. Blue glaciers, old ice. Some don't make it quite to the water's edge, and this worries Steve. It's his third winter in this channel, these waters, and he thinks the glaciers are receding. He nods when Diane mentions global warming, not interested in generalisations but sure of what he's seen. Same down in Antarctica, he says, same all over the place, the ice is receding. He looks hurt by this, says the blue ice is a bad sign, there should be fresh ice on top of it, this time of year.

From west to east the glaciers are Germania, Francia, Italia and Holandia. Italia, to Fed's delight, is the most spectacular, the most beautiful. He's been down to rummage in his baggage for flags – Italian national flag, sailing clubs he belongs to – has us all taking photographs of him, perched on the port side, flags between outstretched arms, huge sparkling grin on him. 'Bit of a patriot then, Fed, are you?'

'Oh yes, yes. I even have the Italian national anthem as the ring tone on my mobile.'

'Not "Avanti Popolo", then?'

He looks horrified, 'No, no. Certainly not!' He looks at me doubtfully, uncertain if I'm going to pursue this. I just smile and shrug, take another photograph of him with his camera.

'*Grazie.*'

'*Prego.*'

'What was all that about?' Tony, eyeing me over his spectacles.

'Ah, an old partisan song from the war,' I tell him, 'Communist, leftist, whatever.'

'Fed didn't like it?'

'No, seems not.'

'Hmm, how does it go?'

So I hum it for him, for mischief, and he starts to hum along.

The frontier between Argentina to the north of us and Chilean territory to the south runs down mid-channel. From time to time we are hailed on the VHF by one side or the other, naval stations monitoring all traffic. Steve says not so long ago that they were firing at each other, not sure exactly when or why. I do remember, though, reading that during the Falklands/Malvinas affair, the Chileans, on the quiet, supplied Maggie with information from a radar station set up opposite Comodoro Rivadiva, enabling the British forces to monitor Argentine air-force movements.

Explains why she stood up for that old bastard Pinochet at the end. Deep waters, these. In any case, we're not cleared for Argentina, so we stay in Chilean waters, something else to be reckoned with by whoever's doing the pilotage.

We spot a schooner going up channel in the lee of Ventisquero Francia. Steve and Debs recognise the boat: French, skipper a Breton, Gaston. Not too many boats working these waters, chartering, and they all know each other. There's a small community down here, I realise, all smitten by the cold and empty south. There's a short conversation on the radio, Steve explaining that after Cape Town, he'll be leaving the boat. Gaston absorbs this for a few seconds, then says, the sense of occasion slight but palpable, 'Ah then, Steve, see you sometime, someplace, good luck wherever you go. Bon voyage.'

She looks so small, I think, heading west under the glacier wall. 'What size is she, Debs?'

'Oh about 70 foot, I reckon, same size as us, more or less.' Ah. The channel doesn't look so narrow now, and when I lean back to look at the wind indicator, the windex, on top of the mast, it doesn't seem so very far up after all.

Soon after the French boat passes, we spot a Chilean gunboat making up mid-channel, great walls of spray flying off to either side of her. Her engines must be thundering away, to be pushing her so hard against this wind. She's making heavy weather of it, all the same. We're running before the wind, 40–45 knots on average, often gusting to 60–65 knots. I've seen 72.6 on the clock, Justin, on the helm earlier, saw 76. I'm happier to be going downwind, for sure; it would be ugly, beating up against this, it must have been ugly for anything coming up in the teeth of a wind like this under sail. Imagine beating into this, and at the same time trying to put boats out, and keep boats out, while surveying the passage. Imagine doing all that without having the slightest clue if there is a way through at the end of it all.

Cold, wet, worn out and unconvinced. What would have driven men like that? What would have kept them going? Maybe what Eluard calls *'le dur désir de durer'*, the dour desire to endure? That Chilean gunboat, now making away on at speed, they have more in common with those old boys than we have, the officers shaped and nurtured by a sense of duty, perhaps patriotic pride, the men, as everywhere, dogged and keeping their heads down, getting through the day, dreaming of small things and keeping out of trouble.

What do they see when they look over at us? Tourists, probably. Why get upset? In a sense that's what we are, though I'm willing to wager we won't feel like tourists in a few days' time.

South of Ushuaia, the southern-most town in Argentina, somebody gets a signal on their mobile – I nip down for mine, meet Steve coming up from the comms suite. 'Eh, Theo, you've got an e-mail.'

I postpone replying, want to phone home instead, craving her voice in my ear. Damn, answering machine. Leave message, then call up my friend Tony Curtis, catch up on the news. Down here at the other end of the world, still hooked into the web of the daily, the habitual and the commonplace.

Meanwhile, more testing. Steve has our watch at work computing course and course corrections, now he wants an ETA in Puerto Williams. The Admiral takes charge, much furrowing of brows, consultation, rechecking. 'OK, Steve,' Justin announces, 'ETA, Puerto Williams, 17.30.'

'You sure?'

'Yep.'

Two hours later, ten minutes early, we land in. Justin looks at his watch, calls to Steve, 'Hey, Steve, we're early, sorry about that.'

Steve just looks at him, unsure how to take this, then grins, gives us all the finger. 'Go on, you lazy shower, what about getting some fenders out, eh? Who's got the lines ready? Come on, come on.'

The wind's died down, the sails are struck, we motor in on a glassy surface. Up above and to the left of us, in an arc along the cliff top, the white-painted station of the Armada de Chile, bristling with antennae, oversized national flag snapping in the light breeze. Below the buildings, docks and storage tanks, a supply ship, two patrol boats. Ahead, coming up on our left as we pivot around a marker buoy, the half-sunken hull of an old coaster, the *Micalvi*. To our right, on low ground, a long wooden hut, looking for all the world like a tennis pavilion shut down for the winter. There are a handful of yachts strung out along the hull of the *Micalvi* and on into the head of the inlet. Away ahead of us, at the end of a long tree-lined valley, snow-covered peaks flashing in the late afternoon sun, the serrated crown of the Dientes di Navarino. The *Micalvi* is where we'll tie up. Years ago she was towed here alongside a flat space, sunk, her hull half filled with concrete. Now her bridge and cabins are used as a bar, headquarters of the Club Naval de Yates Micalvi. Her wooden deck is treacherous by repute, you step carefully as you cross to landside. There's a trim, robust-looking 40-foot ketch moored to the old coaster, *Shenu*, and we warp in carefully alongside her, festooned with fenders. Kevin's not taking any chances of gouging our sides on anything that might be sticking out. We double all the lines back to the boat, Debs kills the engine and we all stand back to consider our surroundings. It's quiet, the first thing we notice after four days of the wind howling in the shrouds and rigging. Inside, on the far side of the *Micalvi*, there's a small pool with a mongrel collection of little motor boats, a few modest yachts and a big old yellow-hulled wooden schooner. I recognise her from the internet – one of my more shameful habits is browsing the net for boats of 'character' I cannot afford and could not, in most cases, handle. Evidently I am not alone in this; Justin peers forward, says, 'I've seen her before, she charters around these waters I think.' As ever, the boat as she actually is looks somewhat more forlorn than she does in pictures. I wonder how long it's been since anyone was aboard.

Puerto Williams is one of two bases for boats setting out for the Horn from this, the west side, Ushuaia's the other, and a few boats around that have the lone adventurer look about them: windvanes, over-engineered masts, the perspex bubble that seems a particular feature of French single-handers – it enables them to keep watch, particularly over the set of their sails, without opening a hatch in heavy weather. So, you wouldn't call this a marina by any measure, and I feel pretty sure that Puerto Williams will be lacking in the lively bar life and reputed whorehouses that form part of the legendary attractions of Ushuaia over on the Argentine side. Well, small, modest and utilitarian suits us fine as it happens.

Simon, with Diane as backup, already has dinner on, a roast of vegetables we will come to recognise over the next few weeks. There's a curious atmosphere on the boat, a restlessness at being back on land, as if we've interrupted something – and at the same time a sense of rest and relief. It isn't as if the past few days have been particularly taxing, though it's been a challenging exercise in pilotage, and the boat does take getting used to; no, what's going on, I think, is that most of us have built up the Horn into something private and alarming, and we know that when we leave here that's where we'll be going. Naturally, no one speaks of this. We're not quite at that point yet, but we want to gather our thoughts, go through another stage of waking up.

Inevitably, eventually, somebody stands, stretches, yawns and asks casually, anyone fancy going up the town for a beer?

Well, duh!

Across the rickety wooden bridge from the *Micalvi*, and up the hill. To the right, ahead, the steep-pitched, double-roofed church. To the side of the church three tall crosses, superimposed on each other, each staggered slightly to one side of the next. Nice to see the thieves get a look-in, I think, the more so when you stop to consider the thieving habits of the Fuegans, and the original European cut-throats who first came by here. Plonked in front of the church, a small Oerlikon anti-aircraft gun, barrels skyward as if the Armada is anticipating the return of the rebel angels. The plaza in front of the church is Plaza Arturo Prat. We presume of English extraction – Justin ventures the suggestion that Arturo's Da was driven into emigra-tion by an unfortunate surname. At the top of the plaza stand the bow of the ship that set out with Shackleton to rescue his men after his epic small-boat voyage. That sobers us up. The town straggles in all directions, mostly following the contour lines around the brow of the hill. Lots of dogs to be heard, houses are bright-painted clap-board with shallow-pitched, corrugated-iron roofs, the roofs almost always green, the walls sky-blue, eau-de-Nil, terracotta, white or yellow. The houses are single storey, mostly set back from the road; at the kerbside, tall iron baskets with heavy lids, standing on poles. These are for household rubbish, left there in plastic bags for collection. There's hardly anybody about, the occasional small open truck goes by, drivers incurious about us. At the top of the town another plaza, Plaza Bernardo O'Higgins; a few shops around the edge, some terraces of stone, a few benches, lots of cats, Diane is convinced they must be the smallest cats in the world. To complete the inventory of Puerto Williams street life, we note: one Pomeranian, bad-tempered in accordance with tradition; one husky, indifferent; and one Alsatian, lugubrious. More by luck than anything else, we find a bar.

The floor is concrete painted red, the stove is ingeniously fabricated from an oil drum, the brandy is rough and very warming, the beer thin and unconvincing. We couldn't care less, thirst is thirst. Off in the corner, two young fishermen are engrossed in some American TV movie, lots of car chases, unlikely blonde female anatomy and quick-fire dubbing. There's a rack of VHS cassettes standing by the far wall, mostly, as far as we can tell, 'Rambo' and Will Smith vehicles with lurid covers. The few trucks and cars outside are mostly Toyotas and Nissans, there's a Ferrari poster on the wall, bare bulbs here and there hanging from a sagging ceiling, the smell of fish frying from somewhere out behind the bar counter and the fishermen are wearing Nikes. Welcome to the bar at the end of the world.

It's probably just as well we're all tired, Justin, Tony, Marko, Diane, Mike and me, I don't fancy waking up with a hangover tomorrow, not on this brandy. One or two of the others may be wandering about, the rest are back in the boat, crashed out. 'Hey, Dorgan, he put you through the wringer this morning, eh? Fair do's, boy, you pulled it off though.'

'Thanks, Tony.'

'Glad it wasn't me,' says everyone else in ragged chorus. I signal for another round before I get a swelled head.

In the lee of *Micalvi*'s wheelhouse, I call Paula on the mobile. Her family lives in McKelvey Avenue in Dublin, I tell her I'm calling from *Micalvi* and count to ten before she sorts through her confusion enough to ask what's going on.

'What are you going to write about tomorrow?' she asks. I've to file a piece for *The Irish Times*, follow up on last week's introductory article.

'Dunno,' I say, 'looks like we'll be holed up here for another day, waiting for weather to go through.'

'Not to put you under pressure,' she says, 'but I met a woman on the beach the other day and she asked me how you were getting on over there. Oh, and Maura Grant rang, the President sends all her best wishes for a safe trip, says she's waiting for the next instalment.'

'Any news?' asks Tony, pouring milk into two mugs of Barry's tea when I go below.

'What? Oh yeah, the President says to wish you a safe trip.'

'The President? What President?'

'Mary McAleese.'

'Mary McAleese?'

'Is there an echo in here or what?'

'What President?' asks Steve, sticking his head around the corner from where he's downloading weather files.

'The President of Ireland,' says Macken helpfully, still puzzled.

'What? The President of Ireland phoned you?'

'Not me. Theo.'

'No, she didn't. She phoned Paula to tell me… ah here, this is getting too complicated, I'm off up for a smoke.'

'I'll join you, mate,' says Steve. 'The President of Ireland! Fuck me.'

All of which, I reflect on the edge of sleep, should teach me to keep my mouth shut.

Puerto Williams, southern-most town in world, 54° 56.2' S, 67° 37' W.

⚓

DAY

# 5

Tuesday, 9 May 2006

Think I'm first up, but find Steve in the saloon, poring over the laptop. 'G'day, mate, grab a cup, eh? Come and have a look.'

He's a good explainer, Steve. First he opens up the GRIB files. The screen is covered with small arrows, pointing this way and that, one, two or three feathers sticking out of the tail at an angle. The head of the arrow shows wind direction, the number of feathers on the tail tells you the approximate strength of the wind. OK, I can see we're in for a bit of a blow; Steve says 50–60 knots early afternoon probably, from the north-west.

'Right, Steve, how do you call up these files?'

'Like this, see? This laptop is for weather only, right? Y'see that big dome on the gantry there aft, up there? Well that's the satellite receiver, like I said, and it's an expensive piece of kit. Mainly it's there to pull down the weather, everything else is a bit of a luxury. Anyway, doesn't matter, this here laptop is just for weather, OK? You guys send and receive e-mails on the other one, OK? Yeah you know that. Now, this here' – opens another window – 'is the satellite picture. Y'see this big dirty system here? Well that's what's giving us wind today. I've been watching this for the past few days, I'm hoping tomorrow it'll track off away up here' – he brings the cursor up to the vicinity of Falklands/ Malvinas – 'cos that'll give us, what?'

'Westerlies? Maybe south-west, depending?'

'Well, yeah, 'bout that, something like that. You get the picture?'

I do, I do.

'So what've we got right now, then?'

'Westerlies?' I venture.

'Corr-ect. The man gets a biscuit.'

Debs comes yawning through from the cabin she shares with Steve, just forward of the comms suite. Kevin bounces down the steps from the wheelhouse, Justin sedately on his heels.

'Righto, Kev, get a cup and get 'em up. Work to do today.'

Kevin is mixing up one of his power protein shakes, grunts.

Debs stretches, cracks her interlaced fingers in front of her. 'C'mon then, Theo, got a nice little job for you. You too, Justin. Up on deck.'

She starts untying the lashings on the RIB. 'Right, we won't be needing this for, like, forever. Grab that halyard, Theo, we gotta get this engine down below.'

I clip a halyard to the grab straps on the engine housing. Debs unbolts it from the transom, steadies it as I take the strain, pulls it after her to the forward hatch, twirls her finger to signify 'lower away'. Justin, below, will lash it tight as can be in the open cage that's to port as you come through the watertight door into the spacious forepeak.

'Now, you two, we're gonna roll up this RIB here and stow that below too.' Out with the aluminium flooring sections, down with 'em, stash them inside the cage. Then Debs produces the secret weapon: a large tin of talcum powder. 'Bet you're wondering what this is for, eh? Well, we'll dry the RIB as best we can and then smother it in this stuff, eh? Keep it nice and dry, keeps it from rotting, eh?'

So we wrestle the ungainly rubber into submission, stopping now and then to dose it liberally with talc. 'Jesus,' Macken on deck now, brisk and bustling, 'Ye smell like the inside of a whore's handbag!'

Justin, sweating and lightly dusted all over, is almost amused. We get the heavy, ungainly package down below all right, but it takes nearly twenty minutes of wrestling and cursing and pummelling to get it stowed in the cage. Tactfully, Debs absents herself from the brute force and ignorance of our efforts, and our language. Sensitive soul, our Debbie.

With the RIB sent down below, you can see how big the deck is now. *Pelagic Australis* is all aluminium, for strength and lightness. Her deck is covered with carefully sited patches of diamond-cut treadmaster, a kind of artificial rubber, for maximum grip. Effective stuff, too: not once in the whole journey will I see anyone slip on deck, no matter the weather. Her three foresails are on furlers, for ease of deployment, and the main mast is stepped between two fingers that project forward on either side from the wheelhouse. The shrouds, holding the mast up, go to the outside of the deck, so that the passage forward and back on either side is between the fingers and the lifelines. In the hollow between the fingers are the winch for the reefing lines and the access hatch to the double bar, an elongated 'H', that keeps the keel down when she's dropped. There are small hatches on top of the fingers that give air and emergency access to the individual cabins off the port and starboard passageways below, and an enclosed space under the deck, between the passages, that the keel can lift into when not required.

There are two shorter fingers behind the wheelhouse, on either side, four winches on each, the insides hollow to take the falls from the sheets, leaving the deck uncluttered. The life-raft is mounted between the fingers, with a hard top over it, a kind of table in good weather. The big wheel is forward of this, and there's a kind of protected porch between the wheel and the door into the wheelhouse. This porch is quite ingenious; it gives a certain amount of shelter to the helmsman, and enables the crew to sit out of the weather, protected from three sides, while the wheelhouse itself is sealed off.

Aft of the life-raft is the open afterdeck, mostly a grid of heavy, white polypropylene which sheds water onto the boarding platform below. This has the useful effect of breaking the force of a boarding sea falling on us from astern, getting the weight of a breaking wave down low, fast, and diminishing its impact considerably. Right aft there's a kind of stainless steel goalpost, the satellite dome is mounted on this, and an array of lesser aerials for GPS, radio, etc.

This is a big, chunky, bullet-proof boat, I'm thinking to myself, when Justin beside me breaks the silence. 'I'd say she's fit for purpose, wouldn't you?'

We hose down the deck, then, bow to stern, a soft brush to get mud from the anchorages out of corners where it's accumulated.

Lunch has materialised, great bowls of salad, bread rolls, platters of fruit, cheese and salami, bowls of olives spread out on the hard top over the life-raft. There's a hint of warmth in the sun, everyone's smiling, joking – not a hint of what must surely be on most of our minds.

Debs is organising a small party to go up the town for last-minute supplies.

Macken pops up on deck, hiking boots, small backpack.

Justin hails him as he steps over the rail, 'Where are you off to, then?'

Tony turns to look north, points, 'Up there, thought I'd take a walk.' Las Dientes de Navarino.

'OK then, off you go. Don't forget you're cooking tonight.'

A twitch of the whiskers, a quick furrowing of the brow, and he's off. We watch him stride away, under the pines where the two kids from the French live-aboard are swinging on suspended tyres from the high pines. 'Think he'll be all right then, Theo?'

'That fella? No fear of him. Wind him up and set him off.'

A bit more life up the town today, small groups of people gathered to chat, here and there someone unloading a truck, hammering at something, dragging the strands of a sagging fence tighter. Neat cords of wood stacked against the sides of houses, wire fences atop low whitewashed walls interwoven with some kind of vine, giving shelter and privacy, dogs everywhere on the dusty streets, in elaborate makeshift kennels in side yards. The people are small, dark, friendly when spoken to, otherwise reserved, perhaps shy.

The store Debs brings us to has a certain frontier air to it, unpainted wooden shelves packed higgledy-piggledy with canned goods, packets, bottles and jars in a dusty profusion, dimly lit from small windows shoved into the walls at seemingly random intervals. There's a stove in the centre, unlit, surrounded by baskets of fruit and vegetables, there are trays of biscuits and cakes on a table near the counter, a cold cabinet packed with cheeses and meats, cooked and uncooked. School must be out, there's a huddle of children with bright-coloured backpacks squabbling over sweets and candies, only occasionally paying us any attention. One small boy in a grey parka is awestruck by the size of Big Mike, backing away against a shelf of canned fruits to crane his neck up at the bearded, smiling giant. The teenage girls in the back of the shop are agonising over a choice of barrettes, stealing the occasional shy glance at handsome Simon. Our booted feet ring on the bare grey floorboards, and, for a fleeting moment, I expect to hear our spurs ring out in the dusty air.

Two brother pups befriend us as we leave, cheered on no doubt by the *empanada*, a meat-filled pastry we divided between them. They pad off down the street behind Debs and Mike, all the way back to the deck of the *Micalvi* as we will discover later, when we find they have taken up residence under a hatch coaming.

Justin and I head on, looking for souvenirs, cards, a post office.

We meet Marko on our way back, snapping away. He's been up to the naval headquarters, he tells us, to make them a gift of one of his Slovak pennants. 'Look, see,' he says, hooding the backplate of his camera, 'Here is the commander and me, exchanging flags, see? A nice fellow, I think.'

When we get back to the boat, Fed is near the top of the mast and Mike isn't sure Steve is a nice fellow. We can hear him hollering, 'C'mon, Fed, put your back into it, man, you're nearly there.'

'I was on the winch,' Mike explains, 'lowering Steve, he was up there checking the windex, the halyard sheaves, you know? So I was lowering him down and the halyard slipped maybe, Jeez, I dunno, a foot? Next thing he's down, cursing a blue streak, makes me go up there; then, when I'm on the way down, he lets it slip a bit, you know? Not a nice feeling. I get down, he tells me, "Now you know what it's like, mate, you won't let someone slip again, will ya?"'

It's getting dark, we've begun to wonder about young Macken when he appears out of the dusk, tramp, tramp,

tramp, over the side, a nod, down below, boots off, into the galley. 'Wow,' drawls Simon, 'who was that masked man?'

In the warm fug as the lasagne cooks, Steve is at the weather again. 'See that? System coming down from the north-west. Hmm...'

After dinner, schoolwork. Marko to do pilotage to Woolaston Island, from there to the Horn; Diane and I to plot passage from Horn to Falklands/Malvinas. Marko's first plot draws some pointed criticism, but he buckles down and produces an excellent pilotage plan, making good use of transits, transit lines, lights, etc. The plan is to make for the Woolastons, anchor there overnight tomorrow, Wednesday, and if the weather gods are co-operating, strike south for the Horn on Thursday morning, round and then on east and north to Stanley.

To be on the safe side, we make two plots for Stanley, one if we do and one if we don't round. Nobody is saying anything, but I can hardly conceive of the disappointment we would all feel if the weather turned against us and we had to run on to Stanley direct from here.

Nobody feels like going back to the bar, early start tomorrow in any case. Tension is rippling just beneath the surface now, a small gesture or a look betrays it, a glance held too long, a sentence tailing off as someone turns away. Fed is overhauling his cameras, Di is listening back to bits she's recorded for her documentary, their heads close at the saloon table, a certain quiet about them. I wonder...

Back in my cabin, I dig out my lucky blue corduroy shirt that Paula bought me all those years ago to go off sailing in; I wear it at departures, landfalls, significant moments, it's got quite a few sea-miles woven into it by now, this faded shirt. I hope to be wearing it on Thursday morning. Something else that has to appear in what photos there might be is my Na Piarsaigh jersey. My father and four of his friends founded this hurling and football club more than fifty years ago. There's a notorious antipathy in my native Cork between northsiders and southsiders, and Na Piarsaigh is the quintessential northside club. I want a photo for the clubhouse to be captioned: 'The Piarsaigh man who ventured farthest into the southside'. It's an act of faith, then, to be digging out shirt and jersey from the bottom of my kitbag, meaning to hang them on the short line over the radiator to air. Juju time.

I sit there on the bunk, jersey in my hand, and find I am thinking about my father. He must have been disappointed that I wasn't much of a hurler, not given to sport. I was a bookish child, not given to rough and tumble. I was a far-wanderer, too, likely to take off walking, down into town or out into the country for the day, sometimes with a few friends, sometimes alone, indifferent, really, even in a gang, to much outside my own preoccupations. I was odd, I realise now, always something held back, always the sense that other people weren't quite real. I'd have moments, like that afternoon with my grandfather looking at the photo of *Rimutaka*, when I'd connect with my dad, or rather when he'd connect with me, see something of what was going on inside my mind, get some sense of who (what?) I was. Those were good moments. Suddenly I have a vivid sense of his presence: I hold the jersey out from me for a moment, a gesture towards his shade, an unspoken claim on his pride. I'm out here for him, too, I realise, for the grandmother he never knew, on his behalf.

On deck some time after, still in a half-reverie, calling to see if Paula got my e-mail copying the piece I've filed for *The Irish Times*, I notice the moon's boat is reversed, and so is Orion. I have the dizzying sense that I'm looking up over the curve of the world towards home. For the first time, I sense the immensities out ahead of us, the great emptiness I both doubt and crave. Soon we'll be out of the channels, soon we'll be out there on the open ocean. Time is beginning to take on weight and depth, to balloon into space, great empty halls of it. Soon now, soon.

⚓

DAY

# 6

Wednesday, 10 May 2006

Up and ready to be off at 07.30. Everyone brisk and fresh, a sense of awakening spreading through the boat. We look drilled and competent this morning, fenders and lines coming in, being stowed, the galley below sparkling, everyone's cabin squared away, a certain surefootedness as people move about the boat. Steve spins us out and into the channel; we get the main up, the Yankee and staysail out and drawing without a word from the skipper. It's bright, blue and fresh out in the channel as we bear down to the east, a 2–3-metre chop, wind filling in from south-south-west. Marko, alas, is in no humour to appreciate the compliments as one by one his pilotage marks come up and take effect. He's seasick, as is Di, a miserable affliction. Puerto Williams falls away behind us, unremarked. You might think we were heading out for a day sail.

Macken's excellent *sopa Irlandesa* for lunch doesn't tempt the afflicted – stock, tomatoes, grated carrot, diced potato, onion, garlic and basil, zapped to a satisfying thickness and served with piping-hot bread rolls. My appetite is awake at last, and not just for food.

It's a day to relish, and I can feel the land, at last, beginning to fall away. The boat likes the wind, lifting and pulling as if she is eager to be off, out of these confines and into her proper element.

The channel is widening out. Around noon, we spot a huge raft of seabirds ahead, and soon we're sailing over a large shoal of fish. To starboard, under the feet of a colourful settlement, there's a fleet of small boats tied up. There are small, powerful seals leaping all around us, and flocks of gulls wheeling and hanging in the crisp air.

To port, on the Argentine side, there's a substantial white house on a rare piece of flat land. Well-gardened, cultivated, it has a tended look to it, a sense of order and purpose enhanced by the large greenhouse to one side of the dwelling-house, the smart fishing boat tied up at a small but substantial dock. Who could be living there, I wonder? Every now and then, coming down channel, we've passed these isolated homesteads, all evidently occupied, some ramshackle, some smartly painted, well-fenced and gardened. I imagine these are the homes of families who keep large flocks of sheep in the hills that roll back and away in ranks to the north, or maybe some industrious fisherman, or a merchant from Ushuaia, a retired naval officer, something like that. Somebody, Simon was it, speculates that these are the homes of Nazi fugitives or their descendants, men fleeing, literally, to the far ends of the earth. Isolation, I reflect, draws invention, stories. I think of when Paula was living in a remote patch of County Leitrim, how her love of herbs and gardening led, by some inevitable progression of the storytelling instinct, to a belief, widespread for miles around, that she 'had the cure' for minor ailments of people and animals. No more immune to this impulse than anyone else, I pass a happy half hour inventing a provenance, a whole exfoliated life, for whoever lives in that sturdy house by the water's edge.

Soon after, there's a semi-submerged wreck away off to port, sizeable and minatory. A freighter, judging by her stooped derricks, maybe 10,000 tonnes or even more, hard to tell at this angle, but, she's big, and she's run aground – whether forced by press of weather or victim of some navigation error, Steve can't tell us. Fed and Di take turns snapping each other with the wreck in the background, Steve looks longingly over his shoulder as we pass by, 'There's a lot of teak on board her still, you know? Got a great big lump of it down in the lazarette.' Inside every sailor there lurks a yearning pirate, a picker-up of unconsidered trifles, a scavenger of all that will come in useful some day, you never know.

Next thing there's a loud splash and a yell of 'man overboard'. Steve's chucked a bucket tied to a fender over the stern. I'm nearest to him, I point to the man overboard and keep pointing, no matter what, as Tony brings the wheel over, Kevin and Fed, hauling the main sheet amidships as we prepare to come about, Simon and Fed centring the staysail. Good man, Macken. He brings us round smartly, drifts us upwind of the bobbing fender. Justin switches off the engine, then lies down on deck, an arm hooked around the lifeline above him, and with Mike pressing down on his legs, he jabs the boathook, first time, into the rope linking bucket to fender. Pretty smart, I think to myself. 'Not bad,' says Steve, 'not bad. Tell you what, though, guys, you gotta remember it's bloody cold in there. Anyone goes in, we've only got minutes to get 'im out or that's it.'

The classes are getting intensive now. This afternoon, as the off watch, we have more navigation; already we've had knots, boat handling and weather. No end to learning.

Towards dusk, Steve brings us in to anchorage at Caleta Martial, Isla Herschel. Kevin takes me forward to drop the anchor; he's a good lad, Kev, his instructions clear and precise. We veer out a lot of chain, there's nowhere here on this low-lying island to put out lines to. The holding seems good, and it will have to be. Steve guns the engine hard in reverse to dig the pick in. We're lying head to wind, a steady 50 knots on the nose, and we really don't want the anchor to drag. The tension on board has ratcheted up a notch or two; when Steve goes below to call up tomorrow's weather, there are so many of us breathing down his neck he has to shrug off his jacket to cool down, use his elbows to fend us off.

We keep anchor watch all night, an hour each in the unrelieved, cold low keen of the wind. Snug in the wheel-house, one eye on the GPS to make sure we aren't moving (it's too dark to see transits), my ears strained for the sound of the chain dragging, I pass my hour sewing a handful of Chilean coins into the corner of a small Irish tricolour. Within minutes of being relieved, I drop into a deep, dreamless pit of sleep.

Anchored in 8.6 metres, Caleta Martial, Isla Herschel, 55° 49.30' S, 067° 17.68' W.

Garton Clay, from the well of St Garton in County Donegal, has this property when bestowed by a male Friel: it guarantees anyone who carries it on his person against death by fire and drowning. Seems to me a sensible thing to carry on a boat. Just in case, I have a few other pieces of the clay distributed here and there around the boat, and in my bag under the bunk, a woven pouch of Paula's with some lucky stones contributed by her and by my sister Margaret, and a charm in German wishing me always 1 metre of water under my keel, given me by a German lad under circumstances I no longer remember – and for full measure, a gesture towards the general good, there's also a woven reed St Brigid's cross hanging there in the saloon.

Not that I'm superstitious, but down there in the lizard brain is perfect awareness that out ahead is the great unknown, something vast and mysterious, full of strange unknowable powers – and the lizard brain never forgets. In nature's great economy, every advance in consciousness is overlaid on what went before it; in the day-to-day, we live unthinkingly in the mode most familiar to us, what we call, with unconscious irony perhaps, the present tense; exceptional circumstances can send us burrowing to the bottom of the kitbag for whatever worked in the past, whatever made sense in the past, not just the personal or cultural past but the deep past of the species. One of the deeper instincts, which is to say one of the deeper survival strategies, is blind propitiation, the recourse to amulets, gestures, signs and signifiers that will attract the benevolence of great forces, deflect evil intent, ensure a safe alignment with whatever powers are in play. Everyone on board, the skipper not least, has made a detailed, rational survey of boat, crew and weather. Equally, I'm sure of it though we do not speak of it, everyone on board has made their own private bargain with the unknowable unknown. Sailing is a science, where informed thought guides decisions about course and weather, informed thought prepares the boat, informed thought estimates dangers, and the counter-moves to deal with dangers. Minute by minute, second by second *in extremis*, the good sailor is thinking, thinking, thinking. But, sailing is also an art, an act of daring and attunement, an aligning of self and boat with wind, water, past and future, a trusting of the vulnerable unrepeatable self to a passage with danger. Sailing is, in the deepest and widest sense, an act of pure faith.

Sailing is also, of course, dressing meticulously for the weather, eating, drinking and working. Climbing out on deck to look at the clouds, the sea state and such of my companions as are already up and about, I reach for a cig-arette and Kevin leans in with a light. 'Looking good my man, looking good.'

I stick my face out into the wind; south-west by God, perfect.

'Come on,' says Kevin, with his evil leer that means something backbreaking in the offing, 'I've got a nice little job for you and Justin.'

The nice little job is stowing the anchor. Great. Bloody thing weighs a ton, it's so well dug in that Steve has to motor forward to break it out, then we wrestle it aboard, careful, careful, clip a halyard to it and very slowly work it across the deck, lower it slowly through the forward hatch. Kev beds it down on a heavy pad of rubber, right forward in the bows – and then spends maybe twenty minutes sweating and cursing and wriggling, half the time upside down, his face and the air around him purple, until the brute thing is so securely lashed down it might have been welded there. It needs to be. For the next four weeks, this boat will be bucking and slamming, climbing and dropping off waves with unimaginable force; if this anchor works loose we might as well be at the mercy of a lunatic run amok with a jackhammer.

'Blimey,' says Justin, when Steve has satisfied himself by jumping up and down on Kevin's cat's cradle of lashings, 'I'd hate to be trying to retie that out there.'

'Ah,' says Macken, materialising overhead, 'the English gift for understatement.'

'Fuck off,' says Justin, wittily.

Everyone's crammed in the cockpit and on the afterdeck when we go up. Nice angle of heel, main, staysail and Yankee set and pulling hard, 45–50 knots of wind from the west now, storm force 10. We're delighted with ourselves. You can smell the open ocean at last, we're getting the first big swells of the trip, locking down and into the great watercourse that circles Antarctica like some mighty river. The wind blows around the bottom of the globe unimpeded, free and mighty, driving the seas before it in an endless pounding flow. We're making good speed, our exhilaration doubled with our sense of relief that we won't, after all, our most secret unspoken fear, be rounding in a flat calm. Up there ahead of us off the port bow, lit by sheets of pale-gold sun, the spires and pinnacles of Cathedral Rock stand jagged and clear.

Salt on the wind now, drifts and gusts of it, we're like racehorses scenting the off, nostrils flared, feet wide-planted, all staring ahead when we're not stealing glances at each other, at the near and far horizons. Steve has his hands in his pockets, riding the roll, enjoying our sense of happiness, grateful the wind has come through for us, happy as we are to be out at last into the open sea.

There's a long plunge to the boat's rhythm, the bow dipping down and in, hesitating a moment, then coming up and on and out before hanging a second in the spumy air, then plunging down and on again, down and on and up again, and on. The water curls back along the sides like a furrow opening to the plough, sheen of black water edged with foam, curling in behind us then roaring out and off in a broad track of turbulent green and white and grey. Fed's claimed the wheel, his gloved hands almost welded to it, exhilaration pounding through him. We bear down like a train on Cathedral Rock, preparing to gybe onto the port tack. Ah now, that's too much, that's altogether too much: a great rainbow flashes into the sky, a great arch over the turning point and we're rocketing into it, right under the brilliant curve of it. Hold it, hold it, steady – now! We leap to the winches, sheet her in hard, Fed spins the wheel and there ahead of us and to port as we clear through and under the great rainbow stands the Horn, a squat grey powerful pyramid against a lowering sky, a faint scribble of foam at its feet. And oh how we're powering along now, the tall sails tilted towards the Pole, the whole expanse to the north of us clear, and ours alone. Out here, immensities. Under our keel, the boneyard of ships that has made this a place of foreboding for centuries. Impossible not to think of them all, the ungainly galleons, the stubby traders, great majestic cloud-sailed four masters and the troopships, the freighters and cargo ships that have foundered here and gone down, down forever into the lightless dark. Impossible not to feel bone-deep cold somewhere inside at the press of those lives smashed under here in terror and cold, in great bellows of despair, whimpers and roaring curses. And we plunge on, the wind from behind us beating our faces if we look behind, muttering and silent, whooping and silent, all of us here together, with and for each other, crossing some line here, each of us breaking through into some private lightening of the spirit that we will never be able to name, never again be able to let go.

Fed is exultant, his face bright with ineffable joy. 'Hey, Fed, will you ever be as happy again?'

He can hardly speak, but he flashes a great smile down at me, 'No never, never...'

He'll be an old man, in an airport somewhere, maybe visiting a grandson, a granddaughter, his bag at his feet, a bustle everywhere and he'll think of this moment and light up like a torch, he'll think of himself as a young man and he'll say to himself, in a whisper, 'That was me, that was me, by God, helming round Cape Horn.' I will always think well of us, all of us, that not for a moment did anyone else ask to take the wheel.

Absurd, of course, to down play the moment, but in truth the cold island peak to the north of us was – just that. Forbidding, yes, grim and lowering even in this clear light, but a psychic more than a physical landmark for all the effect it had on us. The lore of the sea is full of terrors, and most of them are real. This *is* a terrible place when the wind and the seas of winter build up to fury – we are seamen enough to recognise that this would be a cold, implacable hell in the wrong conditions, even if we had no foreknowledge of the place and its perils. Darwin was beaten back from here, even that extraordinary sailor Bligh failed in his three attempts to round it. It's infinitely worse going the other direction, of course, east to west, but even so… We are very conscious of how many men and women have perished here, how many ships, well-found or damaged, have gone down here, but we have all of us on board seen worse days, worse weather. Strange, too, how often the literature is laconic, even dismissive, of what is by any yardstick a defining moment in a sailor's life. Dana, in *Two Years Before the Mast*, stands to his duties below decks as his ship rounds, emerging only to record, 'There lay the land, fair upon the larboard beam, and slowly edging away upon the quarter.' Vito Dumas, in his 1942 solo circumnavigation, broke his nose just before rounding, which understandably preoccupied him – so that all we have of the Horn from this heroic sailor when he eventually staggers on deck is, 'I could not observe the slightest scrap of land; only a bank of clouds to the north indicated its presence.' The great Moitessier (in the wonderfully titled *Cape Horn: The Logical Route*) is even more laconic: 'The cloudy skies of the Pacific gave way to rather clearer weather on the "good side" of South America. The Horn rounded, we had gybed at dawn and were now heading…' – into history, as it happens, but he didn't know that.

The meridian that divides the Pacific from the Atlantic oceans runs through the great Cape, but, it seems to me at this moment, that there is another line crossed here, one that calls to mind the wise old Sufi adage: 'He who knows does not speak; he who speaks does not know.'

Great facts are just facts, in the end. We powered past in a barrage of camera shutters and flashes, the reflex of proof, anticipated memory; I got my photographs with my blue shirt, with my Piarsaigh jersey, with the big wind-ravelled tricolour I had carried on an earlier journey across the North Atlantic whipping over my head. Now we were past, or nearly, the cold truth coming over us that, out there, ahead lies 4,500 miles of rolling ocean.

Nearly everyone's gone below now, busy with one banal thing or another, the ordinary reasserting its honest sobriety.

I lean into the gantry over the stern, one arm hooked round the upright; with my free hand, I rummage in my jacket pocket. The coins feel too light, sewn into the corner of the small Irish flag. I call up my grandfather in my mind's eye, my father, my brothers and sisters, uncles and cousins and aunts, but the pictures are blurred and hard to bring in focus. I hold the small flag for a moment over the turbulent wake and then open my hand. I open my hand and let it go. A long time she's been turning down there in the cold and the dark, great grandmother, mother of us all, the long line of us coming down to now, your mother before you, and her mother… And here I am, I whisper, here I am, named for your son but unhoped for, I'm sure of it, in your last moments. How far it must have been from your thoughts, that one of us would come back, that some day one of us would come here to claim you. And how far back now, too, the child hearing for the first time of how you died out here, giving birth to my grandfather; how far back that child's mind gone cold at the story, unable even to frame the thought that someday, grown old himself, he would stand here on a plunging deck, suspended and shivering over this great empty void, and send skidding down through the cold and wayward currents, down to that dark floor where your bones went down forever, a flag, a handful of coins, this simple acknowledgement, this wordless prayer of gratitude.

Diane calls quietly from the shelter behind me, 'Are you all right there, Theo?' And I nod before turning, once, twice, wiping my face. I'm fine. I'm fine. I go forward on the port side, to the shrouds.

That big old tricolour is still flying, back in the Atlantic again. As I haul it down I call to mind that great sailor Conor O'Brien, the first man to round the Horn in a small boat, the 42-foot *Saoirse*. The Civil War was just over when he set sail in 1923 on his two-year circumnavigation, the flag he carried so proudly through these waters was the flag of a nation still reeling in bitterness and confusion, still reeking of gunsmoke and blood, tottering, battered and uncertain. The very name of his boat, *Saoirse*, Freedom, has a ring of defiance to it, and of hope. My grandfather fought for that flag, he came home from New York, having barely left home, to take his modest part in the War of Independence. I imagine the frisson it must have given O'Brien, to be looking back at the Horn, homeward bound, that flag carried in the breeze behind him.

I look back myself once more, but beyond all flags, to the mystery that will linger forever in these icy dark waters for me and for all my family: we owe our lives, and generations yet unborn will owe their lives, to pure chance, to a random stroke of fate. Had there not been a wet nurse on board the *Rimutaka*, someone to take that unlucky infant into her generous arms, my grandfather would certainly have died, a whole bright line of consciousness would have gone down into the void, and we would have lain forever in the unborn dark of time.

It's cold now. The great Cape is fading back into the distance, the day turning surly, cold and grey. We were given safe passage, I think, and I feel grateful. Something ferocious and ancient and ungovernable took a long, hard look at us, and let us go. This time.

We sail on into the afternoon, twenty miles by the plot, due east, until it's time to turn north-eastward for Stanley. Going down, I check the chart reflexively, the time, boat speed and heading. The same instinct now with us all. Seafaring. Simon hands up a cup of soup, he smiles. I'm grateful for it, the soup and the smile. The comradeship.

⚓

DAY

# 8

Friday, 12 May 2006

My right hand's slightly damaged; I must have knocked it on something, the truth is I can't remember. Odd, that. I have become more than usually conscious of my body. The result is, in any case, a certain difficulty writing.

Since we left the Wollastons yesterday morning, Justin, Tony and Marko have been seasick. It's an affliction I wouldn't wish on anyone, not just for the physical misery it brings but for the energy-sapping battle against despondency that follows it, like some dark twin. These three are experienced sailors, but, as I've learned in the past, this is an illness that strikes where it will. A relative novice like myself can be spared, a hoary old salt be laid low for days on end. Tony and Justin stand to their work when and as they can, but I'm starting to get worried about Marko. For days now he's been a bit lost in himself, abstracted, not quite with us. At first I think it's a language thing, but his English is as good as Fed's, so I end up discounting that. I've been sharing a cabin with him, the foremost cabin of the three on the starboard side, but for reasons best known to himself, he's taken to sleeping on the seats in the saloon. Says he feels claustrophobic in the cabin.

I don't like the cabin much either, too far forward for me. The midships cabin, twin bunks off the passageway, behind a curtain as opposed to a door, has been occupied by Simon and Diane since we set out. In one of those Byzantine manoeuvres that make perfect sense at the time, Simon switches to my, lower, bunk in the forward cabin, Diane stashes her gear up in what was Simon's bunk, I stash mine on the upper bunk in what is now Simon's cabin and Marko keeps the locker space he already had. Now I have what I consider the best sleeping spot in the boat, because midships in any sailing boat is where the motion is least, the noise from the slamming bow as distant as the chatter in the wheelhouse and cockpit. This, of course, is only possible because Diane and I are in opposite watches, which means we can hot bunk all the way over to Cape Town. We each get a premium berth this way, and we're well satisfied. Nobody can quite figure out the advantage to Simon in all this, but then Simon is a law unto himself anyway, so it's probably best not to enquire too deeply into his reasoning. Perhaps it's the banker's inveterate love of being behind closed doors?

But Marko, now, Marko is worrying me a bit. I see he's not eating much but he doesn't respond to coaxing. He stands aside in our watch, does what he's asked and does it well, but he isn't coming forward, he isn't making the effort. Justin is worried, too, 'Have you noticed how grey in the face Marko is getting?'

I have, and so has Kevin, but we say nothing, least of all to Steve. In the nature of things, the skipper is out of the watch system; he comes and goes when needed, and according to some arcane instinct of his own. He doesn't necessarily see what a watch leader sees, or what your companions in the watch see; in this case, a slow but definite withdrawal from life on board. Our instinct is to shield Marko, to give him time, but that can only last so long.

Earlier today, there was a telling incident. Steve and Kevin were up on the foredeck when Steve called back to Marko to ease the sheet on the Yankee. There's a way to do this: you jerk the sheet out of the self-tailer, the rubber jaws on top of the winch; you take two of the four turns off the barrel of the winch and then, one hand holding the tail of the sheet, with the palm of the other hand, you allow the load from the sail to ease the remaining turns slowly, very slowly, off the barrel. The effect when this is done right is twofold: the sheet feeds out nice and slowly, and you keep control at all times. It sounds more complicated than in fact it is; any competent sailor will do it by touch and instinct. For whatever reason, though, Marko lost control of the sheet, with spectacular results. The Yankee blasted forward, and then began to whip wildly back and forth, Steve and Kevin had to dive smartly out of the way – a sail flogging like this has awesome power and could conceivably kill a man, and Marko, grabbing for the sheet, could very easily have lost an arm. I think it was Justin, poor seasick Justin, who managed to get a turn over the winch and tame the beast, but it was an ugly few seconds.

I've done stupid things myself on boats, probably everyone has, but that lapse of attention on Marko's part could have had tragic results. Steve, shaking with rage, came storming back to the side-deck, roaring at Marko. Then Marko began to argue back, and that's when I really began to worry about him. When you fuck up like that, you shut your mouth and take the roasting you've so richly earned. You don't argue – and if you think you can argue with this particular skipper then, friend, you haven't been paying attention.

Nothing much is said, then or later, but long after Steve has gone down and Marko has retreated to the after rail in wounded silence, staring back sightlessly along our track, everyone on the watch, Kevin included, is giving all this some serious thought. Marko's a nice guy, and we know from the e-mails he sent us all, long before we came out here, that he's really been looking forward to this journey. When he's been functioning well, as for instance when piloting us down a stretch of the Beagle Channel, he's been impeccable and clearly enjoying himself. Now, though, he isn't enjoying himself. It might be a health thing, something he doesn't feel comfortable talking about; it might be the strain of living with strangers at such close quarters; it might be, I touch on the question delicately, even when turning the thought over only in my own mind, fear of the vastness out ahead, the long silences and storms we all anticipate. Maybe, to be blunt, this isn't what he thought it would be.

I don't know how to broach this with him, and neither does anyone else. There's another side to this, too, a more brutal, unfair and even savage consideration. Marko's developing that thousand-yard stare: I don't feel comfortable with the thought that he might become overwhelmed out there in the great beyond – as, to be fair, any of us might. I don't want to be on watch some night in big seas in the dark and pitch of things when he loses it, decides he can't take it anymore. There is, of course, nothing in the man's behaviour to suggest such extreme possibilities, but we're jumpy, in a dangerous place, and this is the way the mind works.

The day wears on into the night, the bright banner of the Milky Way streaming out overhead, the Southern Cross flying proudly against a deep black sky. We're over the Burdwood Bank now, and it's ugly stuff. These are comparatively shallow waters south-west of the Falklands/ Malvinas, as little as 44 metres under us at times while we've just come through the top of the Yaghan Basin where depths run to 4,000 metres. That's a lot of water climbing a very high step, and it makes for rough, unpredictable sailing. We're getting lumpy 2–3-metre seas, the boat's being kicked every which way and we're making 10 knots over the ground, the wind still hard from the northwest. Sick as they are, Justin and Tony take their turns helming; weak as they are from the continuous vomiting, they're both better at this than I am. Ah well, I console myself, plenty of time for learning yet.

It's a wild night, our first taste of rough weather, and I go on deck before turning in, thinking perhaps to attune myself to this, to get the feel of what's to come. The Burdwood Bank, the Burdwood Bank... it comes back to me all of a sudden. This is where the ill-fated *Belgrano* was sailing when HMS *Conqueror* sank her with three torpedoes in 1983. *Belgrano,* the first ship to be sunk by a nuclear submarine (that we know of) had, curiously, survived the attack on Pearl Harbour – she was originally the USS *Phoenix.* The sinking, I recall, generated a great deal of controversy at the time, some commentators claiming she had been sailing away from the Falklands/Malvinas when she was sunk – but the tactical manoeuvres of warships change moment by moment, and it would be naive to imagine she didn't pose a threat to British interests. In fact, as Admiral Enrique Molina Pico, head of the Argentine Navy in the 1990s, subsequently said, the ship was engaged in a war and, in that sense, was a legitimate target. In the calculus of war, perhaps, the term 'legitimate target' has a certain validity; to my way of thinking, given *Belgrano*'s vulnerability to submarines (no escort of destroyers, probably little or nothing in the way of sonar to give her warning), the sinking was closer to butchery than to a 'legitimate' act of war. The action is now chiefly remembered for the infamous London *Sun* headline, 'Gotcha' – but that headline only appeared in early northern editions of the paper, and was withdrawn almost immediately when the scale of casualties became known. Nobody knows how many died on the ship, how many succumbed to the icy cold of these turbulent waters, but 323 men perished here, and it's all too easy to imagine their terror, their anguish and despair, their bleached bones tumbling now in the slow current that sweeps through these shallows and out into the black deeps of the Southern Ocean.

Just before the end of our watch, Steve appears silently in the blue glow of the wheelhouse, asks for an ETA for Stanley. I have it worked out, double-checked with Justin. 'About 16.00 tomorrow,' I say.

'Hmm, sounds about right, maybe earlier if the wind picks up. Who're you handing over to?'

'Fed, probably.'

'Righto, make sure you give him the ETA, get him to keep adjusting it if the wind picks up, be a nice exercise, eh?'

Before going down he asks Justin and Tony how they're feeling, has a chat and a smoke with Kev. And then he's gone again. Marko sits in a corner of the deck shelter, silent, his face turned to the sky behind.

⚓

DAY

# 9

Saturday, 13 May 2006

Diane calls from the passageway, 'Come on, Theo, time to get up.'

Stiff, slow, I drag myself into the world. Can't see my watch face, eyes won't focus; ah, 06.50, ten minutes to the change of watch.

Ten minutes to dress and stagger up, be met with a mug of tea. The sacred duty of the watch going off, to have everyone's drink of choice ready and waiting at the handover.

Out in the dark for a cigarette, a blast of cold air. Yo Kev, Yo Debs, Yo Simon – the nicotine solidarity society. Sea, check. Sky, check. Stars, check. Wake, phosphorescent, check. Various dim shapes, sheets and lines, black against black, all in their usual places, check. Right then, still here evidently.

Last night's watch somehow let the wind get behind them, gybing the boat. This is not a terribly good idea, the sudden change of direction causes the foresails to back, the main to slam over, putting big strains on the rigging and mast. Steve, not pleased, was up from sleep as if shot out on deck, yelling and sorting things out. A chastening experience for all concerned, and our comrades are somewhat subdued this morning as a result. I have the good sense, groggy as I am, to bite my tongue and not ask who was on the helm at the time.

The present watch system is a bugger. It looks innocuous if you write it out as a table:

| 1 | 07.00–13.00 |
|---|---|
| 2 | 13.00–19.00 |
| 3 | 19.00–23.00 |
| 4 | 23.00–03.00 |
| 5 | 03.00–07.00 |

Consider, our watch is on now until 13.00, which means that, in theory, the other watch gets six hours sleep. In practice, of course, on a normal day, they'll be foostering about for an hour or so, having breakfast, talking, tidying their bunks and effects, maybe doing some washing. Then they'll be up again at 13.00 for lunch, prepared by us, and on duty for another six hours. The afternoon watch has to clean the boat, top to bottom, stem to stern. Every day. Meticulously. And are we in our cosy bunks while they're doing that? We are not. We're in the wheelhouse with Steve, labouring our way through the next section of the Yachtmaster course. The afternoon watch now has to prepare dinner, while we sail the boat from 19.00 to 23.00. If we've any sense, we're in the bunks pronto then, only to wake again at 03.00. Which means that at 07.00 tomorrow, we'll be milling about for an hour or so, having breakfast, talking… and this will go on for, it will soon begin to seem, all eternity.

None of which matters today, of course, because today we will be in Stanley.

Stanley, Steve tells us, will be the end of the road for Marko, who has decided to leave the ship there. A medical problem, says Steve, something to do with his heart. Marko says nothing. I feel sorry for the guy, but it's clearly better for him to go now, and better for us, too, if I'm blunt. On a passage like this, you're either sailing the boat or you're not. We haven't minded that he hasn't really made himself part of the watch so far, but I'm not the only one, it will later turn out, who has been thinking of asking Steve if he thought Marko was up to the long weeks ahead.

'Well, Marko,' I say to him, when we get a chance to talk, 'I'm sorry you have to leave, but you're going home a Cape Horner.'

'Yes,' he says, 'I know, thank you. You know, I haven't drunk anything since we left Punta Arenas. Really, this is very bad for my health, you know. And also, I cannot eat this English food on this boat.'

And with that he goes below, to pack his bags.

'What d'you make of that?' asks Justin.

Kevin just shrugs, eyebrows climbing to his hairline, 'Beats me, buddy. Beats me.'

'How long d'you think he'll stay in Stanley?' I ask Tony, who's having a rare moment with his pipe.

'Oh jay, he'll be gone in a few hours. There's a flight this afternoon early, Steve arranged it all on the e-mail.'

It's bright now, clear lemon light under a thin blue sky, small clouds racing by high up. We can see the islands low on the horizon ahead of us.

'Right then,' says Steve, mug of tea in one hand, cigarette in the other, 'I guess nobody's going to sleep, eh? Simon, Tony, you guys bring us in. You're in charge now, get on with it.'

We're bang on the course Diane and I laid out all that time ago (was it only two days?) but now, of course, they'll need a pilotage plan for the close work inshore. Scurry, scurry, scurry. Pencils, protractors, dividers, chart, cross-check with plotter, disagree, do the sums again, agree... it's fine entertainment for the rest of us, the more so when Tony calls up a course change to Kevin who's minding the wheel for him, and we can see that we'll miss the harbour entrance by a couple of hundred metres if we follow that bearing. Of course nobody says anything until Tony pops up, Simon behind him with the hand-drawn chart, the calculations and deliberations of two fine minds.

Cap'n Macken is brisk. 'Righto, Kev, I'll take the wheel now, thanks.'

Steve has a wicked grin on his face, the rest of us are poker-faced.

'Eh, Tony? Take a look ahead, mate.'

Macken looks up from squinting at the compass in the harsh light. 'What, oh Jesus. Simon, show me those figures again...'

Just as well, I suppose: strong as she might be, I doubt our fine *Pelagic* can sail through a cliff.

North-east of the harbour entrance, HMS *Liverpool* is riding to her anchor off Mengeary Point, launches coming and going ferrying men and gear. I'm keeping a leery eye on the Seal Rocks and Billy Rock behind them, at the south side of the entrance.

For sport, and because Macken at the wheel is nominally in charge of our vessel, I run up the Irish tricolour to the port spreader. There's more than mild mischief here, though; I'm remembering Conor O'Brien, who called here for coal and supplies and whose notes on the flora and fauna of the islands are still of considerable use. Macken has somehow contrived to get his pipe going while standing to the wheel, so I get a fine photograph of him as he brings us through the entrance, flag fluttering proudly over his woolly-hatted head. And then, because fun is fun but the law of the sea is sober and serious, I take the flag down again.

There's a long east–west channel into Stanley between two low-lying spurs of land, and then the turn to port at Navy Point through a narrow pass into the harbour proper, which also lies east–west. We've a mix of charts on board, some call the islands Las Malvinas, some The Falkland Islands, which is why we've been using the hybrid term (well, not Justin, it has to be said), but it's clear that we're running into the Falklands. The houses are timber frame, planked in shiplap, mostly white or green with red roofs of corrugated iron, many with neat white-painted picket fences; in fact it looks very like Puerto Williams, but with a certain indefinable air of English gentility. As we get closer in, we see vehicles passing here and there, mostly Land Rovers, driving on the left. Stanley faces north, the houses, warehouses and sheds terraced on a low-rising hillside, and the morning sun is flashing off window panes as we turn and nose quietly towards our berth. The deck is a flurry of activity as we haul up mooring lines and fenders, Simon trying to keep order as Steve, who's taken the wheel now, gives us short bursts of engine power; we glide towards a distinctly rough-looking dock, buffeted slightly by offshore gusts.

The guys who take our lines seem afflicted with shyness, all smiles, few words, and when they do speak it's in a curious accent, something of Dorset in it, something of Cornwall, but softer, more hesitant. It seems to take a long time to tie up, lines running this way and that, bowlines, sternlines, springs moving from bollard to bollard... and nobody quite understanding what's going on.

However we manage it, finally all falls quiet. The customs man is so shy and self-effacing, he's been and gone before most of us realise he's even arrived – though of course they know Steve, and the boat, here. And then all the lines have to come off again! There's a big north-north-west gale coming, it seems, and this berth will be too exposed. My turn on the wheel, Steve tells me, so off we go again, if only for a half-mile or so. This time we fetch up in the lee of a giant floating dock, oil-covered, held together by spot-welding it seems to me; it's called Fipass, was brought in here to act as a landing stage for men, munitions and *matériel* in 1982. Later we'll learn it's condemned, but nobody seems disposed to put up the money to replace it. So here, it seems, is home for the next few days, lying north–south behind a big deep-sea fishery protection vessel. Beyond that, looking battered and forlorn but evidently still in working condition, lies a Japanese longliner.

A local friend of Steve's eventually turns up in a minibus and trundles us off to the pub. Well, of course. Do we not deserve a drink? Are we not hardy sailors? Have we not been round Cape Horn?

The Victory seems transplanted in its entirety from some small market town in middle England – Ledbury, say: fake Tudor beams, English bottled beers and cigarettes, darts and pool, laddish raucousness, a big gang of sailors-squaddies-expats hulloing and hooraying, scoffing crisps and swilling pints. With all that, there's a quaintly proper air to the place, a sense of decorum even. They accept sterling, but the change comes in Falkland pounds. I believe it was Justin, the Admiral rising to the occasion, who shouldered to the bar and called the first round, though it might just have been Big Mike, who has a happy knack of unobtrusively getting his own way. So here we are then, legs still rubbery, salt-washed and spray-blown, with pints in our hands, when it dawns on us all at the same time, hey, you know what? We did it, by God. We went to the Horn, down to the great Cape, around and up and out – and here we are!

A kid from HMS *Liverpool* spins into the conversation, a Scottish lad. 'Hey, great, I heard you talking there, are you from Cork? I love Cork, me. I sail National 18s, you know? I recognised your accent. I'm from Findhorn, me, I had a great time in Cork, racing, brilliant! D'you know…?' and he reels off a list of names, young sailors like himself. Of course I don't know any of them, but he doesn't mind, he just wants to tell me how much he loves Cork and Cork people and he had a brilliant time there and, 'Have you lads just come up from Cape Horn? Brilliant! What's it like? I'd love to do that, properly like, sailing it like! Brilliant!' And he spins off back into the boy-scrum of his mates, chock-full of life and happiness and explanations. Moments later, we are treated to a ragged cheer, a wall of glasses lifted high in salute. Nice.

I slip out of the confusion with a phonecard – no mobile signal here – and find a phone box. It takes a while to estab-lish a connection through AT&T. So good to hear her voice in my ear, so strange to be looking out through the small windows of the red box at a row of North-of-England ter-raced stone houses roofed in green corrugated. A melancholy conversation in part; her e-mails have been bounced back to her (and here I've been, feeling fed-up that she hasn't been in contact), and now she's despondent, says don't bother sending me any more… short, painful silences in the conversation, hesitancies, awkwardness. She's been clearing boxes of books out of the garden shed (I feel guilty I didn't get around to this before leaving), getting on with the daily round, while here I am at the end of the world, taking a break from the pub to phone home. How many variations on this conversation have flowed out of this box, I wonder, discomfited to think how banal and not particu-lar our situation here is. 'Look, I'll tackle Steve about the

e-mails, I hadn't realised this was happening, I'll sort it out.'
We put our phones down eventually, unwilling perhaps to
admit just how much our common sadness is to do simply
with missing each other so much.

Justin is walking down the hill. 'Came out for a bit of
air,' he says, and something registers with him, I see it on
his face. 'Phoning home, were you? How's Paula? It's a
bugger sometimes, isn't it, the distance? C'mon, lad, let's
take a stroll.'

Down on the waterfront to our right a visitor centre (!),
some stores, a souvenir shop. Shops to our left, then a stone
church with a huge arch of whalebone ribs to one side of it.
Everything spruce, neat, newly painted. On past what must
be the Governor's house, a Queen Anne affair, red brick set
back in a neat sweep of gardens, the green corrugated roof
more than incongruous. OK, what is it with the corrugated?
On the face of it, a daft choice for this cold wet climate;
unless you paint it constantly it will rust like buggery, so
why? It can only be that here, as in Puerto Williams, everything has to be cheap, and as light as possible. Everything
has to come in by sea. Tonne for tonne, you cover more roof
with corrugated than with slate or tiles.

War memorials are an ambiguous comfort to the living,
and useless to the dead. They make me uneasy. I understand the urge to commemorate, to cast in bronze or carve
in stone the names of the dead. But all too often, that name
there marks a full stop in a family line, the smack of the
bullet bringing a long story to an abrupt end, cancelling
who knows what unknown futures, writing *finis* to a
tangled and rich inheritance. This evening I feel more
painfully than usual the sense of waste, and the precar-
iousness of life. How many never-to-be-born stand in the
ghostly penumbra of each name here? How many lives trail
back into the past, ancestors passing the spark of life on,
blindly perhaps, but in hope, only for that long line to be

guillotined here, casually almost, certainly with indifference. More than all this I hate the great lie, the *dulce et decorum est*, the way brutes like Galtieri and Thatcher spend blood as if it were treasure, theirs to dispose of in the great games of power.

For Justin, though he doesn't speak of it, perhaps fearing I won't understand, this is a place of pilgrimage. We stand there, silently reading the names, imagining how they died, thinking of what they died for. I have Sassoon in mind – 'And when the war's all done, and youth stone dead/I'd toddle safely home and die, in bed.' – but I don't know what Justin is thinking, and I don't want to ask, I don't want to intrude.

Among the names of dead sailors inscribed here, 'C. Chan, laundryman.' Ah you poor fecker, I think, so young, so far from home, so far from your own place and your own people. And then I think that's true for them all, convinced or deluded, simple or brave: they died here, each one of them by himself, far from their own place and their own people. It's full dark now, the wind is getting up, it's cold. Wordlessly we turn back, swinging our arms and clapping our hands. Dispelling the ghosts.

'Where've you been? We've just ordered; looks good.'

The Brasserie has commended itself to our comrades for two very good reasons: one, it's right next door to The Victory and, two, it's the only restaurant open in Stanley on Saturday night. It's doing a roaring trade, and we're lucky to have found a table.

'No, not lucky,' says Simon, 'Steve booked us all in earlier.'

'Where is Steve, by the way, and Kevin and Debs?' Simon nods towards the far corner, where all three are in animated conversation with, evidently, old friends. 'Welcome to the kiddies' table,' says Simon. 'Where've you been?'

The waitresses are Latina, Chilean and Argentinian, bored, disinclined to make conversation. The service is quick, the food indifferent, the wine good. I don't suppose they get too many boats in at this time of year, but I have to hand it to the locals, they make a great job of acting casual, as if we weren't there at all. And perhaps, to them, we aren't. If you make your life in an isolated place, clannish, still mildly traumatised, uneasy about your future, it's easy to slip into a mindset where all you can trust is what and who you know, and everything from the outside is a threat of some kind. Perhaps to these well-fed, scrubbed and indifferent people, we don't seem quite real, as the Scouse sailors next door aren't quite real, nor the soldiers and airmen and women up there behind us on the hill.

Not that it really matters to us – apart from Simon, whose flirting instinct seems to have flared up, to no avail; we're all of us simply happy to be here, chattering and bantering. Bit by bit, we're putting together the trip so far, the mosaic of impressions, the bits of lore, perceptions and hunches and judgements that will flow into the narrative of the trip, the agreed wide-angle version of what we've been doing and where we have been.

The minibus driver pops his head around the corner; we settle the bill, shuffle and circle our way into our coats and make for the door. Simon is last out; he gets a dazzling smile from the young waitress as she holds the door for him and nearly falls down the step in surprise. She gives him a little wave, compounding the damage. I see hope flare, but Simon doesn't know yet that The Brasserie is closed tomorrow.

So difficult to know what is the mask and what isn't. On deck some time later, in the glare of the decklights from the fishery protection vessel, I'm having a glass of wine with him when he says, out of the blue, 'I have immense trouble forming friendships.'

How unfathomable people are. How many times now have I found myself in a moment like this, touched by a con-

⚓

DAY

# 10

Sunday, 14 May 2006

An air of torpor in the boat. Sore heads, the processing of
fading dreams, simple exhaustion. I slept for ten hours,
found Diane in the galley, making breakfast for herself and
Fed. I have the faint but unmistakable feeling that I have
intruded on a domestic moment, Di over-brisk, Fed trying
not to smile too broadly. Ah, I think, saw that coming, but
I keep my face a mask. Truth is, I don't want to know.

'Tony's awake,' says Fed. 'Maybe it's time for some of
your famous Barry's tea?'

'You what?' says Di, 'what's he on about, Theo?'

'Ah, don't mind him,' I say; I'm not going to explain but, speak of the devil, down the steps comes Macken, fresh, brisk and full of the joys, not a bother on him and ready to explain the Creation to God.

'Barry's tea, my dear, is blended in Cork, where he's from and where I now live, have lived for the past twenty years. Barry's tea is mother's milk, it's tea as it should be, the nectar of the gods.'

'Oh,' says Di, 'is it good then?'

I learned a bitter lesson on my last long trip, when we ran out of Barry's halfway between Antigua and Kinsale; this time I've brought a good stash, and so, I discover, has Tony. I confess that one night back there in Punta Arenas we actually counted the tea bags, divided by two, divided again by the number of days predicted for the crossing, and arrived at the melancholy conclusion that, if we're careful, and ruthless in keeping the precious substance for our exclusive use, we should have just about enough to last us to Cape Town. Now amity is at war with greed, of course; our shipmates want a taste, even Fed, who thinks tea weakens the blood and makes the English lousy lovers. Which earns him a look from Di, and a stare from Macken who's intercepted the look and is now looking with frank curiosity from Fed to Di and back again, making them both blush. Now here's Justin, 'What's this about the English, eh?' And then, sensing the atmosphere, 'What's all this then, am I missing something?'

'No, no,' says Tony, resignedly, 'I was just going to make some Barry's tea.'

'Oh, good stuff that,' says Justin. 'Yes please. How are the supplies holding up?'

Oh dear. 'Anyone prefer coffee?' I ask, hoping to ease Tony's pain.

'No, no, tea would be fine.' Right, tea it is then.

'Make it weak,' I mutter to Tony, crowding him in the galley, 'put 'em off.'

I get a wounded stare for my troubles, as if the thought hadn't occurred to him. 'Make sure you take one of these two mugs,' he says, 'these two here.'

The wind's come up into a full, dry gale. 'What we need,' says the Admiral, bluff and hearty, 'is a good walk. Who's for a walk, then?'

All five of us, it seems. *Pelagic*, our sistership, is down in the little cove at the far southern end of the harbour. We'll have a look at her, and at whatever else turns up along the way. Up off the slip road to Fipass, past what looks like a junkyard, we turn left into Connemara. Bleak upland, bleached yellow and green and brown, tussocky with twisted heathers and reed-like grasses, not a tree to be seen, bog and gravelly low banks stretching away into the wind-blown distance.

What a godforsaken place to fight over, to die for.

There's what looks like a totem pole in the distance, far down the gravelled road. Fed brings out a neat pair of binoculars: 'It's a road sign,' he says.

Not far down the road, we pass a small patch of ground where turf sods are lying about, slowly mouldering back into the ground. Turf will never dry like that. Ancestral memory stirs, something in Macken and in myself is affronted. We hop up on the bank, to the mystification of the other three, and start footing the sods, making little tepees of three standing on end, laying a fourth sod horizontally across the top. 'I get it,' says Fed, turning to explain to Diane, 'this way the air gets to circulate between the pieces of mud, and they get dry.'

Mud?

'Blimey,' says Justin, 'can't take you Irish anywhere. Done a lot of this, have you? Cutting turf?'

'Have you?' I mutter to Tony.

'Not at all,' he mutters back, 'but sure we have to give 'em something to think about now and then.'

Right then, we stand back and survey our handiwork: bronze age innovation comes to the Falklands.

A Land Rover sputters past on the road, an incurious finger raised from the steering wheel our salute. The signpost is a monument to military homesickness and thirst. Thirty or forty carefully lettered wooden fingers point north-east, naming a litany of pubs, the distance to mates, family, the comfort of all that is home and the mundane worked out to the nearest mile: Swansea, Shropshire, Newcastle, Norwich, Liverpool, Huddersfield, Mile End, Hull, Edinburgh, Croydon, Inverness and Halifax... the dreams of a garrison at the far end of the world.

The boats, when we come upon them, delayed in thought for a while by the starkly-lettered sign at the head of the cove – 'Danger, Unexploded Mines' – look as if they have drifted to the end of the world. Out there across from us, the rusting hulk of an iron four-master, towed in here on fire more than 120 years ago, canted over somewhat towards the east, her masts still somehow standing. Down here below us, in various stages of time's ravages made stark and real, hulls and half-hulls, dismembered cockpits, ropes, chains, the frames of lobster pots and unrecognisable timbers in a fine confusion. A rickety jetty leads out to *Pelagic*, low in the water, her white paint rust-streaked, her sails sent down below, a tough but forlorn air to her, all set to sleep through an uneasy winter.

The boat we're sailing, *Pelagic Australis*, is one of two boats Skip Novak has sailing these waters, 'little' *Pelagic*, here before us, is older, smaller and altogether more industrial looking. Steel where we are aluminium, 52 feet where we are close to 72 feet. Novak, a famous racing sailor and skipper in his day, built her to prolong his dream of sailing in these southern waters, as an expedition ship to take climbers, sailors and adventurers to these ends of the earth. He tested his ideas on *Pelagic*, and what he learned from her, with the aid of designer Tony Castro, he brought to the design of *Pelagic Australis*. Here are the originals of the line drums that enabled us to tie up in Beagle Channel coves; here is the proof that the drop keel is a sound idea; here the proof that over-engineering is more than an exercise in paranoid caution. We stand there looking at her while Fed climbs aboard. The same thought is in all our minds, and Diane voices it: no wheelhouse.

She might as well say, no home to go to.

Back there to the north, hardly visible against the jetty, her white masts hard to pick out against the white-grey sky, *Pelagic Australis* is a testament to common-sense evolution. Granted, her heavy winches are manual, her hull unpainted no-nonsense aluminium, her fixtures and fittings robust and plain – but she has a wheelhouse, a high, dry snug place where the watch can navigate and drive, in shelter from weather come what may.

No wheelhouse on little *Pelagic*. There's a full gale now, a hard, dry, full gale, and it takes no effort to imagine what it would be like to be out at sea in this boat, rain crashing in waterfalls all around you, green water pouring back from the bow in sheets, the spray so thick you're breathing water, the boat pitching and thumping and lurching every which way, and you out on deck, stood there, helming, exposed to the full furious brunt of it all.

Novak's a hard man, a seasoned racer, a legend in some ways for his hardiness and daring, but he's not stupid, either: there's a certain romantic bravado about standing there and taking the worst the world can throw at you, I can see that, I can even, at a stretch, imagine myself taking it on; but there comes a point where hardiness slides over into masochism, and masochism has no place at sea. Sooner or later even the toughest man is beaten down and, all too often, if his pride has overmastered him, he takes the ship with him.

Good man, Skip, I think, that's a grand wheelhouse you built.

On the way back, we take turns to photograph each other leaning into the wind at improbable angles.

Later that afternoon, in The Globe pub, we fall into conversation with Derek from Glasgow. Derek's a butcher in a local abattoir, out here on contract, due to go home soon. He likes it out here, he says, 'keeps me out of trouble, you know what I mean'. Derek is compact and butty, tattooed, shaven-headed. When you walk into a strange bar, especially in a small closed place like Stanley, you scope out the clientele automatically, trouble radar on full. You'd have thought Derek with drink in him would be in your face before long, wanting to know what's your problem, pal? But Derek, because the world delights in confounding us, turns out to be a real sweetheart, gentle, inquisitive, helpful. 'You're off to Cape Town? Fancy a lamb? I can get you a good price – boned, rolled, jointed, whatever, all delivered to your ship.'

We think maybe Steve has his own source, but sure, we'll ask. 'Aye, whatever you like, pal, glad to help if you need it. Will you have a drink, to celebrate like? Ye're the lads came round Cape Horn? Fuck me, no way, not me. Mad fuckers ye are, still…'

'Listen,' I say, 'it was a lot less worrying than Saturday night in Glasgow.'

'Oh aye, d'ye know Glasgie then? D'ye know a wee pub…?'

After a brisk trot around Glasgow's contribution to the world campaign against dehydration, Justin rises. 'I thought I'd have a look in at Evensong, anyone interested?'

'I'll go with you,' says Tony. 'Sure, why not?'

We'll have one more pint with Derek, and then catch up with them. When we do, the murmuring congregation flowing past us in the dark, Justin has bagged a prize. He's recognised the Governor, marched up and introduced himself on the strength of their having a mutual friend. Howard Pearce is charm itself.

'Well lovely to meet you, Justin, and your friends. Tell you what, why don't you gather your captain and crew and come round for drinks tomorrow night, say 6.45? Cheerio, then.'

'Cheerio, cheerio.'

Paula's pre-departure instructions were, roughly, as follows: eat well, don't fall out of the boat, be careful, don't fall out of the boat, don't get into an argument about politics in the Falklands, keep in touch, don't fall out of the boat. Can I resist phoning her to tell her we're off to drinkies tomorrow with Her Majesty's Governor of the Falkland Islands? Of course I can't. But can I get through from that damned phone box? Of course I can't.

'Very precise time,' I observe to Justin as we head off in search of somewhere to eat.

'What do you mean?'

'Well, he gets the day's work done, then drinks with us, right?'

'Yes, your point, Sir?'

'And then we're off his hands just before dinner.'

'Ah.'

'It's the budget, you see,' I explain to him, 'still paying for Maggie's adventures. And sure anyway, one look at us and you can see we'd eat him out of house and home.'

'Stop spluttering, that man,' booms the Admiral at Macken, 'damn colonials.'

There's a bit of an atmosphere on the boat when we get back: Kevin is low-headed, like a half-stunned bull, Steve all wound up, Debs in tears and looking like thunder. Early night we all agree, unspeaking, as we file past. Let this blow over, whatever it is. Quick check for e-mails. Nada. Di has 'our' bunk, I take the berth above Simon's again, managing not to plant my foot in his face as I climb up.

'You're joking,' he says, when I tell him about tomorrow night. 'Cor, Justin's a cool customer, isn't he?'

'You don't know the half of it,' I tell him. 'Formal dress, of course. Medals to be worn. Goodnight.'

⚓

DAY

# 11

Monday, 15 May 2006

At breakfast, a ramshackle disjointed business of people
coming and going, Steve looks around at us and says, 'It's
true, you know? Harbours rot men and ships. Soon as
you've all finished waking up, everyone on deck.'

Simon, deadpan, is explaining the dress code for tonight
to Fed and Mike. He tips me the ghost of a wink.

Gale still blowing, it's cold, but we're soon in shirt-
sleeves as we set about the business of tidying the ship.
Mike and I get to unroll the long mooring lines from the

forward drums, laying them out in long hanks on the fore-deck, then carefully rolling them back onto the drums in neat parallel lines, the tail tucked neatly in. Wonder how long it'll be before these babies are rolled out again, Mike asks. Then, 'Y'know, I was just wondering. Do you think I should wear my actual medals tonight, or just the ribbons?'

'You brought the medals of course?'

'Oh yeah, you just never know, do ya?'

Fed and Simon have Mike all wrong, I reflect, chuckling to myself. The American laconic is a subtle business, and almost always the mask worn by a lightning-quick mind. Mike, back at the Horn, had asked me to photograph him with a curious flag: white, with the green outline of an oak tree.

'What's that, Mike?'

'Oh, well, that's George Washington's flag, you know? The tree of liberty.' The boy racers looked puzzled, but Mike just gave me that level look of his, waiting to see if the resonances and implications had registered. And then his short, satisfied nod when he saw they had.

'You know,' he says now, looking back at where Fed and Simon are coiling the lines of the aft drums, 'those two guys just aren't going to get along, are they?'

'You don't miss much, do you, Mike?'

'Waal,' he says, playing with the word à la John Wayne, 'I guess not.'

'Come on, then, Theo, Mike, got a job for ya.' We follow Steve out onto the landing stage, up the hill through the chain-link fence into a chaotic junk yard. Wrecked trucks and decapitated Land Rovers, a digger with one track missing, a few tractors, all in army green; crates, rusted containers, piles of scrap, scaffolding pipes, coils of wire, rusted and unidentifiable electrical units of different kinds. 'And this is only what's left,' says Steve. 'Couple of guys got a contract for scrap after the war. Smart kiddies, made a fortune.'

Novak keeps a 20-foot container here as a kind of supply depot; dinghies, filters and spare parts, wiring and tools, outboard engines, that sort of thing.

We pick up two boxes of bits and pieces wanted in Cape Town, and the long, heavy, stainless steel drive shaft from *Pelagic*, going home to be re-machined. We look forward to fitting that down the forward hatch, to be lashed in place by Kevin. That'll sweat a few ounces of beer out of him.

Steve wants Justin and myself to cook up a big stew and a bolognaise, and stow them in the forepeak tomorrow before we set out. This means he's anticipating heavy weather, wants to have nourishing meals ready to heat through, the most to be hoped for in a galley tumbling through big seas. We'll rope down the big pots to the ladder in the forepeak, an exercise in boy-scout ingenuity. There's no hull insulation up there, by design, so that the metal skin of the boat keeps the temperature way down. Up there, in racks, we store fruit, vegetables and meat, the meat laid in vacuum-sealed packs against the hull to keep fresh. Famously, an American guest once asked the skip where the fridge was, to be answered by a horizon-summoning sweep of the hand.

OK, I think, with some relief, looks like we're heading out at last.

Mid-afternoon and the boat is awash with scents – shampoo, aftershave, perfume, soap. One after the other, primped and polished, the salty dogs present themselves for a formal social occasion. Of course, nobody had envisaged the like when packing, so for the most part all you can say for us is that we're clean and moderately presentable.

Howard's house (so far no takers for the E. M. Forster alternative) is Queen Anne via the Caribbean from the uninspired drawing board of some Foreign Office architect. Howard, our new best friend, is affability itself. If we strike him as a rum bunch (and that's how we strike me), he makes light of it. A big man, heavy and strong, bluff and straight-forward but not, I'd say, the sporty type. The interior is generic country house, many over-stuffed sofas and arm-chairs, the sideboard, piano and occasional tables littered with photos of the Queen with the Duke of Edinburgh, the Princess Royal, Charles, Fergie, John Major...

'I don't see Mr Blair, Howard?'

'No, no, I've never met him.'

No Wicked Witch, either. Pointed, I wonder? There's a peat fire burning in our honour, and a Filipina maid brings nibbles and trays of G&Ts.

Howard is career Foreign and Commonwealth Office, former postings include Hungary in 1991, Malta and Argentina. This is his last posting. They wouldn't give him anywhere he wanted, so he's decided to retire, take up farming in Scotland. Seems a bit young to retire, to my eyes, but there you go. It must have been interesting in Hungary, I think, not to mention Argentina, but what I really want to know, without being crass about it, is where do the Falklands go from here?

It's by now notorious that the Falklanders, within days of being 'liberated', were calling on the British armed forces to bugger off home. Not in a hostile way, of course, and not being ungrateful, but this place is deeply attuned to its own isolation, its own ways and customs, and, like all islanders everywhere, the Falklanders just want to be left alone. Howard's view is that the islands are doing well (his remit includes South Georgia), that by now it's a self-sup-porting economy, there's considerable income from fisheries – but I'm finding it difficult to square this with a stray remark he made last night outside church, to the effect that 'most people here work for the government in one capacity or another'.

And how are relations with Argentina? Well, in Howard's view, they are being 'a bit difficult'. He offers the example of a Chilean airline that wanted to fly in charters, but the Argentine government refused them permission to transit Argentine airspace. I know that the vile Chilean dictator Pinochet, in great secrecy, installed a long-range radar opposite the crucial Argentine air-force base of Comodoro Rivadiva, and that this provided the British Task Force with crucial tactical information – indeed some analysts go as far as to say that without this assistance Britain might not have succeeded in retaking these islands. I still want to know, though, what Britain's strategic interest in the islands could be; we all remember Maggie's unscrupulous grasping at the opportunity to have a little war of her own and, to some extent, one can understand that even so hard-headed a government as hers would have felt obliged to defend their turf, however marginal it might have been to the larger interests of Great Britain. What isn't so clear, though, is what, with the demise of Galtieri's regime, in large part due to the fiasco that was the Malvinas, and with the Witch stabbed in the back by her own party, Britain's long-term interest here is. The Foreign and Commonwealth Office, the permanent apparatus of British foreign policy no matter who seems to be in power, is cold-bloodedly mercantile. If 'what's in it for us' could be put into felicitous Latin, I have no doubt they would emblazon it on their letterheads with pride. 'Come on, Howard, it isn't sheep, it isn't fish. What pushes the economic buttons down here?'

He doesn't mind talking about it at all. 'Oil,' he says, 'there are very big oil reserves to be found out in these waters. Very significant.'

Steve, Kevin and Debs arrive, late and cheery. The Filipina maid, a natural comrade I see now, has dispensed with the niceties of trays with glasses and mixers and ice, is ferrying in the G&T, pre-mixed, in great crystal jugs, grinning widely. Clearly we're not the first bunch of sailors to crowd up to the fire here. Steve, the ever-resourceful, has conjured a blazer from somewhere, brass buttons and all. He has a passion for South Georgia, and so has Howard – who is very much determined to prosecute with the full force of the law anyone trespassing on the condemned whaling stations down there. It's a bit of an ecological nightmare, it seems, great stocks of asbestos sheeting, scrap steel and iron, the nightmare junk legacy of a nightmare industry. Steve has a great deal to say about South Georgia, its wildlife, its pristine beauty, and he has Howard's interest now; if there's a record made of this convivial encounter, I suspect Steve's views will be, in the immemorial phrase of the FCO, noted.

Now Carolina joins us, Howard's Dutch wife, clutching a baby alarm so she can keep track of seven-month-old Suzanne. Howard is still astonished that anyone would want to marry him. He keeps saying this, a man still dazed by his good fortune.

'How did you meet?' Diane asks.

'Oh,' Howard answers for Carolina, 'she was backpacking through here and that's how we met.'

She nods, catches my eyebrow raised at Simon.

'Oh I know, I know, what on earth would someone be doing backpacking through this place?' She shrugs, because, well, what are we doing here for that matter?

The wind blew her in here, as it blew us, will presently blow her all the way up to retirement in Scotland, it seems, and, I imagine, rather a large farm for Suzanne to grow up on.

One of the minor arts of diplomacy is getting rid of your guests. Howard and Carolina have a neat line in *divide et impera*; half of us are taken on a tour of Carolina's glasshouse, the others, the late arrivals among them, invited to look at an album of photographs of South Georgia. I admire Carolina's fuchsias, tell her they grow wild in the hedgerows of Cork and Kerry, that some people think they came into Ireland as windowsill plants with the homesick wives of those Cornish miners who were brought into Allihies in West Cork to work the copper mines.

'Oh, I should like to see hedgerows of fuchsia, they must be very beautiful.'

'Oh, but these are gorgeous,' says Tony, 'very fine, very fine.'

And so, when the two groups recombine, it happens that we find ourselves in the front hall, the maid proffering coats at random, and we understand that it's time to go.

'Is that true, about the fuchsia?' Tony asks, as we march down the driveway, past the maid lowering the colours for the night.

And without waiting for an answer, 'Good night, good night, thank you, you work very hard.' We get a last cheery smile, a wave.

'It must be,' says Justin. 'Why would Theo make up a thing like that?'

'And nobody mentioned the war!' says the bold Tony. 'Aren't we very suave!'

At 50p per head to anywhere in Stanley, we have become great supporters of the Falklands taxi business. Back in the boat with no one inclined to cook, we polish off the spaghetti bolognaise – which means of course that now we must prepare another meal in advance.

⚓

DAY

# 12

Tuesday, 16 May 2006

Why are we still here? That's the good question nobody asks; more precisely, that nobody asks Steve. Ask Kev or Debs and you get a shrug, a look heavenward and a change of subject, but we all ask the same question of each other.

'It's like the army, isn't it?' says Justin. 'Hurry up and wait.'

It isn't as cold as it has been, but there are still strong north-westerlies out there. We want to go sailing now, but it looks like at least another day here.

Big Mike has a theory: this trip is a bit of a last hurrah for Steve, Debs and Kevin; Steve especially. He's made his home in these waters for a few years now, on this boat, and he doesn't know what he'll be doing once we land in Cape Town and he signs off. He's saying farewell to what he knows best, and naturally taking his time about it. Might be, might be.

So, friends, what'll we do today? Justin suggests we hire a minibus for a three-hour trip, to Goose Green and Fitzroy, say, noted battlefields. Vote? Agreed.

Souvenirs first, though. Penguins, of course, maps of the islands, postcards, a nice woolly hat for Paula. Bestseller of the day? A chart showing all the known shipwrecks around the islands, and my but aren't there a lot of them? Best of all, though, in the West Store, I buy a local sim card for my mobile, which means I can phone home. In fact there's a sudden rise in the demand for sim cards, everyone wants one. I walk outside into the bright morning and phone home. Joy! She answers on the first ring, 'I knew it was you,' she says, 'I knew it.' Lisa, our friend and neighbour, is sitting at the kitchen table with her. 'Ah, we're both very emotional,' she says, 'we've just been reading your latest instalment for the *IT*.'

'Go 'way out of that,' I say, not so much surprised by the coincidence as to get her to keep talking, just to have the sound of her voice in my ear. If she ran out of things to say, which is unlikely, I'd get her to read the ingredients on a packet of something, just so that she'd go on talking.

'Your e-mails are getting through now,' she says, just as I'm about to ask her how come she's reading the *IT* piece, 'but mine are still getting bounced back. But it doesn't matter, it doesn't matter. Listen, when are ye off?'

'Oh, I wish I knew,' I say. 'I wish I knew.'

Regroup in Michelle's Café, which is exactly what you might expect it to be: full English breakfast all day long.

Jaime, our Chilean taxi driver, says many nationalities here now – Chileans, Georgians (Georgians?), Argentines, Filipinos, lots of Brits rolling through on short-term contracts. It's amazing, really, this rock in the middle of the South Atlantic. The waitress is from St Helena. 'Why come here?' Simon asks, batting his eyelashes at her.

'Oh, I guess to meet different people, you know?'

But alas, Simon doesn't appear to be the different person she was looking forward to meeting.

The tour is a disappointment. Jaime does his best for us, but what can you do with long, blank, loose-surfaced roads, nothing to see on either side except rolling moorland and bog, outcrops of bare rock, long vistas of brown and tan and sludge green. What else? Scarce sheep, a few horses here and there; every now and then a Land Rover goes by, never exceeding the 40-miles-per-hour speed limit. From time to time, there's a marked minefield, to remind us that young men fought and died here in the cold and wet, in the numb terror of a war about, ultimately, nothing much at all. You look at a scrape in the boggy slope of a hill, you imagine a terrified conscript huddled there in the dark, abandoned by his officers; you imagine the terror of incoming mortar fire, the Paras looming up out of the night, cold and wet themselves, burdened by heavy equipment, death spraying from their self-loading rifles. And today? Bare boring hillside that even the sheep can't be bothered to graze.

There should be penguins at Gypsy Cove, says Jaime. There aren't, but there are landmines still among the dunes.

'What's the population now?' Diane asks, more for the sake of breaking the monotony than from a pure desire to know.

'Oh, maybe 2,900, and then maybe 2,000 military, majority of them RAF, then army, then Royal Navy.'

'What do they *do* all day, I wonder?' Justin asks.

'Hurry up and wait, I expect,' growls Mike.

On the shores of Fitzroy Bay there are two monuments: one, a stark obelisk, to the Royal Fleet Auxiliary, one to the Welsh Guards. Farther back at the head of the cove, there's a third stone. *Tristan* was sunk here, and *Galahad*, unloading troops and *matériel* when Argentine pilots came barrelling through that small gap in the hills over there and unleashed their missiles. The memorial to the Welsh Guards, and to three SAS men who died with them, is a large stone with Celtic interlacing in relief. There's a plastic-covered folder at the foot of the memorial, recording not just the names of the men who died, and the circumstances in which they died, but the thoughts of their friends and relatives who have journeyed out here to remember them. You stand there on the springy turf, in this nondescript place on a cold sunny day, in the company of friends who are still strangers, and you try to imagine what it felt like to die here; you try to imagine what went through their thoughts, the officers and men screaming and roaring and cursing and taking cover and trying to organise covering fire, shitting themselves, bleeding in shock, stammering gibberish, the best of them trying to get the boats landed, the wounded into shelter, unbearable noise and chaos all around... and it's all too unreal, too – pointless. All those unique and irrecoverable lives. I look out to sea and remember standing on the afterdeck, praying, was it, for my great-grandmother? And who, in three generations or so, will pray for these, or even remember them, in all their lost ordinariness and beauty?

Fitzroy Farm is still worked, Jaime says, though it looks deserted. The road runs through the farm, a long road between white fences, a gate at either end. There's an Argentine armoured vehicle parked in the lee of a barn, many white labourers' cottages grouped around the main two-storey farmhouse. It looks like a dissolute, half-abandoned Amish community, a cattle station in the outback from an Australian film of the 1950s.

Despondent, hungering for the sea, we doze as the minibus rattles back towards Fipass, in time for afternoon tea with His Excellency on a reciprocal visit. The Land Rover, we note, is maroon, and in place of a number plate sports a discreet but unmistakable gold crown. I imagine the Whitehall committee meetings it took to decide on this, and am once again lost in admiration for the fine minds of the FCO. His Excellency makes his way down the makeshift gangway Kevin has run out for him, brandishing a plastic bag: basil, rosemary and parsley from Carolina. A very Dutch gift, thoughtful and much appreciated. Steve takes our Howard (we're beginning to think of him as a pet by now) on a tour of the boat and when he expresses his admiration, we are all of us as proud as if we had separately and individually designed every last seamanlike feature ourselves.

'So then,' asks Howie, being jolly, 'I expect Stephen is a bit of a Captain Bligh, eh?' (Stephen? Oh, Steve!) Why this is directed at me I don't know, sod's law I suppose.

'Oh, we trust him completely, don't suppose there's anyone out here in these waters knows the run of things as well as Steve does, we're only sorry we won't make South Georgia on this trip, knows it inside out, by all accounts.' (Go on, Howard, offer him a job as a consultant.)

'Well, maybe he hasn't quite adjusted to the fact that we're all grown-ups here, you know yourself what these captains are like!'

Justin, God bless him, almost succeeds in choking back a snort, turns away to fiddle, unnecessarily, with the stern line. The Admiral has been having problems with Steve's attitude, it must be said; and I think the Admiral's accent presses all the wrong buttons with Steve. Steve should learn, of course, from Tony and me; we've had a few more centuries' experience dealing with barking English officer accents. All Justin wants is not to be treated like a junior rating, scarcely unreasonable of him, and, truth to tell, he has a very pleasant accent. Not to Steve's ears, though, more's the pity. All of this byplay washes breezily past Howard, who's soon back on the topic of those whaling stations in South Georgia, the problems of dealing with asbestos and persons breaking the interdiction on landing there. He intends to Take A Very Firm Stand. He's still upbeat about oil prospects, but overnight seems to have come to the gloomy conclusion that Argentina may be 'a bit difficult' about this, too.

Ah cheer up, Howard, you'll be farming in Scotland and enjoying the hell on earth that is having a teenage daughter by the time that comes to pass. If ever.

Waving goodbye to Howie from the deck of *Pelagic* as she slides away from the dock would have been the perfect way to take our leave, but alas it's not to be.

'We're off tomorrow,' Steve promises as we tidy up, gesturing to the stern gantry, 'now that Dolly's here, eh?'

Dolly, delivered in our absence this morning, is a whole sheep, gutted, de-hooved, skinned and beheaded but otherwise entire. Wrapped in muslin and strapped down tight, she'll keep for a week, maybe more, preserved in the salt sea air. Dinners, that's what Dolly represents, fresh meat. Macken is less than entirely pleased, 'I thought it would be a lamb. I don't like mutton, much.'

'I suppose we'd better go to the pub if we're not heading out tonight?' Now who said that? I call Paula with the last of my phone credit; she's away early tomorrow morning; this is probably our last conversation between now and Cape Town. Predictably, the credit runs out as I'm in the middle of describing, trying to describe, the intricate complexities of Kevin's tattoo business.

Having a mug of Barry's with Tony when Simon, enjoying his last smoke of the night, calls me up on deck, 'Theo, Theo, come and see this.'

A Brit platoon is in the process of disembarking from two fast patrol craft at the end of the jetty. There's a Land Rover waiting for them, two officers, maps, side arms. Having briefed the sergeant in charge, the officers hop in the jeep and disappear. The sergeant and a corporal are chivvying the bewildered young soldiers, pushing them about, barking at them trying to get them to form bricks – facing outward, forward and back. Curious uniforms, standard UK camo but peaked soft caps, like Yanks (or Argentinians?). The farcical thing is, all this is taking place under the glare of arc lights mounted on the stern of the Fisheries Protection Vessel across from us on the dock. In a tactical situation, they'd all be dead by now (and why didn't they practise formation back in barracks, anyway?) but then I suppose they're pretending the lights aren't there and, in any case, wouldn't have landed here like this under lights if it were for real. Still, it's a mad kind of situation to land these bewildered lads into, and I'm thinking of offering the sergeant some helpful advice when it occurs to me that, in the dead of night, from a darkened boat, an Irish accent offering helpful suggestions might, shall we say, unsettle him. After all, you never know where he's been.

We watch them form up, eventually, and scurry away, small pale faces turning this way and that, SLRs bristling, and I feel sorry for the poor squaddies, probably destined to be out all night in the dark; hungry, bewildered and cold, training to defend a few square miles of bog and rock, so very far from home.

'I hope they don't bring them past that signpost,' says Tony behind me, 'that'll break their hearts entirely.'

⚓

DAY

# 13

Wednesday, 17 May 2006

## DEPARTURE DAY

At last! Woke, uncalled, at 07.30. A general bustle through-
out the ship, little talk, everyone stowing gear that won't be
needed, packing away clothes that have been drying for
days on the radiators, tidying cabins, passageways, the
saloon, the wheelhouse, the galley; shaking off lethargy
and aimlessness, gearing up into being a crew again. As
we pass each other, going back and forth about our various
tasks, we nod, stop to give a hand if it seems needed;

everyone's alert, aware of what has to be done without having to be told.

Steve's at the laptop, checking the weather, Debs has the chart out, checking the pilotage. In twos and threes, we stand at the shoulder of one or the other, taking it all in, preparing ourselves. Then, starting at the bow, Kevin and Debs walk back each side of the boat, checking rigging and shackles and lines, sails on their furlers, the main flaked out on the boom, ready to be hoisted. Steve takes a bag and a bundle of documents from Alec and Giselle, skipper and mate of little *Pelagic*, who have come to see us off: delivery to Tristan da Cunha. Something archaic about this, the more so as the papers are from the Governor's office, bound for the administration on Tristan. Letters to be delivered from a passing ship.

And so, we're ready to leave. I pour a glass of Jameson's over the stern, Steve pours a glass of wine, now everyone understands. 'OK, Theo, you take her out then.'

Right. Wind's north-west, so we'll fall away nicely off the dock. As we clear Fipass and turn north, we'll stay in close to the port side, then east to go out into the larger bay on 090°. What next? Stand out for a couple of boat lengths, then smartly to 180°, remembering we may have to steer a few degrees up to counteract the wind on our bow. Back to now. What's best? Simon on wheel, I think, a good boat handler. Rig a breast-spring amidships, that will hold us nicely, with some judicious use of the engine as backup, when we slip the springs and then, together, the bow and sternlines. Right, of course, engine. 'Simon, can you use the engine to hold us parallel to the dock until we're ready to slip the breastline? Ta.'

Two large orange balls as roving fenders, Kevin aft, Justin forward. 'Let go springs, let go forward, let go aft. Di! Di! Get that line in smartly, we don't want it wrapped around the prop, for Christ's sake! Right, Mike, let go the breastline. OK Simon, go for it' – and off we go. Smart enough, I suppose, pity some of the lines are in such a tangle they have to be flaked out on deck before being coiled up and sent below.

A hand on the shoulder from Steve, 'Well done, mate. Told you you'd learn something from the last time, didn't I? Any idea where we're going, by the way?'

I recite the cathecism, backed up by Simon who flutters the sheet on which we have drawn and annotated the pilotage. 'All under control here, Skipper,' he drawls.

Steve makes a gesture of mock surrender, 'OK, OK, I'm just asking.'

'Fed, when we get outside, right, when we turn onto, what, Simon?'

'045°',

'OK, when we turn onto 045° you get the sails up, OK? Remember we're getting about 35–40 knots, think about your reefs right?'

Justin and Kevin are the only ones sweating; they've been below in the forepeak stowing the lines and fenders. Macken takes his pipe out of his mouth. 'Now, Justin, I hope you did a good job of securing the forehatch?' Likes to live dangerously, our Tony.

Justin calls Nic, his wife. Nic's father is dying in Mallorca, a long slow process that's hard on Nic, and hard on Justin, too, so far from being able to offer her any real comfort. He hangs up, peers at the phone, then nudges me. 'Two minutes' Falkland credit left on this, you want to give Paula a quick buzz, then?' I leave her a message.

Stanley is dozing in the sharp sunlight; the bright-coloured terraces might be empty of life, there where the low sun lances off the windows. I turn the word isolate over in my mind, *isola* at the root of it, and then we're out past Mengeary point, turning north-east into the empty ocean, keeping well to the east of Uranie Rock, and Fed is marshalling his forces, the sails are running up and out, we heel sharply to starboard and stick in the groove. *Pelagic Australis* puts her head down, a horse let loose into a field, and plunges out.

Away up there to the north of us, a ship is climbing over the horizon. If we can make her out at this distance she must be pretty big, I reckon. Steve sees it too: 'Monthly supply ship for the island,' he says, 'in from the UK.' Such a tenuous lifeline, I think, such a long umbilical for a small child of Empire.

It catches my heart every time, that moment when a boat breaks free of land, turns out into the towering void. I shake off the land like the last of a hangover, I feel a quickening inside me that is part relish, part anxiety. The animal self is exultant, caught up in the blast of the wind, the fresh spray blowing past, the dilation of veins, the quickening in the blood. I crab forward along the port side, the high side, wrap an arm around a shroud and plant my feet. I feel the boat shuddering, her flat forefoot smacking down with each fall, the lift forward as she rises; I hear the wind in the rigging climb in pitch, I squint my eyes against the shifting glare on the water coursing past, I lick salt off my lips, a quick lizard's reflex, and turn for a last look at the island slipping away behind us, stoic and unassuming. I wonder what kind of day it was when the *Rimutaka* slid by here. Did they put in for coal, I wonder, or did they stay far out, driving on from the Horn? Greenstreet, the captain's name was, I remember this suddenly; I call to mind that photograph, seen so long ago. I can see the ship plunging and rising as she goes by on our starboard side, some deck officer with a glass to his eye, wondering what ship we are, and find myself searching the bulwarks for the low spot the captain would choose for the burial, somewhere out of the gaze of the passengers, somewhere a weighted body would fall free and away, not be carried into the vortex of the great bronze propellers.

Bloody hell. I shake myself, not sure for a moment where I am, vividly conscious the next instant of exactly where I am, exactly: here, now, in a great bowl of time and space, in an exact spot. Alive in the very instant, completely and sufficiently and absolutely alive.

God, I could murder a cup of coffee and a sandwich, I think. Two sandwiches, two cups of coffee!

But first, find Diane. 'Hey, Floss, sorry about yelling at you back there, about the line in the water?'

'Oh, don't worry about it, you were right. It was OK though, I was watching it but it's no harm to be reminded.'

'So how come you're not up there watching mister *Master and Commander* at work, eh?'

I get a blush, a laugh and a punch in the shoulder for that. 'Ah here,' I say, 'would you like a cup of Barry's?'

It's lumpy and rolly out here, we've already started picking up bruises. I sit in the shelter behind the wheelhouse, having a smoke with Debs and Kevin. Debs is back to her usual sunny self. 'God, I felt crook in Stanley, I guess I had some kind of tummy bug?' she says, and then has us in fits of laughter as she describes what it's like to vomit up spaghetti. In meticulous detail.

Kev is watching Simon and Fed, up on the raised platform behind the wheel. Squabbling in short clipped phrases, as usual. Simon is back in his tart, abrasive persona; Fed insists on looking away ahead as he steers, talking back to Simon out of the corner of his mouth. As in, 'look, I'm busy here'. We call them the boy racers, constantly vying with each other, seeming unconscious that the tension between them is obvious to us all. I catch Kevin's eye, he shakes his head slowly, pursing his lips, as one who says, this isn't good.

Our Great Leader is also happy to be off. 'This is good, isn't it? Crikey but I'm glad to be out of there. All right, Justin?'

For Justin, closely followed by Tony, has started to feel seasick again. 'All right, Skip. Just the usual. Bloody hell…'

Our Great Leader (or OGL as he is sometimes known) is exhibiting a lighter touch, less masterly, more conversational; direct effect, says Justin, of my remark to His Excellency yesterday about 'feeling like thirteen again, in school'. Now he calls out to me from the wheelhouse, 'Theo, I'm gonna give Stratos a call, see if we can sort out your e-mails, mate. Let's have a look, shall we?' Less than a minute into the satellite phone call to the service provider Stratos we solve the mystery. Steve is calling back my e-mail account as they give it to him, and when he gets to, 'echo, india, romeo, sierra…' I stop him. 'Hey, Steve, that's where they're going wrong. It's eircom: echo, india, romeo, charlie…'

'Bloody hell, I'd say that's it all right,' and I leave him to it, but not before bringing him a coffee now that the kettle's boiled again. So, we'll see tomorrow if that's fixed it.

Presently, Mike comes staggering back from the fore-peak with the pot of stew and, twenty minutes later, we have ample evidence that not all appetites on board are affected by the sea state. Staring into the empty pot as I run water into it before putting it aside to soak, I distinctly remember worrying that we'd made far too much stew, would most likely find ourselves with enough left over to make the base of a good soup later. Astounding, sometimes, the quantities of food consumed on board. Apart from the fresh meat, fruit and vegetables up in the fore-peak, and ignoring for a moment the cadaver above on the gantry, there is enough in the way of dried and canned goods stored under the seats in the saloon to get us to Cape Town from here, and back again; the trick, of course, will be to get there while making minimal inroads into the boring stuff, to husband what's fresh for as long as we can.

Now we go on to a new watch system, with noon as the reference point, thus:

| |
|---|
| 12.00–18.00 |
| 18.00–22.00 |
| 22.00–02.00 |
| 02.00–06.00 |
| 06.00–12.00 |

Our watch comes on at 18.00, so instead of doing what I'd like to do, that is divide my time between dozing in my bunk and sitting out there, just looking at the sea, I'm stuck in the wheelhouse learning flags and their Morse equivalents. The Yachtmaster course was suspended for the duration of our stay in Stanley, and we're like dutiful but sulky schoolkids today, the yoke settling on our shoulders again. Bit stupid, really, since this is, in part, what we signed on for; still, I wonder how disappointed Steve would be if we resigned en masse and said, 'Hey, look, let's just sail the boat, eh?'

Our classroom is the wheelhouse, where we perch or stand, focusing on what Steve is telling us, dutifully scribbling down notes that make sense to us now but will be impossible to decipher in a month's time; we are trying not to let ourselves be distracted by the lift and fall of the water outside, the flash of a bird sweeping past (what was that? Petrel?) – and I swear, it really is like being a child again, and not in any good sense: I remember the grim promises I made myself at twelve or thirteen that, no matter what happened in my life, I would never again, once school was over, permit myself to be 'so cabin'd and cribb'd'. And here it is, unbelievably, the very same taste of copper in my mouth, the same dull ache of time grown turbid, muddy and slow. Ach!

Two night watches tonight: 18.00 to 22.00 and 02.00 to 06.00. First watch is handy enough, we busy ourselves with a bit of helming, some speculative chartwork, a lot of yarning. The big event in the first watch is seeing lights of a trawler, looks like, away off up to port. (On the second watch something big comes up on our starboard side and passes ahead. We fire up the radar when Justin spots her lights, and track it for a while. Warship, at a guess.) I sleep fitfully, wake around midnight to sounds of considerable commotion on deck, somebody running backward and forward, much shouting. I know I should get up in case I'm needed, but then the noise dies down, there's an intense low-voiced conversation going on up in the cockpit. I decide to let it pass, but feel vaguely guilty.

It's 02.00. Kevin is slightly reserved, and I know why. 'Sorry, Kev,' I say, 'I was in a very deep sleep, and then I was getting up when I heard it all go quiet again. What happened?'

'Ah, starboard watch broke a pole, Steve had a kind of shit fit, don't worry.'

Well, OK, I let it go, but I still feel in the wrong. Not a hanging offence, but I know I should have gone up. At 05.00, for something to do and because Tony and Justin are, for the first time today, feeling a bit hungry, I make sausage sandwiches.

'I picked the right watch,' says Kevin happily. 'Yes, sir, I sure did.'

'You poor sad bastard, you mean you had a choice and you picked us?'

'Well, not a choice exactly but, you know, Steve might have kinda got the idea that I'd be comfortable with you elderly gentlemen.'

⚓

DAY

## 14

Thursday, 18 May 2006

Noon. Wake after five hours' sleep, disoriented. Lie there and figure out what's going on. The wind is still in the north-west, judging by the roll and slam. I'm guessing 3-metre seas or thereabouts. Check the time, good, might get a bit of washing done before due on watch. Feel uneasy, why? Oh yeah, last night's business, not getting up and feeling I should have, knowing I should have. Ah well.

Everything that happens on board a boat affects everyone one way or another. A well-handled vessel proceeds in order until some unforeseen circumstance brings change. A good skipper like Steve, with a serviceable boat, will have things set up in such a way that he will make steady progress along a set course, in a prescribed manner, until some outside force – a change in wind speed or direction, engine or gear failure, human misjudgement or accident – intervenes. Think of it as an ecosystem, everything and everyone mutually interdependent under the guiding will and authority of the skipper. When something goes wrong, everyone is affected, directly or remotely. Of course if there is some catastrophic event – fire, a dismasting, flooding, man overboard, something on that level – then the duty watch will call all hands, everyone will be woken and made aware of the situation. When something less urgent occurs, something that wakes you, something you know isn't right, there is an unspoken expectation that the off watch will take note, will signal themselves present and available in case they are wanted, even if they're pretty sure they aren't needed. It's a question of making plain one's acceptance and recognition of our interdependence, a way, too, of signalling one's reliability. With so many on board, with such big watches, there isn't perhaps the same burden of expectation, but nonetheless, absence is noted, a question mark, however faint, is placed in the air above one's head.

I lie there thinking about it. We did the handover, the starboard watch subdued, anxious to get below, to get their heads down. Justin watching them austerely. The wheel-house at night is an intimate place, soft glow from the instruments, men moving quietly, conscious of the off watch asleep. Kevin is tight-lipped, businesslike, out there in the cockpit now, feeding the staysail sheet out a pinch, tightening up. Tony beckons me outside when Kevin goes below to the galley.

'Did you hear all that commotion?'

'Yep, was going to come up then it subsided.'

'Yeah well, what happened was, Steve left them with too much sail up and when the wind built they didn't call him up like they should have, right? They'd about 70 per cent of the genny out, with the Yankee poled out to starboard. Well, Arnie was on the wheel [Arnie is what we call the autopilot] and you know Arnie needs watching the whole time. He kept creeping us too far north and someone should have been watching him but they weren't, then bang, the boat powers up, over she gybes and they break the pole. Next thing you know Steve's on deck, big mayhem, they get the two bits of the pole in and lashed down – see them there on the port side? – and things settle down again but not before all concerned get a bollocking from the skipper. I took a hike at that stage, nothing I could do anyway, and I didn't want to be there while they were getting a roasting.'

Kevin, back up again, is gearing up for a deck check, buckling on lifejacket and harness. Without saying anything I push past Tony, start buckling up myself.

This morning, now, here in my bunk, I understand why I did that; to try to make up, if only to myself, for not having got up in the commotion. Whatever, Kev gave me a considering look, then nodded. 'OK, my man, you take the high side.'

There were fairly big seas out there, racing by in the fitful dark, 4 metres or so, bigger than we've had up to now. You could drop a van in the hole between one crest and the one that hangs there behind it over the dark vault of the hollow beneath. A wild, black, pitching night, the port quarter shooting up then shimmying down with a kind of corkscrew twist, white water pouring off in the starlight, then rising again, coming up like something on pistons, fast and sure.

I see now that it wasn't just compensation for an imagined transgression against the code, I wanted to go out there because it was time to waken my nerve, to call it up and teach it to be steady. I call it up again.

'Here, don't forget your torch.' Justin has a steady way of looking at you when he's reminding you of something you shouldn't have forgotten in the first place. Clear, direct, non-judgemental. A man of tact.

I lean around the backstay and clip my lifeline to the jackstay, the flat tape that runs all up the deck, one end to the other. Then, judging the rise of the stern, moving just as it comes up against me, I swing around the backstay and start making my way forward. Kevin is already pushing forward on the starboard side, timing his progress in little lunges and stops to keep from getting wet; more accurately, to minimise how wet he's getting down there so close to the water. We do a deck check on each watch on this boat, and we check everything we can see: we check the shackles are tight, we check the rigging, we check for signs of chafe on sheets and lines, of wear and tear; we check all hatches are secure, that nothing's hanging in the water; we check the sails, the luff lines, the leech lines, we check the nav lights, we check the split pins in the three furling drums. Tonight, I make a point of examining the lashings that hold the two bits of the broken pole to the guardwires – we don't want those poles coming loose and taking to the air, someone could easily get killed. I meet up with Kevin on the plunging bow.

'Anything your side?'

'Nothing, Kev, all clear.'

'OK then, let's get back.'

'Sixty knots out there,' Justin says, as we unbuckle in the wheelhouse, 'a bit breezy. Seventy in the gusts,' he says, and right on cue we heel over to a sudden blast. 'Everything all right, then?'

'Who lashed down the broken pole bits, Kev?' I ask.

'Simon, why, they all right?'

'Yep, he did a good job.'

'He sure did, checked it myself when I was up earlier. Boy oh boy, did they get a roasting. I'm gonna make coffee, anybody want some?'

So I'm thinking about that deck check as I dress now and climb up into the wheelhouse. Murky old day out there, ugly-looking sea too.

'Morning, young Theo. Up bright and early, eh? Keen as mustard, you are.'

'Fuck off, Justin,' I reply wittily.

'Tell you what,' he continues, not in the least put off by my grumpiness, 'that looked a bit of a lark, last night, that deck check! Do you know, I saw 79 knots true wind at one point. Blimey, that's a bit breezy!'

'I'll bring you up a cup of tea,' I tell him, 'that'll help you to calm down. There's too much excitement here.'

Not much excitement in the afternoon Yachtmaster class. Steve tight-lipped, Fed and Simon sombre, subdued for them. Diane looks unhappy and out of sorts, only Big Mike seems unperturbed. We keep out of the way as best we can – cleaning the boat, sailing the boat, preparing dinner. Halfway through the watch, Tony brings tea and coffee for all hands. And biscuits. Hob Nobs for Steve, his favourites.

'Nice move, Mr Macken,' Kevin murmurs as our watch settles in on the now bright afterdeck to watch Arnie do his work, Steve nibbling contentedly at his biscuits. 'Very subtle.'

I feel, what? Elsewhere. I watch the sea rise and fall, watch grey slide down over blue, watch the side of the boat come up and fall away, come up and fall away, and I have the curious sensation that I'm not here, that I'm seeing all this in another dimension, that, any moment now, I'm going to wake up. I sleep like a stone, entirely unconscious, after dinner; still feeling groggy when I wake for the 22.00

watch. It isn't just me, I'm grimly relieved to note, everyone, even the indefatigable Kevin, seems stupefied. The talk is of solo sailors, how they cope with the stress and strain of it, how they manage sleep. Justin recalls a particularly stupid letter in one of the yachting magazines, some weekend sailor belittling Ellen MacArthur's achievements. I read it too, in a mist of sudden rage; I recall the moment vividly. Not a real sailor at all, was the gist of it, what with satellite communications, computer weather forecasts, specialised sail handling systems and the like. 'Why, the boat practically sails itself.' We look up at the top of the mast, spinning and making figures of eight in 50 knots of wind, the boat pitching, juddering, rolling and bucking underneath us, and we try to imagine the nerve, the stamina it would take to climb up there now. After weeks out here, in seas far worse than this, working all day and all night, every day and every night, having to make yourself get out there and climb, knowing you don't want to, knowing that, very likely, your life depends on doing it. We are not terribly impressed by that letter, or its author.

'Jeez you guys are rough, who'd a thought it? Remind me not to get on your wrong side.'

'Ah no, Kev, don't be worrying. We're not going to *actually* kidnap the letter writer. That would be wrong. And it would be wrong to shoot her full of sleepers, chopper her out to an Open 60 in mid-ocean and tuck her up in a bunk with a weather forecast taped to her forehead in mirror writing. You couldn't do that to someone, sure that would be illegal.'

'And a little note to say, "Good luck, you're on your own now",' adds Tony helpfully.

'Mirror writing?' asks Kevin. 'Mirror writing?'

⚓

DAY

## 15

Friday, 19 May 2006

Tiredness has become the dominant theme of daily life. In part, this is because of the disruptive effect of the watch system. In an age of relativism, we have lost touch with certain ancient fixities and definites, and one of these is the body's insistence on what it considers appropriate sleep. This varies from day to day, naturally, but the grid system of fixed watches makes no allowance for individual needs. We're not stupid people, we can see why this is necessary, you can't be constantly adjusting a watch system to allow for how any one person is feeling at any one time. But the fact is, all too often, someone is only nominally present for his watch, the bones present but little else.

The mind is accustomed to overruling its symbiote, the body. We arrange our days, more often than not, to satisfy the fickle appetite for mental stimulation, and we fall out of touch with ourselves. We are misled by the clock, by artificial measurements of time. Because of the need to regulate the social order, we have divided the day into twenty-four equal segments, and we apportion, usually, eight of those segments to sleep. Body time, however, is a more complex and sophisticated phenomenon. The body negotiates between sets of complex demands, including demands of the mind for processing time in dream states. It takes into account general metabolism, nourishment levels, light inputs, demands on musculature, ligature and nerves; it monitors blood sugars, enzymes, carbohydrates, oxygen levels and toxins, and then sets out its programme for *its* day: so much time for robust activity, so much time for repose and thought, so much time for the ticking over of routine work, and so much time for sleep. In this demanding and relatively novel environment, with big physical demands on our resources, and complex demands on emotion and mentation, I know my own body has very definite ideas about when, and for how long, it needs to sleep. The watch system, alas, cannot allow for this. The alternative to the body's holistic analysis of its own shifting needs is to train it to accommodate its processes to the non-negotiable watch structure, to teach it to live, for a while at least, in firmly structured time. This can be done, it is already happening, but it's a dulling and sometimes disheartening business.

So, fuck it; grin and get through. The seas out there are still lumpy and unpleasant, 5 metres maybe, but there are cross-seas running, remnants of some blow down there in the south, cutting into the long swell from the north-west. The result is that we lurch all over the place, making our course steadily north-east but, at any one moment, moving up and down and sideways all at once.

God but this is one big empty ocean. I've crossed the North Atlantic, Antigua to Ireland, admittedly in better weather than this for the most part, but I didn't have then anything like the sense of abandonment that I feel out here. In the North Atlantic, you are never too far from a ship of some kind. I don't think, for instance, in that thirty-one-day crossing, there was ever a day when we didn't see some other vessel – a yacht, a cargo ship, a tanker. Down here in the South Atlantic, we are crossing a great void. No amount of advance reading prepares you for this. I feel it today, strongly, the sense of being isolated, an island, in some great booming void space.

It seems nuts, in this great empty space, to spend the afternoon studying tidal heights. Land seems already unreal, the idea of closing with it, of needing to know what the tide will be doing at the moment of your approach, seems faintly absurd. The body says, there is only the sea and the wind, this small world moving through a larger world, that's all there is, that's all there ever will be. We plough on, through the lesson and through the day, feeling somehow thin and insubstantial as big seas hammer the hull, and light over the water falls in mountain-sized chunks, this way and that, mindless, haphazard and indifferent.

Night, a sunset of long flattened bands, purple and orangey-yellow, dark clouds piling up above the stripes of colour, the long flat run of the swell. The sea's gone down; we're grateful for the respite, for flat decks and easier movement as we go about our business, but we already know this won't last, and not just because we've all had a look at the oncoming weather in the GRIBs. We know in our bones that this ocean doesn't do calms, not for long.

We've had a consistent 60 knots all day, the log records a gust of 78; anywhere else this would be crazy weather, nobody in his or her right mind would be out in it, but we seem to have adjusted, and very quickly, to a new norm. What would puzzle and disturb us now would be a drop to what, in our previous lives, any one of us would have considered a good stiff sailing breeze, 20–25 knots.

'No chance of that,' says the thoughtful Mr Macken. 'If you told me a month ago I'd be sailing away without a bother on me in 60 knots, I'd have called in the guys with the white coats for ya. This is mad, isn't it?,' he says; meaning, this is the normal now, and we're all right.

Still tracking remorselessly north-east; another day, maybe two, and we'll hope to pick up the westerlies that should blow us all the way in a straight line to Tristan da Cunha, and on to Cape Town.

The clouds have gone, there's a low quarter moon out there to port, a great swathe of stars trailing overhead, the Milky Way with its myriad worlds, the Southern Cross blazing away on the beam to starboard. Diane points out Sirius, Canopus, Orion. We star bathe for a little while longer, then Debs calls Diane into the wheelhouse where she's settling her watch for the night, and I say goodnight to Tony, goodnight to the watch, and head below.

On a long trip, a man's bunk is his cave, his own private world, his refuge from the elements, and from whomever he's sharing the voyage with. Diane and I have worked out, more or less by tacit, unspoken agreement, how to manage our little cabin. The lower bunk is for sleeping; she keeps her gear on the upper bunk, racked up at an angle and with the lee cloth hoisted to keep everything in place, I keep my gear on the upper bunk in Simon's cabin, similarly racked up. Our bunk has a 12-inch lee-board in place, to keep you from falling out when the boat heels, so that when you lie there you are enwombed between hull and lee-board, you can roll as the boat rolls and roll back again, rebounding off one side or the other, as she recovers. I stretch out my sleeping bag, fold a fleece beneath my pillow, undress, climb up and over and in, pull the curtains closed, stretch myself into the down bag and, for the next four hours, I am completely at home, in my own world inside the greater world of the boat out here on the big lonely ocean. It is a moment of exquisite luxury, this moment when everything in the immediate world comes to a stop.

I might read for a bit, or make some notes in my journal, I might recast some small drama from the day, playing it over from different angles. I settle to the boat's motion in small increments, a rolled up blanket beside me, ready to be deployed here or there as a cushion against lee-board or hull. And then, settled and ready to go over, I look for a moment at Paula's picture taped to the bulkhead and wish her goodnight, absurdly, before turning off the light.

⚓

DAY

# 16

Saturday, 20 May 2006

Left to ourselves, with an eye out to see that Arnie is doing his job, we like nothing better than to pore over the chart, see how small a portion of the ocean we have traversed, estimate how far we have still to go. We get the weather from Steve whenever we can, one of us always at his shoulder when he connects to the satellite, storing away the information for the others. We can eke out a watch very nicely doing this, passing between time at the chart table and time outside, just gazing dreamily at the ocean in its infinite variety.

Our reference matrix is *Admiralty Chart 4003, A Planning Chart for the South Atlantic Ocean*, what you might call a topographic chart except that there is no *topos* to speak of out there. We steady ourselves in the grid of latitude and longitude, we point to a spot on the surface of the chart and say *there*, there is where we are. And we look out the window and try to make that agree with the overwhelming *here*, here is where we are.

One of the things we like to do is to go back over the log, plotting our present position as an estimated point in the vastness. We take our point of departure from, say, the 06.00 entry, blanking out the position column, and then from the record of courses followed and time taken and average speeds between then and now we work out a dead-reckoning position. There are arcane minutiae to be considered: there is a slight eastward flowing current to be taken into account, and then there is knowledge particular to this boat, this crew. On a beam reach, for instance, you have to ask if she's been set sideways, made leeway, since the last log notation; we examine the record to see who was helming, if not Arnie. Both Fed and Simon have a tendency to chase the wind a bit, hunting for speed, sometimes at the expense of course made good. They may have made a bit of a loop between two noted positions, added a little distance, or even saved a little on time. This can distort our calculations of average speed. So we scribble and measure, measure and scribble, and calculate and then we compare the results with the actual position as revealed on the GPS.

We're very rarely out by more than a mile or two, but Justin is almost always the closest. Today he's been projecting our course, time and speed to Tristan da Cunha. At our present rate of progress, he tells us, we should arrive there in a week plus twelve hours. Well, that's something to bear in mind, but he could be out by a day or more either way, through no fault in his calculations but depending on what the weather chooses to give us. A big south-westerly, for instance, would drive us on nicely, shorten the journey, but then we might equally get headed by an easterly (unlikely, we think), or we might run into a fast-evolving weather system that will knock us about a bit, or…

The other chart we like to consult is the *Routeing Chart for May, South Atlantic 5125(5)*. This is a fascinating piece of work, issued by the British Admiralty, one of a large number of such charts for all the oceans of the world, at all times of year. Along the principal shipping routes, wind roses are marked at regular intervals, giving the likelihood of wind directions at the particular point. The nearest to our present position, for example, tells us that, statistically, the likeliest wind we'll have is north-westerly; in fact, this afternoon, right now and for most of the day so far, it's been south-westerly, but we suspect it's going to swing before long. Consistently since we left the Horn, we've been getting unlikely winds, according to this chart. This, of course, leads us into baroque and arcane speculation about long-term weather change, global warming, the whole kit and caboodle. The 'norm' winds at a given point at a given time of year are derived from countless reports furnished to the Admiralty, voluntarily, by the masters and navigation officers of ships that have passed this way over many decades. We think it odd that we should be getting abnormal winds so consistently, and not just in terms of direction: the rosettes also give wind speed averages, and we've been getting winds appreciably higher than, and sometimes much lower than, the specified norms.

This chart also gives recommended routes for sailing vessels, not with the likes of us in mind, of course, but based on the commerce and naval considerations of the eighteenth and nineteenth centuries. Thus, as we deliberate on these weighty matters, like some ponderous court of admirals on whose decisions the fate of empires, commercial and political, may rest, we find ourselves in communion with all those who have gone this way before us, depending on precedent, experience and their own powers of direct observation to manage the passage with all speed, economy and precision. For all that we're linked by satellite to advanced weather-prediction technology, to the wonders of GPS, we are still all alone out here, at the mercy of what may come, from any direction, at any time. Our command of the situation is always held under temporary and all too revocable licence. We have developed a healthy respect for all who have gone here before us, the hard way; at the back of our minds, of course, is a healthy and selfish interest: it is all too easy to envisage some crash in our electronic systems, it does us no harm at all to have some familiarity at least with how it might be – what we would need to know, if we were cast back on these time-proved resources.

We have more or less a following wind all day, a few points above our port quarter, so the Yankee's poled out to starboard. Steve, coming up as usual when you least expect him, draws deep on a cigarette and says she's drawing nicely, pulling away good-oh. 'Enjoying yourself, Theo?'

'I am,' I tell him, 'I am.'

And it's true. Feeling a little fresher now, body clock making its peace with the watch system, the sea relatively (very relatively) calm, so not having to brace and grab every time I want to move. Steve, I think, is beginning to overcome his suspicion of me. Now he volunteers information sometimes, calls me down to look at the weather, talks a little about himself, his past, his ideas for the future. I try to see myself through his eyes: not terribly fit, middle-aged, sharp-tongued, watching everything, missing little. He knows I wrote a book about my last ocean trip, knows I must at least be thinking of doing another out of this one. He sees what I lack in experience, too, the discrepancy between what I know out of wide reading and what I've learned, directly, at first hand. I imagine it would be all too easy for him to see me as one of those too-smart-by-half types who, by sacred tradition, are the bane of all men and women whose bent is practical and whose relationship with the world is to be always doing something in it, with it or to it.

Of course, I may just be projecting all this onto his blameless head. For all I know, he scarcely thinks about us at all, except to assure himself we're not doing any actual damage to his boat. I remember a moment, heading down the Beagle, when I was on the winch, putting in a reef or taking one out: I must have tranced off for a second or two, and the halyard dropped maybe 12 inches before I stopped it. Big bellow from the cockpit, 'Watch it, for fuck's sake, don't break my boat.'

A flash of temper, I was about to roar back, 'It's not your fucking boat', when inspiration saved me, and I yelled back, '*Ná bris mo bhád!*'

'What, what did you say?'

'It's Irish, Gaelic for don't break my boat.'

'Oh, cool, how do you say it again?'

An honourable draw, then. What was that flash of temper about? Being yelled at, of course. Had enough of that for years in school, am not disposed to put up with it again. Is that what I'm projecting onto Steve here, the role of the hated authority figure? Oh please, banal or what? I never expected my teachers to like me, never *wanted* to be liked by most of them anyway, and, to be fair to them, they obliged me in this if in little else. The result is that, ever since, I rarely put myself in situations where anyone has authority over me, even authority voluntarily accepted, and I lack the experience of dealing with it. More specifically, I assume that anyone having to deal with me from a position of authority won't like me.

It could very well be, I tell myself severely, that Steve is a very nice guy, and you're, essentially, just not likable. So now! Would this bother me, if true? Probably not.

Dear me, the things that cross your mind at sea.

Which reminds me... 'Hey, Steve, my e-mails are all still fucked up. Do you think we could try to get 'em sorted out, once and for all?'

'Really? Sorry, mate, I thought that was all sorted out. You must be missing your Sheila then, Paula, yeah? No worries, I'll get that sorted out for ya.'

There's a relatively festive atmosphere in the wheel-house, for no reason I can discern. Steve turns, 'Hey, Justin mate, what're you up to?'

'Well, I've just worked out that if we keep going like we are, we'll end up in Tristan about midnight next Saturday night.'

'Yeah? Well that wouldn't be too good, now, would it? The thing is, with Tristan, you can't land there. Too much of a swell. So, what we do, we drop the hook off, if there isn't too much of a swell for that, otherwise we just stooge up and down for a bit, right? Till it gets light? Then, whatever, we land half the crew in the dinghy – their dinghy mind, they gotta make a few quid out of us haven't they? – that lot have a tootle around then back on board, the other half go ashore and then by and by, all done, off we go. If you're right, mate, we get to spend a night going up and down, up and down, off Tristan. Hope that doesn't happen, be dead boring, eh?'

Steve, delivering this, is quite a sight. He's in his normal attire, blue tights today (could be black another day), khaki shorts, bright orange rubber boots with thick blue soles, black fleece and sleeveless navy windproof jacket. Skinny arms and legs (but watch him run up the mast with those skinny legs, feel the power in those skinny arms when he joins in with you on the winch); top that off with a thin face, a shock of blond hair and a Marlboro Light sticking out of his mouth, and that's Steve. Now we're used to these eccentricities of dress, we take the attitude that it's Steve's business what he wears, and, hey, obviously it works for him, but what's this? Mr Macken pops up the ladder from the port side passage where he maintains his sleeping quarters, and now he's getting in on the act with a blue top, yellow shorts, black thermal tights and sea boots. What next, we wonder, Kevin in a bikini?

'Justin,' I say, pompous and brisk as I can manage, 'take that man below and see he returns properly dressed.'

'Aye aye, Sir. You, that man…' but even Justin can't keep this up. It's too much for mortal flesh to bear, he scurries below for his camera. Macken, completely unmoved by all this, calmly lights up his pipe.

Southern Ocean chic, you saw it here first.

Everyone's up now, early for dinner: Debs is below in the galley, 'supervising' as Kevin concocts a beef stroganoff; Mike has come into view, taken a cool, slow look at Tony and gone back below for his camera; Simon, having carefully inspected Dolly's wrappings, edges in beside me to shelter as he lights up.

'Well, the love birds are having fun,' he says. Fed and Di are up in the bows, taking photographs of each other.

'Ah now, Simon, Simon, don't be jealous.'

Jealous, judging by the look I get, he isn't.

The mellow mood drags on late into the night, Arnie ticking away contentedly, the wind skittering a bit as we come on at 22.00 again so we haul in the Yankee, neat and quick, and shortly after the wind swings firmly into the north-west. The skipper, ever alert to wind shifts, says decisively, 'She'll go north before too long now.' And she does.

Just before midnight, then, to round off the day, I'm out watching stars when Steve calls up, 'Hey, Theo, you've got e-mail, want to have a look?'

A rush of elation, made all the sweeter by this unexpected relaxing of discipline, his invitation to read and reply to e-mail when on watch. It's a hit, a real hit; her words on the screen ringing in my ears, my fingers flying over the keys as I reply. I come up into the fresh night and everyone's smiling at me, at this rush of energy, well being, joy. It's made known that everyone knew how much I was missing her. I feel borne up and shy, suddenly, to be with such good people. The wakefulness is worth gold to me, everything feels, for the first time, right and good and measured; I fall asleep, eventually, more at home in myself than I have felt for, it seems like, weeks.

⚓

DAY

## 17

Sunday, 21 May 2006

It has begun to seem as if this will go on for ever. Long ago, way back there in Punta Arenas, I was walking with Tony through the dusty, silent back streets of that mysterious closed town and he asked me, 'What's it like, to spend that much time on a boat?'

I had no easy answer. I remember saying, 'You'll feel as if time itself has changed. You'll get back that sense of time you had as a child during the holidays, when you'd run out onto the street in the morning, the endless day before you.

Remember the sense that teatime, bedtime, could be days, weeks, months away, out there ahead of you at the far side of a day you would never grow tired of? The idea that time out ahead of you was limitless, unbounded?'

'Yeah, yeah, I remember that.'

'Well, you'll get something like that feeling, but we'll also be constantly reminded of who we are, where we are, where we *really* are. We'll be having to cope with watches, structured time. And there will be days when we'll have a pain in our heads trying to get the two feelings into some kind of balance.'

'Yes,' says Tony, 'I can see that. You know, when you did that trip, you kept talking in the book about that sense of time, but you didn't say much about having to balance it with other stuff?'

'I know, I've been thinking about that; there were only four of us on that trip, there was enough space for what you might call dreamtime. Here there will be eleven of us, and it will all have to be much more ordered, I have a feeling that will change things. Maybe a lot.'

Well, that conversation had restarted in my head, it feels, even before I woke up this morning, Fed in the corridor calling softly, 'Hey, it's time to get up.' Dressing, stumbling around in the narrow space, chilled already after the snug warmth of the burrow, I realise there is something I should have added in that conversation: this will be a different kind of ocean.

And, coming up heavily into the wheelhouse, I realise something else. That trip was different, too, because I was sailing with people I already knew.

I stand out in the shelter, braced against the not-too-bad roll, looking in at the slumped bodies, the near-sleeping and near-waking faces of the watch going off, the watch coming on, and I feel myself among strangers. It's an eerie feeling: there, for a moment, a precise pointed awareness

that I am in the middle of nowhere, in a hostile environment, with nine perfect strangers, and no way to escape, no
possibility of walking away.

It's as if there's a bowl of cold air around my head.

A shiver runs through me.

I light a new cigarette from the butt of the one I'm fin-
ishing, something I rarely do, and Kevin sees it. His
shoulder jammed in against the port side wall of the shelter,
he's been watching me, I realise, for some time now.
Unexpectedly, he reaches across with his free hand, the one
not cradling his mug of coffee, and taps my shoulder with
his knuckles. 'Just hit you, huh?' His eyes are shrewd.

'What?' I say, but regret it immediately, because I see he
has understood exactly what's going through my thoughts.

He smiles, says, 'Ah c'mon, you know what I mean. It's
funny, I've been thinking the same thing since I got up. It
sure is strange, out here in the big ocean, when it hits you
that you don't know any of these people, that you're a bit
sick of the bumping and the banging and the boredom;
that maybe tonight you'd like to go have a beer with some
buddies, you know, just hang out, shoot the breeze, drive
home on a flat road, with streetlights, past all them houses,
just pull up in your drive, kill the lights, sit there a
moment, happy to be just about to walk in the door, climb
into that warm bed with herself asleep, you know, wriggling a bit but not mad at you or nothing that you smell of
beer and cigarettes, lie there for a while before falling
asleep yourself? That's what you're thinking, right?
Something like that?'

'No,' I say, softly because I can't trust my voice right
now, 'not something like that, exactly like that.'

He mock wrestles my neck for a moment, shouldering
past. 'Yep,' he says, going through, 'hits us all, buddy, hits
us all. You want another cup there, Theo?'

'Sure,' I call after him, 'sure. Thanks.'

'Bloody hell!' says Justin, materialising at my shoulder. What is this, the Day of Apparitions? Where did he come from?

'I was out there on deck, around the side of the wheel-house. Feeling a bit blue, are we?'

'Yeah, a bit, you know?'

'Yes, I know, it's beginning to get to me, too. But, gosh, Kevin! I mean…'

'Yes,' I say, 'full of surprises, eh?'

'Who is?' Kevin asks, a hand jutting out through the door with a mug jammed in a fist of rock.

'You are,' I say to him, looking him in the eye, taking the mug. 'Thanks.'

His face lights up, a sarcastic gleam in his eye. 'Oh yeah, sure. You know what? When herself says that to me, I duck; sure to be some kinda storm in the offing.'

But he knows he's got through to me, and I let him see that he has, and he winks over my shoulder at Justin and disappears again, saying, 'You guys be careful now, don't break my boat.'

The albatrosses come in over the leeward side usually, always from behind, about half mast height, banking slowly away from us, then in again. A pair this morning, in no kind of hurry, up to nothing much at all, just cruising alongside with no particular intent. They'll hang about for a while, then disappear. There are Great Petrels, too, as most mornings. I like them better, the cut and swoop of them, the greater live-liness, but best of all I like the Cape Petrels, with their black and white camo markings on the upper wing. I have a thought half-formed, about totem animals, how people elect or are elected by their totem spirits, but I haven't the energy to pursue the thought right now, and besides there are no Cape Petrels this morning, at least not yet, and the wind's getting up and Justin wants to harden in the sheet on the Yankee. 'Come on then, young Dorgan, lend a hand.'

If we are all struggling to reconcile actual time with the artificial time of watches, I don't know what clock Steve is on. He appears at seeming random, disappears as quietly and with no warning. Of course he's attuned to the boat like nobody else is, in part because to be so is his responsibility, in part because, in some sense, he is the only one in touch with the whole of what is happening at any given moment. While he's asleep, he's aware of any and all sudden changes: let there be an increase in noise level on any watch, a rise in wind speed and force, a different feel to the boat's motion through the seas, and he's out of sleep and instantly awake. I think, too, there's a predictive element to this: before going down he'll check the log, looking for the pattern of things, he'll check the barometer, calculate where it's going in the next few hours, he's memorised the GRIBs for the day, he might double-check if there's a fast-evolving situation, some imminent likelihood, and then he'll close the door of the cabin behind him, vanish into the dark only to surface when he knows he needs to, or, as I say, when there's a sudden alteration in the totality of things.

To one extent or another, all skippers have this facility, part natal instinct, perhaps, part ingrained by years of experience and learning, but Steve has it to an advanced degree.

Does he accept or does he covet this sense of total responsibility? That's a hard one. Duty or appetite? Something of both?

We've been motor-sailing a lot, sails and engines, pushing on to keep to our schedule. The boat's due in the yard at Cape Town; we have some leeway, of course, but there's a date beyond which it would not be acceptable to arrive. We know this, so, much as we would like to sail the whole way, we accept that this isn't possible.

One consequence of this, there's more maintenance to be done on the hard-working engine. For a day or two now, the cutless bearing, through which the shaft passes to the propeller, has been overheating. Apart altogether from the high-pitched grinding whine this produces, a source of considerable stress to us all, there is a danger here that the overheating bearing will distort the shaft, and that could have very serious consequences. If we lose the power of the engine, it isn't just that we are likely to be late in Cape Town, we will also be unable to pick and choose our weather, an option we currently, even if to a limited extent, enjoy. I know that deep down we would all of us love to sail the whole passage, to take what chance brings us, to beat into or run before heavy weather, to pit our wits against the weather gods, make our peace with the elements – for the experience, certainly, to test ourselves, of course, and for our store of memories. There are sailing purists, I'm sure of it, who would disdain our use of engine on passage, and I might agree with them, were I snug in a firelit bar somewhere or coasting from one sheltered anchorage to the next, and not down here in this powerful ocean as it actually is; I'm digging out the toolbox for Steve now, and thinking: let them come down here into this and see what they have to say.

The cutless bearing is water-cooled, so the idea is to find some way of getting water to flow to it. First plan, run a pipe to a pump in the lazarette, back of the boarding plat-form, under the afterdeck, see if that works. OK, we get the pipe through, connect it to the vane pump, but this can't supply sufficient pressure and quickly overheats. Steve sits back on his haunches, thinking, and while he's thinking his hands are moving, acting out what he's thinking of, fitting part to part, tracing a run of pipe here, a valve fitting there. Nothing occurs to him, his hands waver, fall still. 'Let's have a look in the workshop.'

Up he springs, through the wheelhouse, on past Tony and Fed's cabin, past Mike's, through Kevin's, always tidy and squared away. There's a kind of lobby then, between the ends of both passageways and the forepeak. All kinds of everything stored here – tools, valves, filters, runs of pipe and rolls of cable, washers, nuts, screws, bolts, nails and God knows what else, all meticulously stored, shelved, named and numbered. I've passed through here on numberless occasions, never really stopped to take it in. 'The thing is, Theo, you have to be able to find what you need immediately. The way it is, when you need something you almost always need it in a hurry, right? I know people think I'm a pain in the arse about this, but it's really important that everyone knows where everything is, all the time, yeah? You know where your survival suit is, right?'

'Yes, in the small locker beside the head of my bunk. In fact, had a look yesterday to make sure Di hadn't moved it. Then had a look to make sure hers was where it should be, too.'

'OK, you put it back, right? You know where it is. But suppose we lose a through-hull valve then? Want to be bloody quick about fitting a new one, or a bung or something, right? So, you gotta know where everything is; when you take something out, if you don't use it, you put it right back where it should be for the next guy. Simple!'

While he's talking, he's picking up, looking at and then putting back various small bits of pipe, ball joints, valves and the like. The whole time he has a clear picture in his mind of the run of pipework, the feeds and diverters and pumps available to him back there under the sole of the saloon. 'Nah, mate,' he says finally, hands still, gaze far away, 'nothing comes to mind, does it? Looks like we're buggered. Any ideas?'

I have no particular aptitude for mechanics, I don't even drive a car, but I've been paying attention, following the logic of what he's trying to do, and I've grasped one salient fact: he needs to get water flowing through, in or around (I'm not entirely sure which) the overheating bearing. 'Can it be sea water?'

'Yeah, course.'

'Well whether or not the engine is on, we're moving through the water, right? Suppose we trail a wide-mouthed funnel over the stern, a pipe at the outflow of it leading back to the bearing, right? Maybe the pressure of water forced into the funnel would be enough to get it flowing back up the pipe to the bearing?'

'Yeah,' says Steve, 'we might try that, mate.'

But his face says for him what he's too polite to say out loud: daft idea. We never do try it, and he never does find a solution. As luck will have it, we will sail more for the rest of the trip, and motor less. The bearing doesn't seize up, the shaft doesn't distort, but whenever the engine comes on and that infuriating whine cuts to the roots of my teeth, I'll be muttering darkly to myself: well it might have been a daft idea, but we could at least have tried it.

'Any luck?' Tony asks.

'Nah.'

They're scrubbing the decks, himself and Justin, happily splashing buckets of water about, leaning into the long-handled brushes. Amazing what builds up, especially in the cockpit, considering the wagonloads of water that fall on us when it rains, that come pouring back from the bow in heavy seas. Bits of sandwich, scraps of meat and cheese, half a biscuit (how come that hasn't just dissolved and washed away?), an occasional cigarette butt, tea and coffee stains, general grime. It's a kind of relief, I realise, scrubbing at some recalcitrant mysterious stain, bringing our focus down to the smaller scale, the mundane domestic. We are all the time struggling to accommodate ourselves to the vast scale of the weather, the tumultuous and constant pile-driving winds, the great lifting and falling mountains of water all around us, the sudden cloudbursts, the violent movements of deck and hull, table and seats and bunks; we are all the time lurching, falling, banging into things and each other, hanging on to things, launching ourselves across open spaces; our hands, hips, feet and elbows are battered and bruised, our heads are in a constant whirl and spin. It's curiously soothing, then, to be engaged in something as familiar as brushing and mopping, hosing and scrubbing. This late morning, the wind a calm 40 knots, the seas a trifling 2 metres, we are enjoying an interlude of familiar domestic peace. When the afternoon watch comes up for lunch, we watch everyone sharply, tut tutting when a crumb falls, darting in with a paper napkin when a soup bowl leaves a damp smear on a gleaming surface. They watch us warily, sensing that some kind of madness has seized us, unaware that we have become, for the moment at least, houseproud. Neither wives nor companions, of course, will believe a word of this.

We plod through the coursework for the afternoon, breaking off early in a last spasm of the day's domesticity to wash clothes, to shower, change sheets and pillowcases, tidy our cabins.

We change worlds on the 18.00 to 22.00 watch, sailors again. The engine's off, we've a bit of wind, and we take turns helming, giving Arnie a break and ourselves a treat. Justin's the best helmsman, effortlessly reading wind and wave and the motion of the boat, only now and then checking the compass to see he's not gone off course. Macken is good, too, but tense, watching the compass more, a picture of determination. It takes me a while to get the feel of it, up on the box behind the big wheel, clipped on, of course, ship's orders at night, head up over the shelter in the cold onrush of wind. It's harder than I thought to settle into the feel of it, and when I get knocked off, by a wave out of the ordinary, say, or a sudden fall in the wind, I tend to over-compensate, spinning the wheel too far to one side, then too far to the other. Charity prevails, no one says anything much, but their faces say enough for me to wish they would all go away and leave me alone until I get back into the swing of it. Kevin says nothing almost as eloquently as Justin does, but in the end he takes pity on my annoyance with myself, and offers some coaching tips. 'Close your eyes,' he says, 'think back to earlier, with Arnie on the wheel. Listen to the tick, tick, tick. Small adjustments, you see? Small constant adjustments. Don't wait for her head to fall off, anticipate, let your hands feed the wheel.'

'That's it exactly,' says Justin, 'small movements. Don't wait for things to go wrong, don't be obsessive about keeping to the exact compass course, stay five to either side of it as an average.'

Macken sits staring off into space, felled by a sudden energy drop. Says, 'Steve's awake below, I think I'll pop down and see what he says about the weather.'

As he unclips, moves towards the stairs down, Steve sticks his head up. 'E-mail, Theo, Justin. You too, Kev. Been having a look at the GRIBs, going to get a bit nasty in the next four hours or so.'

A sudden grip of ice in the stomach. In Steve's private lexicon 40 knots is 'a bit breezy', 60 knots 'breezy' – what does he mean by 'a bit nasty'? A bad storm, I'm thinking, very awake now, nervous. Turns out he means the wind is going to go south-east, heading us – an ugly way to go sailing, smacking head-on into the oncoming swell and wind. A longkeeler would carve her way through, to some extent at least. *Pelagic*, with her flat sections, will rise and slam down, rise and slam down again, on and on for as long as we make into the wind and waves.

'Right then,' we say to Kev, 'if that's what we're looking at, might be a good idea to plan some low-maintenance dinners for the next few days, eh?'

Big pots in the forepeak time again. Yes, and we'll have to think about the sail plan, won't we? The kind of man-oeuvres we'll have to deal with? A brisk bustle of common sense, a making of lists, a self-assignment of various responsibilities. Agreement, a plan.

'My boys, my boys!' Kevin is pleased, and not least because Steve down below can't help overhearing this conversation. Kevin's watch does its teamwork bit, and Kevin's grin would do credit to a Swiss clockmaker as we slip effortlessly, unprompted, into the next gear. Mind you, down in the shadows of my mind, I'm still scolding myself for my clumsy helming; it's good to be part of a functioning team, but my quarrel, in the end, is always with myself. Another ten minutes and I can check my mail. Tony puts the kettle on for the upcoming watch; Big Mike needs a head start on the others, a slow awakener, he says, 'always was, guess I always will be', so Kevin goes up to give him a shake. Justin starts taking notes prior to filling in the hourly log. The long watch is nearly done.

⚓

DAY

# 18

Monday, 22 May 2006

So much for being headed. I come up well-rested for a change, expecting wind, expecting to be banging about a bit, and, instead, there's not enough wind to have us put out more than the main with three reefs in it; not for power, just to hold us steady.

After yesterday's adventures with the cutless bearing, I am much more attuned to the engine than before. Now it's obtrusive beyond belief, running sweetly to be sure – Steve is meticulous about maintenance schedules, and so are

Kevin and Debs – but monotonous, monotonous, monotonous.

'I don't know,' says Justin, as we lean in over the chart table, tracking back along our route to date, tracing finger lines on towards Tristan, 'I just don't know.'

'What?' I ask, when the silence has gone on long enough. 'What don't you know?'

'I don't know that this is quite what I expected when I signed on for this trip.'

'Ah, I know what you mean,' Tony says. 'I think when I heard about it first all I could think of was Cape Horn. I got it into my head that that would be huge, a huge experience, like. And in a way it wasn't, you know?'

'I agree,' says Justin, 'well, sort of. I mean, it was blowing a hooley, you know, only for some reason that didn't register with us. It really was blowing you know, I mean that's storm force 10 for God's sake!'

Kevin is sitting back in the small seat to the side of the chart table, taking all this in, Tony is perched on the two-man bench seat opposite, on the port side; the Admiral and myself have our elbows hooked over the chart table. Arnie is driving the boat, but each of us, unobtrusively, is watching the course, watching the wind speed, watching the sea state over each other's shoulders. Parliament is in session, and we know without thinking about it that Our Great Leader won't be popping up like a jack-in-the-box for some time to come.

'So, Tony,' Kevin leans forward a little, wickedness in his face, 'are you trying to tell me you were disappointed in Cape Horn?'

'Ah jay, no, no, not at all, it's just…'

But Justin has something else on his mind. 'That lot got a right bollocking from Steve this morning, did you hear?'

Yes we heard. This time, I'd scrambled into my gear, got as far as the steps up to the wheelhouse, close enough to make out what was going on, and decided this was one time I definitely wasn't needed.

'I ran into Macken on the other side,' says Justin.

'And I could see the two of you at the end of the passageway when I stuck my head out,' Kevin says, 'but, to tell you the truth, I didn't even get dressed, cos I knew this was coming. Hoo boy, was it coming!'

'I never saw you,' says Tony, sounding almost wounded, but we're not to be deflected.

The starboard watch had been getting the full Captain Bligh treatment from a very pissed-off Steve. 'What the fuck are all of you doing out here, eh? Why did you come on this trip if you're not even prepared to work together for fuck's sake! All I hear is bitching and moaning, picking faults with each other, why can't you pull together, eh? Answer me, go on. It isn't fucking rocket science, you know! All you have to do is work together, is that too much for you? What're you doing out here, anyway? What are you doing this Yachtmaster for? Do any of you seriously think you're fit to skipper a passage with this attitude? Simon, Fed, you guys are sailors, you know what it's about, eh? So why can't you do it right, then? Diane, I know you've no experience, sorry, I don't mean that, but you've only got some sailing experience, right? But you're a teacher in a fucking university for Christ's sake, you're not stupid, are you? And Mike, Mike mate I know you like to do things in your own sweet time but this is about team building, this is about you all working as a team isn't it?'

Round about then, I decided I didn't want to add to anyone's woes by being seen, by letting it be known I was aware of what was going on, so I crept back to bed without hearing the rest, without really needing to hear the rest.

Kevin is lugubrious, listening to us piece Steve's harangue together. 'I don't know, guys, maybe it's an age thing, you think? I know Mike's the oldest guy on the boat but Fed and Simon now... and Diane... I mean, you guys have your shit together, you look out for each other, I see it, Steve sees it. Theo says he has much less experience than you guys but you all pull your weight as far as I'm concerned, you think it's because you're older, got a little more sense?'

Justin, much younger than Macken or myself, might justifiably bridle at being called older, but he sees what Kevin's getting at. 'I think it's a generation thing, in part anyway. Mike excepted, those guys are used to thinking me, me, me, it's what the culture encourages, isn't it?'

Tony is nervous that we're drifting towards psychobabble, as he calls it. 'I just think Fed and Simon are never going to get on. They haven't a good word to say about each other, or to each other. You know the way Simon got christened Spice Boy? Where did that come from, by the way? No matter. Well, you know the way Simon is, he makes a joke of it, calls *himself* Spice Boy. Fed puts an edge on it, I think, there's that feeling of a put-down.'

'Yes,' says, Justin, 'and then there's the Fed and Di thing.'

We let that one hang there in the air a moment, and then let it go by. Nobody's quite sure what's going on there. How serious it is, whether or not it's romantic-sexual or boy-girl pairing in a small gang, but we're not comfortable with it. Equally, we try to respect their privacy, we try to mind our own business, and though everyone has a definite private opinion about the business, we keep it to ourselves. Tact? You could call it that. Something larger, too, though: what keeps a boat together is some sense that everyone is in it together, the weak with the strong, the experienced with the inexperienced, or less-experienced. Everyone has something to give to the boat, and nobody is ever blamed for having less to give than anyone else. In a sense, a good skipper encourages a kind of ideal communism, as long as it's accepted, of course, that he's ultimately in charge – from each according to their ability, to each according to their need. In a good boat, anyone with a particular skill is always prepared to teach it to someone lacking that skill; equally, in a good boat people take care to get along more or less equally well with everyone else. Over and above that, while it's natural that individuals will gravitate towards others with whom they feel some affinity, it can be corrosive if some people start thinking in terms of 'us, and then those others'. And that's the destabilising effect of a pair bond in a situation like ours: one natural consequence of pairing is protective withdrawal, and you can't be coming forward to others, as you need to for the good of the watch, if your deeper instinct is to pull back into your protected space.

Tony's uncomfortable with the turn the conversation is taking. 'I don't know, I think we're being a bit judgemental here.'

'And maybe a bit smug?' I suggest.

We think about that for a while.

'No, I don't think we're judging people here,' says Justin, 'but there's a real difference between the watches, we're just trying to figure out what it might be. And bear in mind, nobody's claiming to have the right and wrong of it here, we all know we could be completely wrong about this. For all we know, they might think *our* watch is dysfunctional. Isn't this a bit like rival teams here, each unable to see the good in the other?'

We think about that for a while, too.

'Kevin, you're being very quiet, what do you think?'

'What do I think? Well all's I know is this watch is working and them other guys ain't. Debs is trying everything she can. Y'all heard Steve last night, he's tryin' to figure it out too, I guess. Y'know what's weird, though? All cooped up like this together, you'd think we'd get to know each other better, wouldn't you? Back there at home you'd imagine, hell, I'm going to be locked up with all these people in a small space for five weeks, and you imagine all you might learn about someone in that time, right? But it ain't like that at all. I haven't a clue about those guys. I'm beginning to figure out you three gentlemen, but, take Simon now. Someone like Simon, I just can't figure out. One minute I see him being kind and thoughtful, next minute he's saying something sarcastic to me, and thinking I won't get that he's dissing me, right? I mean nothing out-right, OK, something that would get him a sock on the jaw in other circumstances? But, the little dig, you know? And then the others? I like Fed, I guess, he's a good sailor, too, but he has to be numero uno, doesn't he? I mean, Steve's the skipper, right? What, Fed doesn't get this? Thinks he knows better? Di, well Di's a nice kid, I like her – I guess we all do, right? But this isn't her kind of territory, is it? She tries, give her that, she tries, all you can ask, really. Big Mike now, hoo boy, he's a character, ain't he? World of his own, that guy, but steady as they come, steady as they come, man.'

'Wind's coming up a bit,' Justin says into the silence. 'Oh look, time for the log.' Tony springs into action: 'Tea!' He shoots off down the stairs.

'Like a bloody ferret,' says Justin, grinning. 'Whoosh! He's gone!'

Time for a deck check, 'Theo, my man! Buckle up!'

Simon's lashings are still perfect, the poles haven't budged an inch.

We meet at the bow. 'All clear my side.'

'All clear mine.'

We turn to look forward, rising and plunging as *Pelagic* ploughs on. 'Sure is an empty world out here.'

'Sure is, Kev. And that's why I like it.'

A wolfish grin. 'Me too, buddy, me too. Kinda puts things in perspective, don't it?'

We take tea in the shelter, me watching the wheel thoughtfully, the ceaseless, small ticking corrections of the autopilot as we fall sideways down the face of a wave, as the wind dips for a moment, comes up again a point or two off.

'See,' Justin says, 'just small corrections, no big turns? You start to come back against it as soon as you sense it beginning to fall away?'

Tony juts his chin towards the stern. 'Dolly's looking well today, the dress suits her.' Our muslin-shrouded sheep is still there, lashed to the gantry, rising and falling to the swell, the tiniest of flutters where a small corner of her wrapping is coming loose.

'Our turn to cook dinner tonight, isn't it?'

'Oh yeah,' says Kevin. 'Steve says to ask you guys how you feel about leg of lamb.'

'You mean mutton dressed as lamb,' mutters the epicurean Admiral. 'Still, we'll do our best with it, eh, Mr Dorgan? Don't suppose there's any rosemary, Tony? No? Thought not. So, roast potatoes I imagine, green beans, how're the green beans, Tony?'

'Fine, fine,' says the appointed keeper of fruit and vegetables.

'Yes, red wine for the gravy, I think. Onions, lots of garlic of course…'

A thought occurs to me. 'Justin, have you seen the forty-eight-hour forecast?'

'No, why?'

'Well, there's a bit of dirty stuff up ahead. My guess is tomorrow we'll be cooking for the forepeak, for the day after, right? So, we should keep the bones from tonight for tomorrow's soup, and make dinner for Wednesday while we're at it.'

'What day's today?' Tony asks.

'Monday?'

'Never mind that,' says Kevin, 'anyone know what date it is?'

'May 22nd,' says Justin, promptly. 'Kevin, do you ever look at the log?'

'Only at the good stuff, my man. How many miles to go and what's the bar doing?'

Lunch is a silent affair today. Steve is remote, has his lunch outside with Debs and nobody's minded to join them. Mummy and Daddy, I think, looking around me at the subdued faces; forms keep repeating themselves, now we're being the tense children of unhappy parents, unsure when to speak, or what to say.

Butchery lightens the atmosphere, later in the afternoon. I've a basin of sudsy water on the afterdeck, wrestling salt and dirt out of some socks and a fleece, an acrobatic fling with the homely, when Steve pops up with a knife and iron, whetting the blade, swish-swish-swish. Simon has elected to be deputy for the dismembering, peels back the muslin, exposes the marbled blue-cold hind leg of poor Dolly. Fed's on camera duty, Di is both fascinated and, perhaps, slightly appalled, murmuring into her microphone, asking Steve to give a running commentary on what he's doing. Our chef de cuisine for the day looks grave when ceremonially handed tonight's dinner.

'I don't know, looks pretty tough to me.'

'She'll be fine, mate, don't you worry. In the old days, this would have been captain and officers only, you lot would have been left waiting for soup from the bones. Luxury grub, this.'

In the old days? On some of the ships I've been reading about, a sheep hung on the quarterdeck wouldn't have lasted kissing time unless the captain had posted an armed guard, and maybe a guard on the guard as well.

We could, of course, have done what we do with the rest of the meat: had Dolly butchered and dressed in Stanley, the various cuts vacuum sealed and packed away against the hull up in the forepeak, but Steve enjoys the atavistic touch, and so do we all. It's a primitive but effective way of carrying meat and it recalls an age long past, it's a kind of connection to all those who have crossed this ocean before us in far less comfort than we enjoy, grateful when they could get it for fresh meat, dry clothes, some respite from the weather. We have it easy, I think, and regret the thought immediately. Don't go tempting fate now, I admonish myself, you should know better.

And besides, it's a bit of fun. Fed enjoys himself, photographing Steve and Simon at work. Simon and Steve enjoy mugging for photographs. Di enjoys seeing Fed enjoying himself and Big Mike is enjoying himself photographing them all.

'Happy families, eh Debs,' I call, but she looks at me blankly, she is not amused. Ouch! Kevin, behind her, shakes his head.

We eat out of bowls, in the wheelhouse and in the shelter, perched on steps, on seats, hunched on the floor. Ridiculous even to think of eating at the saloon table, the boat always at an angle, swinging this way and that, banging up and down, never still. Some nights are better than others; tonight's not so bad but forget roast lamb with all the trimmings, a glass of wine, civilised conversations. In the half-dark, you chop up whatever food is in your bowl whenever you find a more-or-less horizontal moment, and then it's fork or spoon the rest of the way. The green beans are *à point*, the roast potatoes brown and perfect on the outside, soft and floury on the inside, and Dolly, God love her, has done her best to rise to the occasion, tasting almost convincingly of lamb. Mumbled praise for the Admiral and his *sous-chefs*. It's a photo finish for seconds between Steve and Kevin.

This period of relative calm has gone on for too long, we feel. Things are being tidied away – we're all at it, I notice, a general tightening up. Whenever you go into the cockpit now, there's someone out there, looking up, looking around, checking the wind, the sea state. As if on some deep cellular level, no matter what seems to be going on in our talk, we have given ourselves over to some primal sense of being locked into the lift and fall of all that lifts and falls. Change coming, we feel it. There's something out there; we all sense it, but we know it's best not to speak of it. Not yet.

⚓

DAY

## 19

Tuesday, 23 May 2006

There's a small but noticeable cooling of the air. The barometer is still pretty high at 1016, but we note this with a sceptical eye: can't last, we know this. The hairs on the back of the neck have flattened; whatever was circling us last night has moved away somewhere, out beyond the firelight. Nevertheless by mid-morning the boeuf bourguignon for tomorrow is already cooked and cooling, soon to be sent forward to the forepeak for tomorrow's dinner. Kevin is often amused by the culinary inventiveness on our watch, but boeuf bourguignon, as far as he's concerned, takes the biscuit.

'What the hell's that?' he asked, when Justin proposed it. 'Sounds like some fancy-dancy dish from the French Quarter in New Orleans.' He pronounces it, to my delight, N'Orlins.

'Spot on,' says Justin. 'It is French, just a beef stew with red wine, really. Got this red wine left over from last night's whatyamacallit—'

'Lamb,' says Macken, helpfully.

'—Not lamb, bloody mutton. So I thought we might as well use it up.'

'Well use it up, man, use it up. God but I love this watch. Ya hear that, Steve? We're having beef boorgeenyon for dinner tomorrow.'

'What's that, then?'

'Oh, just a beef stew with red wine,' says Kevin, as one who says everyone knows *that*...

'Cool bananas,' says Our Great Leader. 'Sounds good.'

I watch him go. Kev knits his eyebrows, 'Our Great Leader? Who christened him that? No, let me guess, that would be Mr Dorgan, right?'

'Sometimes, for short, we call him Oscar Golf Lima, or Oscar Golf if we're in a hurry,' I tell him, being helpful. 'Or OGL.'

'No, no, get me out of here!' And up he goes too.

'A cup of Barry's tea, gentlemen?'

'Why thank you, Mr Macken.'

The Admiral unbends to go rummaging under the port side seat for biscuits.

The wind's about 30 knots, the sea is coming up. It's a shredded blue sky this morning, high winds up there tearing the clouds apart. Just cold enough that, when you ease back your fleece hat, the tips of your ears begin to tingle after about a minute. We keep putting gloves on, taking them off, putting them on again. Steve is helming, for the exercise presumably. This is the good stuff for him, you feel, driving the boat. I watch him for a while, for the sheer human pleasure of watching a man do what he was born to do. He braces a knee against a spoke of the big wheel, leans out and down to ease the mainsheet, one hand cupping the coils, one hand tailing. 'You want a hand there, Steve?'

'Nah, mate, I'm fine. You just enjoy your fag.'

Two minutes later. 'Theo, you want to ease out the stay-sail a smidge? Ta. Got a light?'

Something is out of place here, I feel it, I just can't see what it is, then I get it: no orange boots. Instead OGL is wearing some rather fetching knee-high sheepskin lined boots, flat soled like slippers.

'What's with the boots, Steve?'

'Oh man, you got to get yourself a pair of these, they're so fucking comfortable, you wouldn't believe it.' Then a flurry as something catches us broadside, kicks the wheel in his hands. 'Oops! See that, Theo? This kind of sea's a right bugger, never know where you are with it. And the wind? Fuck me, look at it. Just where we don't want it, eh?'

Just where we don't want it, is right. It's gone round south-east which means, as our course is north-east, that it's driving the seas, 2 metres and rising by the look of things, smack into our starboard bow. This makes for a very uncomfortable motion, partly because we keep slamming our flat forefoot, partly because *Pelagic* is fairly slabsided, and waves on the beam tend to smack us the way a wave hits a vertical wall. To the usual rising and plunging, rolling and yawing we can now add a repetitive shock and shudder, as if our starboard side is being slammed repeatedly by some mindless brute with a hammer.

He's still at it, the brute I mean, as I try to catch some sleep later. It makes for an interesting addition to the usual fun of trying to sleep while every minute or so someone picks up your bed and drops it 6 feet or more onto a concrete floor. I like this boat in many ways, she's strong, buoyant, reassuring in a blow, she's a boat to inspire considerable confidence is what I mean, but she doesn't do the knifing through with grace bit very well. And, I remember as things finally get blessedly fuzzy, seemingly she doesn't heave-to, either.

Woke mid-afternoon to hear Steve at it again, getting stuck into the starboard watch about not pulling as a team. Ah, this is bloody stupid. What's the point of roaring at them? If it was me, it would just get my back up. And I just know they're all thinking rebelliously, I didn't pay all this money to be abused and roared at. 'I'd be fucking thinking it myself,' I mutter crossly, wondering where the hell my other sock has got to, and why the hell one of my sea boots smells and the other doesn't. All this shouting and roaring, for fuck's sake.

A raised eyebrow from Tony in the galley, a shake of the head. He doesn't think this is such a good idea either. Justin, who's also up, is more forthright. 'Steve's out of order,' he says. 'If they're not getting on, and obviously they aren't, what's the use of telling them that, over and over? Be better to work out a way of leading them towards getting on, wouldn't it?'

It's unusual to have both watches awake at the same time, apart from meal times. We're in the cockpit, saying nothing much, just looking at the sea, and Steve, Debs and Kevin drift in until we're all standing or sitting there, nobody saying anything. Steve is no fool, he knows what's on our minds. He ducks his head into the wheelhouse to see where everyone else is at – the other watch are faffing about the boat, cleaning or preparing dinner – and says, 'Look, guys, nobody likes this shit, ok? Nobody likes being bollocked, and I don't like bollocking people. Stands to reason, don't it?

Be nice if we were all some big happy family, everyone pulling along nicely together, all cool bananas, eh? But, look, I've tried being sweet and reasonable, with them all as a group, with all of them as individuals, but fuck it, nothing changes, you know? I mean, what'm I supposed to do, eh?'

We slam off a wave sideways, Arnie whirrs and ticks, ticks, ticks; Steve takes a quick glance at the compass, forward at the sails, steps around Kev and adjusts the Yankee sheet slightly, doing a quick all-round scan of the horizon at the same time. I know that, in a minute's time, he won't remember this small blur of action, of readjustment, but it frames his dilemma perfectly. He's got a monster of a boat to sail, a grotesque set of powers and influences to command, cajole, sidestep and manage. He has a fixed set of forces available to him, to pit against these: in essence, his own experience, the boat's systems and two watches. Now one of those watches, to use one of his own characteristic phrases, has gone pear-shaped. Out here, today, right now, in these building seas, this rising wind, if it were me I'd be very concerned. In fact, I am concerned, but there is very little I can do about it.

It's all very well, I reflect, for me to be thinking, if it were me, I'd handle them differently, but that's too simple. If I had Steve's experience of this boat, this ocean, I'd be a different person. Even if this experience were grafted on to my self as I habitually think of it, having lived through many such crossings in such an environment would have changed me anyway. Certainly, now that I think of it soberly, command in these circumstances would very likely advance the authoritarian streak I sometimes recognise in myself. Under pressure of weather or danger, living by day and by night with the ever-present need to have an answer at all times to whatever arises, responsible not just for the ship but for the lives and well being of all aboard, myself not least, I concede that my instinct towards consensus would very likely be overruled by my equally lively instinct to take charge.

It occurs to me that we have become mesmerised by this ocean, by the passage of days, each much like the next, by the ceaseless rise and fall, the sense of being driven onward by an unrelenting wind. We rise, we work, we fall back again and sleep, only to rise again to more of the same, day after day, night after night. The body's wisdom is to adjust to whatever norm is prevailing at a given time, and the mind's instinct, especially outside the comfort zone of the daily habitual, is to follow the body's lead. We are confined in a small shell, conscious of two great facts: the boat is all that is the case, and the boat is out there in a gigantic, sometimes monstrous, void.

In a sense, we have put to one side the idea that we are making irrevocable progress in a fixed direction, down the long line that rejoins the world at Cape Town. It's as if we believe in the chart more than in the planet, in the two-dimensional reduction rather than in the full-blooded actuality of being here, now, on passage from a known, real place, Stanley, to a known real place, Cape Town.

We accede to being carried forward and, to that extent, our focus turns inward, to the small handful of people on our watch, to the four-hour or six-hour span of the watch. We work out our little social worlds, and the wild card is the skipper, the one who comes and goes on some other schedule of his own, in some other unknowable dimension. Time happens to us in little bubbles, begins again with each watch, disappears again as individually we go to sleep.

The thing is, I'm starting to grasp this now, Steve has no world of his own to retreat to, as we take refuge in our other lives, or rather his is the full true world here, the boat in the present moment, and the boat on passage from one known place to the next. Minute by minute, waking or sleeping, he has to keep everything in mind, past, present and future. And he will have to find some way of conveying his sense of the passage to us, some way of recruiting us into this sense of a common departure point, a common destination towards which we voyage moment by moment in the here and now. All of us, together.

We sit there, assembling our thoughts, Justin and Tony and I, after the others have gone about various bits of business. Justin says, thoughtfully, 'Isn't it interesting, that he would include us like that? I mean, you could understand him talking it out with Debs and Kev...'

Justin and Steve haven't managed to hit it off, and it's clear that Justin would make a very different kind of skipper, but he is a man of grace and fairness: as much as Tony and I are, Justin is struck by the simple honesty with which Steve has brought us, the term amplifying even as I hear it coming, into his confidence.

Yesterday, after bollocking number one, as it were, I was thinking of how much I enjoy sailing with these two, and with Kevin. I remember thinking, 'we could sail this boat, we could finish this trip', meaning by 'we' ourselves and Steve. Now the thought comes back to me, and this time I find myself wondering if this might become, in some sense, an option. Yeah, I think, I could sail anywhere with these two guys – if they'd have me, of course.

'With you, too,' I say to Kevin, as he emerges into the sunlight again.

'Me too, what?'

'Ah never mind,' I say. 'I'll explain it later.'

'Jesus, sometimes I think you guys are nuts. Never mind, never mind, no doubt all will be revealed. Sometime.' He has a sextant in his hand. 'I'm going to take some sights, I reckon; one of you gentlemen care to mark for me?'

'I will,' says Tony, hopping up briskly. 'I was thinking of going for a walk, but sure this'll do.'

No point looking at me, guys, I don't understand him either.

'You know what?' Kevin says, taking a long slow look around while Macken ferrets out pen and paper. 'It appears to me, yes it does, that it's going to come on to rain. Yes sirree.'

And it does. By late afternoon, it's bucketing down rain, a cold wind has come up, there's foam on the grey waves now, an undertone of black where the swell rears and turns over before sliding greasily under us. It's got dark early, not the true dark but that kind of lowering dark in daytime that makes you uneasy. Steve and Debs head up to the foredeck, in full wet gear, life jackets, harnesses clipped on. It's lashing down now, and I admire, not for the first time, the dogged tenaciousness of Debs, her stocky grace and matter-of-factness as she goes about her business up there. I'm watching them from the step behind the wheel, cold spray hitting me from the starboard side, rain falling near-vertically on my face. We do this automatically, no one's ever said anything about it, when someone goes forward, day or night, one of us always stands watch, just keeping an eye out. Debs, swinging back into the cockpit, ruddy-faced, laughing at something that happened or something that Steve must have said up there, sees me, gives me a quick squeeze on the elbow, a smiley wink as she goes by.

'Nice one, Theo.' Steve pauses a second, looks at me, nods and passes on.

Simon comes out for a cigarette. We sit on opposite seats in the shelter, not saying much, not needing to say much. We hear Steve inside say, 'See that, you guys? Anyone notice anything, no?' He's slipping out of his sodden jacket, looking for somewhere to hang it. 'No? How'd you think I got wet? Anyone notice Debs and me up there on the foredeck?'

'Well I did,' says Di.

Steve doesn't hear her. 'No? Well Theo did, out there having a smoke I suppose, so he stood up on the box, to keep an eye on us, right? Well, who's on watch? You are. So how come it never occurred to one of you to keep an eye, eh? C'mon, answer me? Tell you what, you gotta start thinking like that, right, if you're ever going to make a team? Ah, sod it.'

I wish he hadn't done that, I really wish he hadn't done that.

Simon leans over. 'It's cool, man, don't sweat it. Anyway, he's right. We should have been looking out for them.' Then after a short silence. 'Steve's OK, you know. Steve's cool.'

I could manage an hour's kip, I reflect, still plenty of time before we're actually due on watch, but I don't feel like walking through the wheelhouse just now, so I light up another, sit back and think of the weather.

We've been stealth-sailing for the past day and a half. We're making more north than north-east now, two big lows out there, one more or less behind, one more or less in front of us, and we're slipping neat as we can between the two of them. Steve has a particular fondness for this kind of work, balancing the need to make progress towards our immediate goal – Tristan, I remind myself, Tristan, Christ, I'd half-forgotten about Tristan – against the hammering we'll get if we aim into a low, and the fall off in speed, hence distance made good, that will inevitably follow. So, we sail farther, and slightly more easily, off our best course in theory but making better speed, hence gaining in time what we lose in distance.

I enjoy this myself; I don't have a very good grasp of what the GRIBs and forecasts are telling us, but when Steve or, say, Justin, explains to me what I'm looking at, I have a knack for figuring out where we should be in order to take advantage of the predicted conditions. When someone has helped me decode the graphics, I will happily decamp to the chart table to scrutinise the log for trends, check what the barometer has been up to, have a gander at wind speed and sea state, and take a long look at the chart. The fun is in laying a course, waypoint by waypoint, that lies as close as possible to our ideal projected track but gives us the optimum heading at any given time. It's a kind of four-dimensional predictive geometry, I think, and immensely satisfying – until of course someone else comes along and derives an entirely different course, or series of tactical moves, from exactly the same set of data.

The wind has been treacherous all day, moody, strengthening and dropping at seeming random. By contrast, and following some law I don't quite understand, the seas have been steadily building so that it's lumpy, bumpy and awkward moving around.

Towards midnight Steve pops his head up, says, 'Hey Kev, if it was me I'd maybe drop in the last reef, maybe take in 50 per cent of the Yankee, eh?' And then he's gone again.

'Right, gentlemen,' says Tony, forestalling Kevin.

'Ah, get the hell out there, lemme see if I can't git you guys good and wet.'

'Ah, you're all the same,' says Justin, 'you bloody slave drivers.'

'You betcha. Out!'

One of those moments when everyone's in good humour, sober, aware of exactly what needs to be done. Justin takes charge of the reef, scuttling wet-backed up the high side, me trailing, while Tony and Kevin take her head up into the wind a tad before they start grinding in that Yankee. Justin takes up the topping lift, flips off the line clutch in the boom; I have the reef line on the coffee-grinder winch amidships, over the keel hatch, and as Justin eases the main halyard I start to grind like crazy, my damaged shoulder giving me hell but so what? We need to do this fast and clean and right.

OK, he signals, OK, and I lock off the reefing line on the drum, drop the tail down through the grating at my feet into the basket below decks. Justin meanwhile has hard-ened in the topping lift, and is now putting his back into getting the main halyard bar taut. I glance over my shoul-der from time to time and always either Tony or Kevin is there, torch in hand, keeping an eye on us.

'OK, let's get back.'

Justin has to put his face nearly in my ear to be heard, and this time he follows me aft as Kevin feeds us slowly off the wind again and we settle to a more stable ride, a more fluid and comfortable motion.

'Nicely done, gentlemen, very nicely done indeed.'

'Ah, we do it for love of you, Kev, you know we do it for you.'

'Why thank you, Admiral, yes I do know that, and it makes a girl all shy, it does. But hey, seriously, you guys notice anything just now?'

'Well, yeah,' says Tony, rain pouring down his specs, 'a few things, what did you have in mind?'

'Well, old Steve there, you notice he just comes popping up says do this, do that, and then heads off down again?'

'Well, yeah.'

'So, it ain't that long ago he'd a been up here like a hawk, watching you guys, giving you ten kinds a hell. Do this, don't do that, don't break my boat and what all? You see him do that tonight? Uh huh. See, he knows you guys are OK. You getting me here?'

'Tea,' says Tony. 'Barry's for all.'

'Make mine a double,' says Justin.

I turn my back to the sun, and down there where my shadow is pointing the next land is Antarctica. Nothing between there and here but a great cold waste of water. I look back west, and, with an effort, grasp that the nearest land in that direction is the long tapering tip of Argentina, a fleck of Chile dangling beneath it; I turn east, and out there ahead, if we can bring ourselves to believe it, is that other Great Cape, the Cape of Good Hope.

All over the air behind us are albatrosses, Cape Petrels, Great Petrels. Are we sailing over some great shoal of deep-water fish? Some cloud of plankton? The birds come and go; they appear out of nowhere, disappear into nowhere, that's how it seems to us, but of course they are driven by the great blind imperative, the unending search for food. They are here every day, patrolling great swathes of ocean, and we are but a momentary apparition, we appear for an instant and pass on. The old sailors used to think themselves sometimes befriended by a particular albatross, just as in warmer waters some have been known to imagine themselves befriended by a particular shark. It seemed to us obvious, at first, that the albatrosses latch on to us as a possible source of food, but now we think differently: I have never seen one go for anything we've thrown to them or let fall over the side. They'll coast up alongside for a while, then fall back, dip, and appear on the other side, keeping station for a while before peeling away indifferently about some business of their own. Very occasionally we'll see one flip down close to the water, but never so close as to let us see if it's feeding when it does. The petrels are more of a border-line case: time after time we'll see them plunge into the disturbed water we leave behind us, but whether to scavenge something we have let fall, or to profit from something brought to the surface in our wake, we can't really tell.

I find myself looking forward to these birds when I come out on deck on morning watch. This is partly to do with the weather: the better the weather the greater the number of birds we'll find hung there in the bright vault opening behind us. This morning the sun is out, so the birds are out in numbers.

Scale alters fact. I look at this albie, hanging here to the south of us, maybe 50 feet off, maybe 50 feet above the surface of the water. Its wingspan is 8–10 feet, but in this great immensity, my eye will not accept the sheer size of the bird, it registers as a sea gull would in home waters. I'm not very taken with the albatrosses, truth to tell. I can watch them for long minutes on end, the minute adjustments they make in their flight, the soaring effortlessness of it all, the way they allow themselves fall behind a wave so that you expect a splash – but then the wave crests and falls and there is the albatross, inches from the surface, almost insolent in its ease, the precision of its flight. Wonderful, and yet for a totem I'd take the petrels any day, the cut and swoop of them, the lively, darting aggressiveness of them; the petrels seem more alive, somehow, that the albies, more full of the quick of things, and somehow more vulnerable. There's something woolly and ponderous about the alba-tross, more meat on the bones as it were, more of a sense they are capably built for the long haul, while the petrels, thinner, more nervous and peevish, seem more at risk this far out, with less to fall back on, less recourse in a storm, say, fewer reserves if the pickings should prove thin. So, for one reason or another, I identify with the petrels.

Absurd, of course, each is as fitted for this environment as the other, but though the strict biologists will frown, it is a natural human instinct to identify with creatures, to sense some affinity with one or other of the many kinds with whom we share this world. There are few phrases in common use as facetious and shallow as 'ah that's only pro-jection'. I think it is a considerable achievement, to be able to project your consciousness into some other being, to know, if only for a fleeting second, what it is to curve and dip as the petrel does, to soar as the albatross does. I'm not talking here about what's called 'anthropomorhic projection', of the kind that gives us the inane imbecilities of a Disney, say; I'm talking, rather, about *identification*, what it is to find in some other creature a quality or behaviour that you recognise in yourself. And watching that creature, intent as you can be, emptying out the self for one brief instant, to *be* that creature.

Diane hasn't gone down yet. She comes with a cup of tea, stands in beside me. We watch the birds hang there, glinting and gliding, the petrels flashing away in a sudden flurry, the albies coasting softly now this way, now that.

'You doing OK,' I ask her, not turning, 'you hanging on in there?'

'Whew,' she says. 'Steve can be very heavy, can't he?'

'Yeah, he can, but I have to say I can see his point.'

'Oh I know, I know, that's just it, isn't it? So can I, I mean we all can but, I don't know, nothing seems to work. Well today I've made a list, what needs to be done during each watch, and who should be doing it. I think if we have a list there won't be any arguing, none of this "whatever" from Simon for instance. Don't you think that will work?'

'Well it's worth a try,' I say. 'Sure, and good for you, taking it on.'

I like Di, she wants to think well of people and she has kind instincts; it isn't her fault that she finds this all a bit bewildering: she has little experience of the sea, in some sense has no business whatsoever being this far out on a merciless ocean, but she's determined to make the best of it, determined to give the best of herself, and I admire that.

The list won't work, of course. Most likely it will only give them something further to argue about. Mike and Diane are facilitators by nature, willing to listen, to give and to compromise. Perhaps in other circumstances, Fed and

Simon have this capacity, too. Here, though, in this watch, on this boat, I can't see it happening. There is a mind-trap where compromise equals surrender, and it seems to me that neither of them can see surrender of the ego as precisely what's needed.

Easy for me to say, of course, but antipathy is only rarely amenable to common sense and besides, I remind myself severely, you could be getting this all wrong.

'Come on, Di,' I say, 'you think we don't have arguments on our watch? Petty resentments, little things people do or say that drive us mad?'

'No,' she says, 'no I don't actually. And even if you do, it doesn't seem to matter. You all just seem to get along somehow.'

'Ah, that's just cos we're grumpy old men.'

'No,' she says, 'I don't think you're grumpy at all.'

'Ah, go on out of that,' I tell her. 'It'll iron itself out, you'll see. You know what you should tell 'em the next time there's an argy-bargy?'

'What?'

'Tell 'em to shut up and sail the fucking boat.'

'Yes! Yes, that's a good one. Shut up and sail the fucking boat. I like that. Well I'm off to our bed while it's still nice and warm. See ya!'

Justin comes out as she goes in. Leaning back against the gantry, looking up at the peak of the main, then off to one side, the other, taking it all in.

'Blimey, changeable, isn't it? I was just having a look at the log, wind's been from everywhere for the past seven hours. And look at it now, half an hour ago it was south-west, now it's what, almost south? What next, I wonder?'

For once, we're rising and falling regularly, if you time your movements you can walk about almost normally.

'Gentlemen! Any idea what's for dinner?' We all three turn to look thoughtfully at Dolly. Kevin, I swear, actually licks his lips. He's destined to be disappointed: dinner proves to be one of Simon's vegetable roasts.

'Very nice, Simon,' says Macken. 'Steve, do you think now are we maybe neglecting Dolly?'

Later, cloud after stars and rain, we're below with Steve, calling up the weather. We've been watching all day and all night for a wind shift, not the swinging gusts we've been having at seeming random but a deep shift, and preferably firmly to the west. We're still making north, slipping stealthily between two big lows, but by dawn tomorrow we'd need to be making a decisive bend to the east and Tristan. Last night we were expecting the wind to back south-east, but instead it veered 60 degrees west without warning, then came back down south-west again later.

We're studying the satellite weather picture, Kevin above keeping an eye on things. The two big systems we're avoiding are spinning slowly clockwise, moving slightly ahead of us.

'Watch this,' Steve says, 'this is cool.' He drags the cursor diagonally to select a system, taps a few keys, and up pops a 3D radar picture of the low off to starboard, the one we may yet have to run into. We can see mountain ranges, the varying heights in the centre of the cell; there's a succession of undulating ridges all the way into the centre peak. Here, now, the bar is at – 'What's the bar, Kev?' – 1015, right. It's been between 1014–1016 all day.

'See that,' says Steve, 'pressure in the centre of the low? 995. That's what? A drop of 20? What we want is the lowest gradient high to low, OK? That way we get lower winds.'

He looks up at Tony, who looks at him over the top of his glasses. Steve laughs, 'Well not *low* winds, Tony, *comparatively* lower, right mate?'

'Oh great,' says Macken, 'for a minute there I was disappointed, thinking things were going to maybe calm down a bit.'

'Not out here, mate, not out here.'

Not everybody gets Tony's sense of humour.

'Right,' says Justin, clapping his hands together at the handover, 'lots to report, lots of bugger all that is. Wind's still dicking about, Steve hopes we'll be getting westerlies about 06.00.' ('Booked 'em specially, has he?' Simon murmurs.) 'In the meantime we just keep going as we are. Questions?'

Fed has a question, several questions, studying the chart thoughtfully as he accepts Justin's report on behalf of the watch. 'We don't want to get above the latitude for Tristan, correct?'

'Correct.'

'Do you think that big low up ahead will make for a big swell at Tristan?'

'Let's see, we thought we'd be due Tristan Saturday, and it's Wednesday–Thursday now; my guess is it'll be Monday, Tuesday we get to Tristan so yes, I'd say the answer is there'll probably be a big swell still running at Tristan.'

I see where Fed is going with this, and then he voices what he's been leading up to. 'So, if this is right, OK, then we might not be landing at Tristan after all?'

There's a general silence as we process this thought.

'Good question, Fed,' says Steve, 'good bit of analysis, mate.' Fed beams. 'Come on down,' says Steve, 'and I'll show you what I've been looking at just now with the others. Anyone else? Mike?'

I have two e-mails from Paula to read and respond to – two! Of course I've half an ear out as Steve explains the 3D picture to Fed and Mike, and I'm smiling to myself as Simon joins them and Fed starts relaying to him the information he's gleaned. Steve catches me smiling, grins himself and winks; towering to one side of his murmuring watch-mates, Big Mike is smiling fondly down on all of us.

⚓

DAY

# 21

Thursday, 25 May 2006

Back there in Stanley, aeons ago, still moored up at Fipass, when I was getting ready to take the boat out, I went down to the saloon for my gloves and found Steve with his head in the bilges under the saloon table.

'Whatcha doin', Skip?'

'See this diverter valve? I'm switching us over to salt water now: you want to wash, shower, whatever, it'll be salt water from all the taps from now on. We want water for cooking, for tea, coffee? Switch it over to this one, see?

Actually, there's anyone up there not actually working right now, send 'em down and I'll show them this.'

So, today begins, up early enough for it, with a salt-water shower. Wedged against the wall in the starboard heads, I examine myself in the mirror over the washbasin. The beard gets a cursory look, still scrubby, but I couldn't care less what I look like at this point. Clean and dry is all we aim for these days. Now I get a fresh perspective on why my left upper arm feels so bloody sore: there's a yellow-blue-black patch on the muscle, the size of a saucer. There are other interesting bruises, too, but this one is, as Mike would say, a doozy. Back to the cabin, shivering in the icy hallway; arnica from the mini-medicine chest Paula packed for me, tea tree oil for the bruised toe, lavender for the burn on the knuckle from cooking yesterday. Where would you be going!

Not once since we cleared Stanley has it been possible to move about the boat without holding on to something. Sitting still involves wedging yourself in somewhere, bracing yourself against something or someone – even while sleeping you are in constant motion, rolling this way and that, jolted awake from time to time when the boat falls off a wave or something nasty slams us smack in the bow or from one side or the other. This takes a toll in bruises – stripped naked and photographed we would, I imagine, resemble a random group of Pinochet's prisoners, back there on Dawson Island in the Beagle Channel. (And why, I wonder again, is it still forbidden to land there? Mass graves, torture chambers? Or could it be there are still prisoners there, unknown, unacknowledged, long since presumed dead?)

Well, you go out sailing and you pick up a bruise or two, nobody minds that, it's expected. Down in these waters, though, it's a different story. This is a violent place, and it takes some getting used to. Oddly, perhaps, most of the nastier knocks we take happen in either the galley or the wheelhouse. Out on deck you know damn well you're in a hostile environment: the wind is howling around your face, lashing into your eyes; everywhere you look is water in motion, great slabs of it barrelling past, tumbling and falling like blocks of ice in your squinting vision, banging the deck out from under your feet, sluicing back over your boots when you go forward or pouring over you in foamy cataracts when it isn't sweeping down torrentially from the black sky overhead. Outside, you know where you are, and the body's prepared for it: braced, crouched, pugnacious and hyper-aware.

Inside is where the damage happens. Inside lulls you, not only because it's dry, not only because with the heavy door in the wheelhouse shut the incessant howling switches off; we converse in normal tones, we roll up our sleeves, our foul-weather jackets hang on hooks or lie bundled in a corner, ready to hand for when we need to go outside – if you avoid the instruments, if you're wedged into a corner on one of the two side seats, perched on the midship stool with a grip on the inside wheel or hunched over the starboard-side chart table, your elbows firmly planted for grip, you could forget what it's like outside. It's comparatively warm in here, too: stairs go down forward to port and starboard to the passageways on the lower levels where the cabins are, and there are radiators in the passageways, radiators, too, in the cabins. Aft, on the port side, a third stairway gives down to the saloon and galley level, the diesel stove with its permanent garland of drying socks and tea towels on your left-hand side as you turn towards the computers and, around the corner, the engine room. It's warm down below, and heat rises, so the wheelhouse is never actually cold. This lulls us, as I say, and sometimes we let our guard drop; sometimes, perhaps, we relax for a moment, and that's when the damage happens, instantly.

Take my arm, for instance. It was, what, two days ago? Kevin was on the high stool, yarning away, punching a button now and then to bring Arnie under finer control. Justin was leaning back against the chart table, elbows hooked high behind him, I was on the high port side bench seat, Tony was holding the handrail looking out aft through the wheelhouse door. 'Watch the roll!' he shouts suddenly, and then I was catapulting across the wheelhouse, bouncing off Kevin, head low and coming up under Justin's jaw. I had a fraction of a second to decide what part of the body would best absorb the impact, twisting away from Justin – no time for the arse, the usual cushion of choice – and then my upper arm slammed into the edge of the chart table. Had it been my elbow or forearm I would certainly have smashed a bone. I say 'decide' here but that isn't, perhaps, quite accurate: there was no thought involved, merely the body choosing its option, positioning itself at unbelievable speed, 'me' just observing. Then me bloody sore.

If the wheelhouse is bad, the galley's worse. Cooking with us is a two-man job. We've usually decided on dinner the day before, so when it's time to cook we have all the ingredients planned out. An Irish stew, for instance. Tony, sometimes known as Ferret for his ability to winkle out the choicest vegetables from the boxes up in the forepeak, will come staggering back the passageway, his basin laden with onions, potatoes, garlic, carrots, such herbs as he can find (sometimes we suspect he has a secret stash up there only he knows about) and a big bloody chunk of vacuum-sealed beef. The galley itself is quite a confined space, a U-shaped enclave to the right of the stairs going down. Two deep sinks are set in a unit running back to the hull, then at right angles to this there's a stainless steel work surface, deep-fiddled, cupboards beneath it, racks for mugs, spices, tea and coffee above, running along the side of the hull. Up against the bulkhead there's a deep, lidded storage box set into the work surface for pots and pans. Turn right to face forward now and there's the cooker, the oven door towards you, heavily gimballed to stay level in all weathers.

I turn on the gas, check the gas alarm's working. Justin gets down on the saloon floor, one arm wrapped around the table support, lifts the board and reaches down into the maze of pipework, scrabbling for the diverter valve to get us fresh water from the tanks. Tony parks himself with some bowls at the saloon table and starts peeling. Justin chops vegetables while I chop meat, or vice versa, while the big pressure cooker comes to the boil on the stove. In go the vegetables, in goes a stock cube or two. Meanwhile fry off the meat to seal it, in with that and, presto, stew on the way. Sounds simple, eh? But Tony has been at every kind of angle while peeling, Justin and I have a forearm each jammed down over the work surface fiddle, pulling ourselves up against the cupboards, cutting laboriously, with infinite slowness, so that some lurch or other, some lift and crash sideways or up or down doesn't lead to fingers among the ingredients. Tony needs three hands to keep everything on the crazily tilting table surface, we're being banged this way and that and the other way until the lid goes on the pot and we can uncontort ourselves, and stretch cramped muscles; we're all bucketing sweat, battered and bruised and sore. By now, of course, we're so used to this that we wash what we've used, stack it to drain, wipe everything clean and climb back up again already forgetting what it's been like for the past thirty minutes.

Days later, we'll wonder where the bruises came from.

This afternoon, nearly twelve hours later than we'd anticipated last night, we finally turn and bear away east after two days plugging north. Much palaver with sails, bang that bloody elbow again, a shooting pain that brings an involuntary start of tears, a red mist. On this boat, you need the protective armour of a skateboarder, an ice hockey player and an American footballer. Plus the agility of a chimpanzee, the stamina of a bull and the sang-froid of an albatross. I say this to Steve, when he's satisfied with the set of the sails, the new course and the general tidiness of things. He looks at me for a second, then says, 'Nah, mate, you just need to be a sailor.'

'Ouch,' says Tony, laughing his head off.

Steve winks at Kevin and hops off forward, light footed and nimble. Fuck off and fall in, I say crossly to myself, and then spin to look for a piece of wood to touch. Macken's head is handiest, so I rap him on the forehead.

'What's that about?'

'Don't ask,' says Kevin, 'don't ask, you should know better, just don't ask.'

'Oh yeah,' says Steve, swinging back past us, 'nearly forgot. E-mails for everyone today. Hallo, Simon mate, you got one, too.'

'Oh good,' says Simon, 'cool bananas.'

Two e-mails from Paula, one before she set out to walk the dog up to Burrow Beach, one after returning. Valerian plumes, she says, on the walls of the Burrow Road. I see them vividly. She's been re-reading the book of poems I published soon after we met. Such a time, she says, remembering how we were.

Justin's had a long e-mail from his beloved Nic; she's well, he says, missing him, so are the boys. Kevin is checking his mails now, chuckling away at something his wife has written.

'All good at home, Kev?'

'Oh boy, yeah, tell you what, though, I ain't sharing *this* with you guys.'

'Kathleen's in great form' – Macken tamping tobacco into his pipe – 'it's all go at home.'

'Would you look at us,' I say, when we're sprawled in the cockpit with coffee. 'The tough guys, the hard men, round the Horn in a force 10 and raw meat for breakfast.'

'Ah feck it, lads,' says Tony into the happy silence. 'Isn't life great?'

I have the word 'companionship' in my head, revolving it idly, lazily, as we all settle to dinner, sprawled every which way, inside and out, when it comes to me, looking around, that this is what's meant by that hallowed term 'ship's company'. I must have spoken the words out loud, because Justin across from me grins suddenly, looks around him and says, 'Yep, that's it. Ship's company.'

We're crossing thin cloud bands now, the light high up fitful and faint. The wind is north by north-north-west, the forecast says it will go north-west before morning. We'll see, we'll see. Meanwhile we plunge on, on into whatever the night brings, under fleeing stars, their light and the gleam of our running lights flashing the water the bow turns aside, a long furrow to starboard as we lean towards the east at last.

This gives Justin pause, as he has a flight home booked on 10 June, and we've seen already how even our most sober predictions are liable to buckle and fluctuate under press of weather. For myself I don't mind, I'm booked to fly out on the 14th (a rare example of prudence and foresight on my part), and if we arrive in early I'm inclined to rebook: much and all as I'm looking forward to having a dekko at Cape Town, I'd rather be flying home.

Tony, mulling all this over, is the most thoughtful of us. This journey will only bring him halfway home: waiting for him at Cape Town will be his partner Kathleen, some friends and two very large BMW motorcycles. The plan is to ride overland up through Africa, and then across Europe to Ireland. Put this simply, it has an air of the nonchalant to it, and truth to tell Tony seems pretty calm about it all. Justin is perturbed by this. 'Tony, you'll be wrecked when we get to Cape Town, I hope you're planning a long rest before setting off?'

'Not at all, I'll be fine. Two days if everything goes according to plan and we'll be off.'

'What if the bikes haven't arrived?'

'Ah they will, they will. I had an e-mail, sure, from Kathleen, to say they're gone off in the container, sure what could go wrong?'

Kevin looks at Justin and shakes his head in disbelief: what could go wrong? Out at sea? Why nothing at all, Mr Macken, nothing at all. The thing is, Tony's doing this for the fun of it, of course, but also to raise funds for a women's refuge in India and an ambulance for a hospital in Malawi. To borrow a phrase of his own, he's 'some man for one man'.

I turn away to look at the heaving, slanting sea, shrivelling down a little into my collar, squinting into the white sun ahead, my breath frosting in front of me. I try to imagine the long stretches of dust road and mud road, the tarmac stretches with their overladen lorries, the pitiless brazen we are bewitched, as always, by the tumbling and sliding of water everywhere, out right to the edge of the world.

Yachtmaster class today is knots and splicing. No matter what they tell you, everyone who goes sailing is half in love with the old skills, the old ways of doing things. It only takes a riding turn on a winch, where the sheet wrapped around the drum climbs out of its place and locks hard so that it can't be freed, and everyone on board is scrambling to get a rolling hitch on the sheet to take the tension off, so that the riding turn can be eased without letting the genoa fly. Somebody burns a hand on a pot handle? There'll be a whipping on that handle by sundown. Handling lines and sheets is half the fun of sailing for many, and we are far from immune to the boy scout fun of it. On a quiet day, the true obsessive will sidle up to a coiled line and furtively flake it out, in order to coil it again in what he's convinced is a more seamanlike style. We're no different, of course, and today we take particular satisfaction in learning new ways of splicing an eye into a line. It's tradition again, I suppose, that coveted feeling of doing something you know generations have done before you, men and women like you who have gone down to the sea in ships, stepped out beyond the bounds of the known into a world with its own traditions, its own lore and perils and musty secrets.

After that, we're given a large-scale chart of the Falklands, and challenged to work out the pilotage through a tricky passage. There's a great deal involved in this: scanning for obstacles and shallows, figuring in the set of the currents, the state of the tide, the draught of the boat and hence its clearance in particular places, likely boat speed and so on. In the middle of this, preoccupied, I reach for a propelling pencil, draw in a line and discover, to my horror, that the pencil is in fact a pen. There are few crimes so heinous in chart work as drawing a line in ink, and this lot aren't about to let it go by. I'll never go near a chart again on this boat without someone or other checking me: 'Are you sure now that isn't a pen?' It doesn't help that I think it's daft to use propelling pencils, vulnerable things, when ordinary pencils will do just as well. I drag up the story of the millions NASA spent developing a pen that would write upside down in zero gravity, while the Russians just used a pencil, but they're having none of it: when you pare a pencil in a space capsule, where does the graphite dust go, never mind the shavings? I'm too annoyed with myself to think of the obvious answer: you bring spare pencils, so you don't have to do any paring.

Mine is not, however, the worst crime of the day. In a moment of madness and misunderstanding which he'll never be able to explain, Kevin tosses a half packet of Steve's precious Hob Nobs overboard.

'What were you thinking of, Kev?'

'I have no idea,' he says sorrowfully. 'I really have no idea.'

An hour later, the levity is overwhelmed by horror.

Steve's at the laptop, all colour drained from his face, silent, unmoving. I'm coming out of the engine room after a routine check and see him there, frozen, staring unseeing straight ahead of him. I stand there and watch him until he lifts his head, rolls his neck slowly as if his head might fall off. Whatever it is, it's bad. I step closer to him, and he sees me finally.

'Jesus, Theo, I can't fucking believe this. Man, this is bad, this really is bad. You know the Volvo 70 race, right?' I do, big state-of-the-art boats, carbon and kevlar, thoroughbred racing machines. 'It's a fucking disaster,' Steve says. 'They're US to UK, right, eastbound, not long out. Wind comes up from 10 to 25 knots in a couple of minutes? Skipper calls for harnesses, guy is coming out into cockpit to clip on and bang! Overboard. *ABN Amro 2* it was. Jesus, I know a few of the guys on that. They bash round for him of course, fast as they can but it's blowing a hooley now, I guess; time they get to him, get him back on board, poor bugger's dead. Oh fuck, I wonder who it was?'

'What's up?' Justin's here now, senses something terrible. Steve gives him the gist of it, shaken, really shaken. This is his world, he's a racing skipper himself, he's sailed boats like this, in these conditions, he knows the horror they'll be feeling now, a comrade smashed dead out of nowhere, in minutes.

'Oh Christ,' mutters Justin, 'I've got a mate in that race, navigator on *Movistar*.'

Steve looks up at him now, right in the face: 'Jesus, yeah, *Movistar*… they've had some trouble too, mate, it's a right go round. *Movistar* has had problems with that fucking canting keel, eh? She started to overwhelm her pumps, right, and *ABN* turned round and came back for 'em. Dead guy on board and all, turned around and came straight back for 'em. Well, you would, wouldn't ya? Have to. Still and all…'

'Can I… ?' – Justin gestures towards the laptop.

'What? Oh yeah, sure, Justin, go ahead, go ahead.'

Debs has woken, is standing in the doorway of the cabin she shares with Steve. Kevin is down, taking it in. They close in on Steve as he heads out on deck, protective, stricken. Justin has an e-mail from Nic now. She's spoken to the wife of their friend Andrew Cape, on *Movistar*. He's OK, they're all OK but the boat's a write-off and everyone's in bits about losing the guy on *ABN*. Justin doesn't say so, but I know damn well there's more to the e-mail than that; it takes no imagination at all to guess at the outpouring of concern from Nic, so closely touched by death at sea, missing her man down there in the South Atlantic. As if she were there in the cabin with him, I leave them to their conversation.

Night watch. Nobody talking much, Kevin on the high stool, staring away ahead through the toughened glass screen. What he sees isn't out there, at least not out there through the glass. I see his face in reflection, blueish, greenish. I glance at my watch, reach for my jacket. Justin is making the hourly entry in the log – he turns at the sound of the zip, looks at me, nods, reaches for his own jacket. We take our life jackets from the row of canvas pouches on the after bulkhead, unfold them, fit them tight. We snap on the harnesses, and Kevin slides off the stool, slow and smooth. Tony goes down quietly to put the kettle on, to whip up one of his life-sustaining fruit salads. We take a torch each, flick them on and off, then move outside. Kevin stands in behind the wheel, takes a long slow look around. The wind is fresh, the waves no more than 2 metres, Milky Way bright and clear up above, long skeins of pale cloud running south-east ahead of us. Still nobody says a word. I take the low side for a change; a quick look from Justin, then a nod. We clip on, stand there a moment, braced to the rise and fall, then Kevin says quietly, 'OK, guys, I got your back.'

We flick on the torches and go forward.

⚓

DAY

# 23

Saturday, 27 May 2006

During the day, we are rarely, if ever, really aware of exactly where we are in the world. How many mornings have I sat here, slowly coming to, shreds of dream and lethargy spinning away with the cigarette smoke, and never until this morning have I looked at the sea as something profoundly and dangerously cold. We 'know' about hypothermia, we know the survival suits in our cabins are designed to ward off that insidious and lethal danger. We 'know' the water is cold, of course it is for God's sake, it washes the shores of

Antarctica, there are icebergs not far down there over the starboard horizon. My skin tells me the air is cold, every morning, most days, and if the air is cold then... but today, I'm thinking morning but of course it's afternoon, I'm getting confused, today it feels as if I am really *looking* at the water, all that stuff just there beside us and underneath us every minute of every day, waking or sleeping, and thinking: that stuff could kill you, snuff you out like a match flame in a gale.

That swell is not just beautiful, not just a threat to our balance as we race along, nor is it just mindless, a great mass in constant movement: that sea would kill you. Today, looking over the stern rail as the petrels cut and skip past unheeded, I am imagining what we take care not to imagine – the sudden lurch at the wrong moment, a rogue wave climbing suddenly aboard and then flash, you're gone, tumbling bewildered, perhaps unseen, into that deep roiling pit of liquid ice.

We take care not to dwell on such things, we take care to see such things do not happen to us, or to others, but today something comes creeping up on the wind and puts its chill voice to my ear.

'Ten minutes,' Steve says, when he's warning us to be careful always. 'That's all you have. You go in, you've got ten minutes for us to turn her around, get back to you, get you aboard. Otherwise...'

I'm thinking of course of that poor soul lost off *ABN Amro 2*. He might have been asleep below when the sudden commotion, the boat heeling over to that big gust, the roaring and shouting on deck, brought him scrambling into the cockpit. A good guy, by all accounts, solid sailor, experienced, competent. The skipper was roaring to get harnesses on, it seems he was reaching for his, or he had it and was reaching to clip it on, when something massive and unexpected rumbled aboard, a great wall of roaring blue-black water that swept him into its backwash, tumbling him, beating him down, flushing him over the stern in a tumble of foam. They'd have crash-gybed the boat, risked everything and everyone to come about, to beat back to him in the climbing wall of wind, but the cold would have frozen his heart, convulsed his lungs so that he breathed in great lethal gulps of water. He was dead when they got to him, the waters up there in those latitudes, at this time of year, much the same temperature as these waters here.

Their grief and shock as they retrieved him, panic of resuscitation, letting it go, finally, accepting that for this friend and companion everything was over.

All that a life might yet have been, cancelled abruptly by the icy, uncaring sea.

I imagine us here, in similar circumstances, the furious urge to care for his body, to get him home – one of us, gone. And then, then, over the radio, a sister ship, taking water, their keel sheared off maybe, they're not sure, the pumps overrun, overwhelmed. Ten souls in the balance. Mayday. Mayday. From the French (*venez*) *m'aider*, come help me.

And the skipper of *ABN Amro* came about once more, every man in the crew with him, I'm sure of it. Back through the maelstrom, back through those plunging seas to pluck ten men off a stricken boat, to steady the ship, to come about again, his head full of weather, survival sailing, men to be cared for – and then the cold, brute logistics of death: contact to be made with the dead man's family, with the race authorities, with the nearest rescue elements, for there's a body to be taken off, ten men to be taken off, and a boat to be sailed in ugly rising weather because they're not out of it yet, not by any means.

Justin has pieced together what happened to *Movistar*. She's been having trouble with her keel all through the race. Had to put into Albany for repairs to an hydraulic ram, discovered new problems in Wellington, started taking water aboard near Cape Horn, so severely they thought they might sink. What happened then? Guy called Chris Nicholson dived on her, hitched up two bilge pumps direct to the batteries; they limped into Ushuaia. Fixed her up. Headed out again. So what happened in the end? About 300 miles off Land's End the aft keel bearing broke away from the boat, water started pouring in. *ABN* came back for them, stood by. The crew got into the life-raft when they saw there was nothing to be done, *ABN* took them aboard. Calm seas by then, but forecast for 35–40 knots, gusting 50. Nothing to be done.

What can you say? We sit there, letting it sink in.

Somewhere back there, on some night watch or other, Tony I think it was, or it might have been Kevin, asked me if I believed, in the sense of professing some formal faith. A desultory question, just something fleeting that had come up in the talk. Not really, I said, if I'm pushed I always describe myself as an agnostic Buddhist pagan.

'What're you doing, Theo?' Steve standing beside me, looking back into the wake as I am.

'Saying a prayer for that guy,' I say, 'and for his mates.'

'Yeah… good one,' he says. We don't look at each other. 'You all right, mate?'

'You mean with all this' – turning towards him, sweeping in sea, sky and boat in an upturned palm – 'Oh yeah, no worries, Skip, no worries.'

'Tough deal, eh,' he says, 'Hans Horrevoets his name was. A good guy.' He shakes his head, bumps me for a second with his shoulder, turns and goes back inside.

So we all shake it off in our different ways, we have to, and get back to being here now.

The conundrum of the moment is this: there's a big system still hammering Tristan; even assuming it moves away soon, which it might not, there will be a great swell running, which means we won't be able to land. Now, we want to land there, no question, even those who, like Justin, have appointments to keep, flights to catch, whatever. All things considered, Steve wouldn't mind landing in there, and besides, he has stuff to deliver, taken aboard in Stanley. So, we have to sail slowly and carefully, riding the weather system, time our arrival for, say, the morning of 1 June, departing twenty-four hours later. Simon and Fed can't get their heads around this at all. Sailing slowly, deliberately? Nobody asks them straight up, though I'm tempted to. 'Lads, what would you prefer, sail fast past Tristan or take it easy and land there?'

Justin, who's keen to see the place ('When will I ever get a chance again?') has nonetheless calculated that leaving Tristan on the 2nd gives him very little chance of making his flight. Normally the most equable of men, he's turning decidedly cranky about this. In fact, he's squaring up for a good row, I can sense it, so can Tony and Kevin. Our Admiral is inclined to dig out his contract with Novak, in which the envisaged date of arrival in Cape Town is given as 5 June. To be fair to all, Novak makes it plain that this can only be an approximate date, and Justin, long-time sailor, knows sail boats don't run on rails. 'However,' he says, 'however, five days' leeway is more than enough, surely?'

'Listen,' I take him aside, 'listen, why don't you mention to Steve that on foot of assurances given you entered into business commitments ('I did, I did') and if you don't make it back in time it's going to cost you a lot of money?'

Justin nods, goes in to talk to Steve. To be fair to Steve, he's pretty understanding about things, when he's calmed down a bit. Justin ruffles his feathers, somehow, and Steve can certainly get on Justin's nerves; the last thing we need now is a confrontation between them.

'Tell you what,' I say, happening to overhear their conversation, 'why not aim to hit Tristan first thing in the morning, and bugger off at midnight, eh? We gain twelve hours that way, don't we?'

'Yeah, yeah, we could do that, couldn't we? What d'you think eh, Justin?'

'Yes, seems like a good idea, Skip. Worth a try certainly. Thanks.'

Macken is sniggering over the kettle below.

'What?'

'Would you look at the innocent face on you,' he says, 'go away, you bloody chancer.'

'My dear Mr Macken,' I say, 'I have no idea what you could possibly mean. Is the Barry's tea prepared? Oh good. I'll take mine in the after lounge, if you please.'

Next step, now, is to plant the idea that after Tristan, a fast run to Cape Town would be the thing.

In fact, I think everyone aboard would like that. This boat can fly on some points of sail, you feel it in her, her quickness to come up, her urge to accelerate. Simon materialises, must be getting to time for the handover, dinner. 'Wouldn't it be good,' he says, 'to see the full main up? The stay and the Yankee and the genny? On a beam reach? Can you imagine, man, can you imagine what she'd be like? That would be awesome, that would be truly awesome.'

'You get on well with Debs, don't you, Si?'

'Yeah, so?'

'Well, if Debs is saying to Steve we ought to put the foot down after Tristan, and Kevin is saying it, and we're saying it…'

'You sly dog!'

'Ah, think how happy it would make you and Fed, eh? You could fall in love again, run away and get married, even, when we hit Cape Town!'

The level Simon look – then, clearly enunciated, 'Fuck off, Theo.'

But he's laughing. Here's Fed. 'What's so funny?'

'Come here and I'll tell you,' says Simon. 'Walk this way…'

'Them two are talking, crikey!'

'Hiya, Debs.'

'Hiya, Theo. What's up with them two then?'

'Debs,' I say sorrowfully, 'I could tell you, but then I'd have to kill you.'

mind, you could call me, say, ten minutes before the others? If that's OK?'

Mike has the midships cabin on the port side, curtained off from the passageway as I am on the other side. 'Mike, Mike!' The great form stirs, turns ponderously over.

'Who's that? Oh, Theo. Good morning Theo, thank you for waking me. Be up in a minute.'

Call Fed on the way back, 'Eh, Fed, *é l'ora!*'

'Huh? Huh? OK, OK, *grazie.*'

Justin, working his way up the starboard side, is a touch more brusque; he rattles back the curtain, 'Morning, Floss! Wakey, wakey!' Then he pushes open Simon's door, 'Morning, Spice Boy, it's that time again!'

Tony is in the galley, a rattle of insulated mugs on the work surface, kettle just beginning to whistle. When we set out, everyone was asked to name their wake-up drink of choice, now Tony's preparing strong coffee, weak tea and boiled water with a slice of lemon for the newly awakened. Debs is always wide awake by the time she comes up, Di generally looks startled and still dream-struck, Fed is all business, taking the handover from, usually, Justin; Simon, my doppelganger, moves through the mill in the wheel-house like a zombie, collecting his mug en route to the shelter outside and that first necessary cigarette. Big Mike has a whole routine for these morning calls. He comes stumbling and fumbling up, lurching, grabbing on, wide-eyed and blinking. We always think he's going to go crashing over, especially when there's a big lumpy sea running, but I notice he never has, that this seeming awkwardness is deceptive. Sometimes we wonder if he isn't putting it on, some form of private amusement? If it isn't raining outside, he'll stand in the doorway looking back down our track, 'Yep, still there. Do them pesky Fuegans never give up?' Or, if it's lashing rain, which it often is, he'll peer out and say, 'Can't see 'em, pesky Fuegans. But they're

Since the various readings of the Riot Act, Diane has taken the initiative of making up lists of what's to be done by whom on each of their watches. We consider ourselves finally off duty when she begins to read from the list, Fed standing close in beside her, reading over her shoulder.

I go down to check for e-mails, my hands searching fleeting handholds of their own accord as the boat lurches and pitches on into the dawning light. Without thinking about it, I pause at the foot of the steps, wait for the starboard side to rise and cant the floor towards me, then scuttle forward against the incline. There's a strict rule, no wet trousers on the upholstery. Even when it's not raining my chest-high trousers are usually wet from spray anyway, so I unhitch the shoulder straps, peel the trousers down around my knees and slide onto the fabric-covered short bench. All this on automatic pilot, so inured have we all become to the exoskeleton of the boat as it has closed around us. Now I am in the boat, on the boat, but also in some liminal space, some null zone between here and there. Home is calling, real home, not this hard-charging capsule of aluminium, this micro-world of intimate strangers. I log on, call up Paula's e-mail and her words begin to sound in my ear as I read them off the screen. Then, I am not on the boat reading, hearing, these words but at home, hearing her sound them in my ear. My attention, I mean to say, is there, not here. This is a long-distance version of what happens when some business has taken me into the city, and I phone home. Talking to Paula, then, I am acutely conscious that she is in place, that I am in some sense *displaced*. Real time is home time, the little world of Moyclare, the time of the dyad. All other time is just that, other time. Wherever I am, if I'm not at home, that's exactly where I am, *not at home*. It has taken me many years to learn how to be conscious of where my attention is placed at a given moment, to learn that attention, conscious directed awareness is not always where the body is. To learn this, and to learn to use this, to work with this.

Out here in space, it can be dangerous for the mind to dwell too much on home. The boat is in constant motion, moving always in three dimensions of space, and moving also through time. It's a complex unforgiving environment: there are hard edges in here that can do damage to the fragile body, huge forces out there that can whip off an arm, or whip you off the boat, without any warning. We've all learned that the true root of exhaustion on this voyage is the unrelenting need for perpetual attention, physical and mental, to where *exactly* at a given moment your bones and mind are in time and space. The irruption into this zone of awareness of that other life, the life you left behind long ago, that life you may yet rejoin, is fraught with dangers. The phrase 'be here now' has a deep bronze resonance out here on the vast ocean; it rings in your mind like a spiritual direction, and as the most prosaic and useful advice that common sense can give you.

You can split yourself for a time, as I am doing here now, immersed in her words, contorting myself to stay with the bench as the boat rises and falls, dips and shudders and lunges this way and that. It is even possible, using some sense I am barely aware of, to know when there will be a short lull, a brief period of grace, and then my fingers can fly over the keyboard, sending words home, answering her questions, joining new words to our stretched but un-broken flow of talk. Then I log off, close the lid down on the machine and sit there for a moment, collecting myself.

On *Spirit of Oysterhaven*, from Antigua to Kinsale a few years ago, we didn't have e-mail, but we had a satellite phone that would occasionally, at unpredictable times, pick up a signal. I remember vividly the mixed feelings after a call, the delight of having been able to talk and then the emptiness after, the sense of dislocation. Our skipper, Zafer, would never phone home, nor would Anne, his wife, ever ring him. 'No, no way,' he'd say. 'I'm out here, and that's all there is to it. I prefer it this way, and so does Anne. I get on with things here, she gets on with things there; sure we'd drive ourselves mad, thinking about each other's problems and not being able to do anything about it. Of course, if a shark gets me, you might want to give her a ring, so's she'll know, like!'

I go get my sleeping bag from Simon's cabin, roll it out in the snug burrow, undress and climb over the lee-board, all without thinking. Her photo there on the bulkhead; see you in a few hours I say, catch myself in my foolishness, smile and fall asleep.

Lunch al fresco, soup from last night's beef (the last of the beef, did we take that aboard in Punta Arenas or in Stanley?), Kevin's beer bread and a variety of cheeses courtesy of the Admiral. In civilian life, the Admiral is a cheese and wine vendor, and down in the saloon bilges, cool and dark, lie some samples of his wares, including a once-great wheel of Parmesan, now considerably diminished, which alone would have long since earned him a particular place in our affections. It has also, alas, earned him the alternative nickname of Cheesy, but as it's mostly Macken who calls him that the pain is not, perhaps, overwhelming. At any rate, he scarcely winces at all, now, when addressed as such.

Classes go on, but first we must clean our world. This we take very seriously indeed. We don't care for the job, but we take care to do it thoroughly and well. All the floors get scrubbed and mopped – saloon, galley, wheelhouse, passageways, cabins, steps. Then the port and starboard heads are scrubbed, the washbasin and toilet given particular attention, every surface is scrubbed and disinfected. On a good, that is to say a relatively calm, day we do the windows of the wheelhouse, inside and out. We wash down the cockpit with buckets and buckets of seawater, scrub off the tea and coffee stains that have accumulated – we toss the dregs of our tea or coffee over the leeward side, not always successfully. Pretty mundane stuff, really, but that's the point: this is our world, and our health depends on keeping it as clean as possible. You see sailors lurching ashore after a long passage, unkempt, bearded (the guys at least), wild-looking, and you might imagine a filthy mess below decks, the more forgivably if they've come in out of severe weather. There may be a mess, but only if water has made its way inside in some recent emergency and there hasn't been time to clean up yet. Of course it depends on the skipper, pretty much, but any kind of a decent and competent skipper will make a fetish of hygiene and cleanliness, for very good reason: poor hygiene leads to illness, illness leads to exhaustion, may spread to the whole crew and lead to diminished capability – so on, down through the cascade into genuine danger of loss of vessel, loss of life. It sounds hyperbolic, put like that, but we are, right now, two days' sail from Tristan, which in any case has limited rescue resources; after that, unless there are naval elements of some kind nearby, if anything goes seriously wrong we are between nine and eleven days from the nearest meaningful land, Cape Town.

On the basis of 'shut up and sail the boat', we usually buckle to and get on with it, some with perhaps more enthusiasm (or resignation) than others. Today I'm down on my knees in Fed's cabin when he rolls over, looks down and smiles as I scrub, 'You really like this, don't you?'

I give him a venomous glare, convinced he's dissing me, doing his I'm-a-real-sailor bit, that what he means is really, 'Yeah, this suits you better than trying to helm, this is more your level.' I'm really mad at him, so much so that later, when he comes up for dinner, I tackle him about it.

I have, of course, got it wrong. Fed is hurt and puzzled that I would take him up like this, 'Maybe my English isn't so good, you know? I was trying to say, "You really *don't* like this, do you", understand? The way you have in English, hey, it's in Italian too you know, of saying something such a way it comes out meaning the opposite?'

I do understand, and I am vastly embarrassed at having misread the meaning, more so at having embarrassed Fed now, too. 'Look, I'm very sorry, I got that completely wrong, you mustn't mind me, maybe it's cos I'm so tired, I get things arseways sometimes, I'm sorry.'

'Hey, man, don't worry, man. We're all fucking tired, me I want to sleep forever feels like, don't worry.' Then, because he's a good man, he says, 'Hey, you know what, I'm glad you said this. That's a lot better than just keeping shit to yourself, saying nothing, you know? Thanks for that, Theo.'

Then I hear what he's saying behind what he's saying, he's studying my face and when I nod and my eyes flick outside for a second he nods too and says, a little sorrowfully, 'Yeah, exactly.'

Tension on board, after Simon is somehow taken with the idea that it would be a lark to strew Dolly's dismembered remains (bye bye Dolly) on the floor of Justin's cabin. We know Justin's pissed off about this, but we don't learn that he's made a formal complaint until Kevin and Steve corner me and ask what's going on. Steve is obliged to take a formal complaint seriously, but he's uneasy about the consequences. What to do? It's fair enough for Justin to be angry, and Steve is certainly prepared to give Simon a bollocking about this, but a formal complaint entered in the ship's log is no trivial matter, however trivial its occasion. 'So, Justin, Steve is taking this seriously, and he'll deal with it, but maybe a formal complaint is taking it too far?'

Justin agrees to withdraw the formal complaint, having made his point, Steve is mightily relieved, Simon is contrite and, now that Justin has been so gracious in the interests of greater harmony, it's a good moment to impress on Steve that Justin really does need to make that flight. 'Yeah of course, mate, I can see that, been thinking about that, y'know. I don't see why not, eh? Bit of luck, we might even get some good wind the far side of Tristan, eh? Be able to crack on the white flappy things, get the old girl going eh?'

'Eh, Justin. Steve has been saying that, after Tristan, he's of a mind to crack on for Cape Town see if we can't get this thing up and running.'

'Has he now, well that's good to hear. Here's hoping, eh?'

We're playing cat and mouse with the wind all day: it comes up, we set the appropriate sails; it dodges off somewhere else, we trim to compensate, and so on. According to the GRIBs it was due to go south-easterly this morning and stay there, a big and useful shift, but it doesn't do this until after dark. Macken and I have worked out a fiendish new way of switching the preventer blocks (the preventer is to stop the boom swinging violently to one side or the other) and we get to try out our new system; it works smoothly and quickly, and we are very pleased with ourselves. 'Tea, Mr Macken?'

'Why, thank you, Mr Dorgan. A spot of Barry's would be just lovely.'

Kevin is a bit down in the dumps, most unusual for him. 'What's up, Kev?'

'Aaargh, I'm just fed up with sailing so slowly!'

'So are we all, Kev. But be careful what you ask for!'

Even with the log, which we fill in every hour, on the hour, it's all too easy to lose track of the days and dates out here. Have just realised there's an *Irish Times* article due tomorrow or the next day, and am wondering what to write about. Flicking through my journal, I find the following: 'Roman virtues – order, discipline, hygiene; Greek virtues – find the gods, trust fate and intuition.' Dull-headed now that the day is dying, it takes me a few minutes to work out that taken together, these are the virtues necessary for a successful sea voyage. Are they, though? If your taste runs more to 'the powers in play' than to 'the gods', perhaps they are. I'm too tired to puzzle it out now.

An uneventful day, still stealth-sailing as best we can, staying between those two systems, the huge one and the smaller one, but it's colder than yesterday, longer and somehow more sullen-looking seas, the wind a brisk 30 knots. We've seen this before, of course, morose days and nights where you buckle down and set yourself to get through the watches. There's a certain monotony about all this, grey skies, grey water, conversation flagging; every-thing on the boat feels damp, everyone has gone inside

⚓

DAY
# 26

Tuesday, 30 May 2006

Slowly, slowly, things begin to deteriorate. I see that now, looking back, but we didn't much notice at the time, or at least I didn't notice.

We came on watch last night at 18.00 to 30 knots, expecting a major wind change in our next duty period, around, Kevin says, 03.00 – 'that's according to the *forecasts*'. Four hours later, we're heading down to the bunks again, and Justin is briefing the oncoming watch that she's now blowing 40 knots. The bar is dropping, he tells them, the wind has been building steadily. Looks like a bit of a blow. Fed is studying the log intently. At 02.00 we're back again, it's today, so to speak, a new day though it feels like the same day, and Steve is awake, says she's been gusting 55, holding more or less between 45 and 50. It's a cold, baleful wind out of the south, ice in its teeth, a feeling of considerable depth to it, weight behind it. Steve's been on for much of the watch, Debs tells Kevin, but now he says he's going to grab some shut-eye. 'You all right then, Kev? You know to call me if you need to, right mate? See you later guys, remember my mantra now!'

'Yes,' we chorus, 'watch the roll.'

It's 03.00 and a steady 55 knots, storm force 10. It's gusting 60 regularly, nobody wants to go outside if it can be helped; there are bloody big angry waves out there, rolling up on us from behind and to starboard, black, grey, a heavy green, all this seen close in to the wheelhouse side, flashed for a moment in our sideways light as we roll heavily, sullenly, and out there behind those – we sense their brute weight, we 'see' them as they blank out chunks of what sky there is – even bigger waves, rolling with a long thunder over the high banshee howl of the wind. The crests we can see are being flattened by these torrents of wind, white-grey spray blown down into the hollows and then flaring out until the roiling surface is laced with cold foam.

We brace ourselves as best we can as her head goes down deeper than we've seen before, comes up with an effort, rolling back walls of water that split on the windscreen and go by to each side. We look at Kevin, we look at each other, nobody saying much now, we look at Kevin and he straightens and says, as much to himself as to us, 'Better call Steve, this looks like a bit of a nasty.'

Steve takes a moment to come up, he's checking the latest satellite, and when he does come up he's in full foul-weather gear and that's when we realise this isn't over, this is serious. All he says is, 'Get everything out of the way that isn't secured, this looks dirty.'

Half an hour later, she's blowing 60–65 knots, and gusting well in excess. How much in excess? *Well* in excess. We're at the stage where the pure desire to know is balanced against 'better not to know'. This big heavy boat is canted over at 45 degrees, not wallowing exactly, but making heavy weather of it, a heavy pounding resounding through the hull, a sense of having to shoulder through many tonnes of water, moment by moment.

Steve's like a cat, I mean really like a cat, I see where the simile comes from. Tense, rangy, all concentration and bony delicacy, looking inside himself for memory and precedent while never, not for an instant, losing his total sense of the boat, his feel for what's coming on to us; he prowls – down to the laptop, back up into the wheelhouse, his eyes flicking from wind speed to bar, looking now forward, now sideways, now back, as immersed in this storm as if he were out there in the heart of it, naked and unprotected. Big walls of water are roaring back the deck, one after the other, a bright green waterfall smashing up from the angled windscreen, roaring across the roof over our heads, crashing down to each quarter and then off. As we roll we ship great weights of water, now port side, now starboard, now we're not on the water, we're in it, coming sometimes up for air – but the air, too, is washed through with water, a thin grey aerosol of water and foam, you know you can't breathe that stuff.

For the first time in my life, I *feel* the full weight of the sea.

'All right there, guys?' Steve looks around, in what passes for a lull.

We are, we tell him, one after the other. Fine. Thoughtful, but fine. He searches our faces for, what? Fear? Well of course, any good skipper would be looking for signs of fear in this, and me, I would be worried to be out here with anyone not touched by fear in these circumstances, but he's looking for something else too. I see it in their faces just before he does, because I'm more used to these men than he is, but he grins when he sees it, a big cat now, raw power in his blood; he sees that under light of exhilaration, primitive exultation that here it is now, the weather we dreaded but coveted, too, when we signed on for this; here is the real deal, big weather. He grins at me now, and I feel the same hair-raising exhilaration whispering through me, while my mind continues to process the objective and undeniable truth that this is a very, very stupid place to be right now for any animal with a healthy interest in survival. 'Oh yes,' he says, shouldering Kevin, feinting to shoulder Justin the other side of him, 'yes, yes, this is a storm all right.'

At 05.30, an express train slams into us on the starboard side. Just as Steve roars, 'Watch the roll!'

Everyone's knocked off their feet by this, a whirling of arms and legs, bodies cannoning into bodies, books, charts, pencils and mugs flying every which way. Kevin and Steve, that fraction more alert than us, grab the overhead rails, to steady themselves, to keep their feet, the rest of us are like drunks hit by a fire hose. Regaining our balance, we regard each other thoughtfully. Wouldn't fancy too much of this, I think to myself, and I see in their eyes that much the same thought has occurred to Tony and Justin.

We're bearing east, remember. This wind is over our starboard quarter, from south-west, and the deep swell is from there, too. Hence, the waves roaring by are coming, more or less, from behind and to one side. But down there below us, down towards Antarctica, is another great system, and that's making weather of its own, shoving its own great swells out and up. When the swells intersect, the weaker waves will be overpowered by the stronger, generally the most recent, and then deflected if not subsumed into the prevailing rolling direction. Every now and then, predictably but not regularly, two waves will combine and either change height – a monster in the prevailing wave train – or change direction: a bloody big wave from another point of the compass. That's what hits us now, broadside on. The noise is terrific, thunderous, overwhelming – as if something enormous, born in a foundry, had slammed us in temper with a huge iron club.

'Yep, this is a blow,' says Steve.

'Oh yeah, this is a storm all right,' Kevin adds.

I marvel that the others are still sleeping, and then wonder if they are.

I go down to help Tony make the hot drinks for the next watch – just because we're getting our heads kicked in here is no excuse for abandoning hallowed custom – and it's extraordinary how different everything seems down below in the galley. It's quieter, for one thing, that nerve-shredding howling whine reduced to a keen moan, and the motion is far less, too – of course it is, my brain contributes, you're closer to the water, the roll is far less. Still, we bang, climb, fall away, judder, shudder, slam, yaw and pitch more than enough to remind us that it's a bit breezy up there. We put the mugs in the sink, keep a wary eye on the kettle, swinging crazily on the gimballed stove. 'Don't forget to switch off the gas at the tap,' Tony reminds me.

'It's already off.'

'Good man, good man – you think Mike will want his boiling water and lemon this morning?'

'Give 'em what they asked for,' I say, 'there's a time and place for innovation.'

'It's a bit breezy,' Justin briefs the upcoming watch, 'otherwise nothing much to report. Tristan the day after tomorrow, looks like. Any questions?'

For a terrible moment, I think they may fear the Admiral has lost his marbles, looking about them, clutching at anything and anyone they can to stay on their feet, staring at him, white-faced. Mike peers out astern, 'Pesky Fuegans, paddling up a storm today.'

Justin relents. 'It's blowing 50, 60 knots, it's been gusting well in excess of that but it's eased off very slightly in the last half hour.' (Eased off! – you can see the disbelief dawn in their eyes as they come more fully awake to what's out there.) 'Bar's still dropping, course 085°. No questions, then? Right, I'm off to beddy byes.'

Simon is gazing stonily over Mike's shoulder, I know he's wondering what the chances are of a cigarette out there. Di is looking tense, and why wouldn't she? Sensible of her, if you ask me. Fed looks – thoughtful.

I'm in the starboard head, brushing my teeth, when there's another tremendous crash and I am all but thrown off my feet, dodging a fistful of darts flung at my face (tooth-brushes, I discover seconds later), flailing for a grip, for balance, for not to go head over heels. Spinning-light chaos for a few seconds, bouncing off metal walls, and then back to the normal as we know it. I slump down on the toilet cover, elbow locked on the high vanity unit beside me and take a moment to catch my breath, figure out what's just happened.

I go up, Tony in the wheelhouse is all outrage and indignation, 'I was sitting there on the throne when next thing you know, bang, over she went and when she came back I was sitting on the vanity unit!'

There's a moment's silence, and then a chorus of shrieks, 'I hope you wiped it!' A treasured memory in the making.

'What happened?'

'A fucking big wave,' Simon's description, 'a *fucking big* wave, big beam sea, just hit us on the starboard side and rolled us over. Mast hit the water. Then we rolled back.'

'Oh.'

I suppose I should go to bed now. I stand for a moment at the wheelhouse door, my hands welded around the hand-grips on either side, looking out through the armoured glass at great walls of water roaring up behind us, listening to the high moan of the wind as it climbs ever higher, into a register I've never heard before. I allow myself, briefly, to frame the thought: we are a very, very small boat in the wild roar of a very big storm. Then, smoothly and firmly I shut the thought down. Instinct, or something even stronger than instinct, says: put that thought away. Put it somewhere deep and silent and dark and leave it there. I claw and bundle my way across the heaving wheelhouse and go below.

I sit down on the passageway floor to get my foul-weather gear off, no other way to do it, hang the gear up over the radiator, wriggle my boots off, wait for the roll and then tumble over the lee-board into my bunk. On cold nights, I usually finish undressing on the bunk, I keep fleece and tracksuit pants and socks on top of the sleeping bag, dry them if they're damp, keep them warm in any case for when I wake. Tonight I wriggle into the green cocoon fully clothed; this is partly for comfort, mental and physical, and partly because I could very well find myself heading up in a hurry at any moment. I lie there, the reading lamp on, and look for a long time at the photo of Paula.

Then I switch off the light and think about dealing with fear. This is a bad night on a bad ocean, and it could get worse. I've been in a storm before, and I didn't like it, too many dark things flooding unbidden into an overheated mind, too many vivid imaginings of disaster. I have to deal with this, with everything I've been putting off thinking about for the past four hours. I have a mercurial disposition, I know this, I know I fly into sudden passions and rages; emotional weather passes through me at high speed. I also know that, right now, this is a time to slow down, to catch myself feeling whatever it is I'm feeling, and to examine it, deal with it. Anxiety, then, I tell myself, anxiety first. Well, what of it? Of course you're anxious, anything could happen here, anxiety is the body's way of being prepared, it's a by-product of adrenalin. OK, then, anxiety we can handle. How? Well, like this: you're in a good boat, strong, designed for bad weather, designed in the *expectation* of bad weather. Go through the boat: forward, strong bulkhead to forepeak, big heavy watertight door, one on each side behind that, into Simon's and Kevin's cabins. Above? Strong hatches above every cabin, all dogged down, checked every deck watch and, besides, each of us always checks his own. OK, next, centreboard well? Permanently sealed? Yes? Good. Up then, wheelhouse, door sound as a pound; windows, well what could be thrown at them worse than they've already handled? Good point. Aft, finally. Anything there? Nope, all well sealed off. Right then, what're the chances of water getting into the boat then? Can't see it happening. So, the boat can't sink, right? Well I wouldn't go as far as that...

Come on, it's not going to sink. Well you never know. All right, say something does go wrong, she won't go down immediately, right? No. So, the life-raft. Yes, and...? Well, you're always reading about people being rescued, aren't you? You get the Epirb (emergency position indicating radio beacon) triggered, for God's sake there'll be plenty of time to send a mayday, you'll be grand. Maybe so. But what if the life-raft gets swamped, what about hypothermia, drowning?

(Now this is a truly odd experience, this conversation with myself, so odd, in fact, that a part of me is standing back and actually enjoying it, insinuating the equivalent of 'go on, go on...' into the 'conversation'.)

Here we go now. The life-raft gets swamped, well then you die. Just like that. You die. And of course you don't want to, no living creature wants to die, but suppose there is nothing else left except to die, are you afraid you won't be able to deal with that? Yes, I am, I'm going to go crazy with longing for everything I'll never experience now... Well, natch. But if there really is no other choice, if you really are going to die?

(I don't know how I got to this point, I'm feeling bizarrely detached from everything, from the boat, from myself, this conversation, I keep wondering why I'm not floundering in chaotic anxiety.)

And out it comes: surrender. I'm afraid I won't be able to surrender. To let go. To let what will be, be.

(I'm very warm now, cosy even, I'm feeling very comfortable, rocked here in my padded cocoon, my face against the photo on the bulkhead, the specific feel of warm coated paper against my cheek. I'm *enjoying* this conversation, for fuck's sake. I tell myself – yes, well, you're also avoiding something; that mysterious familiar *I* says, would you ever get back to it.)

Well, Paula – that's it, really. I don't want to be without Paula. There it is, stark and simple.

But (this thought crowding and somehow completing the previous one) can you find it in you, if it really comes to it, to let go – to be grateful for all you've been given in this life, all you've touched, tasted, seen, walked through (this all in a blurry rush now), all who have loved you and shown you some kindness, your family (I see them all), can you imagine, there, at the point of it, letting it all go with a feeling of gratitude? Paula, even Paula?

A lick of anxiety now, taste of copper in the mouth, and then – well, what's been happening since I went down? ('I' is back, I notice.) Nothing much, I realise, the usual slamming and banging and howling winds and lurching and rolling – the usual. Perhaps, OK, slightly more than the usual, but not, shall we say, by an order of magnitude, eh? And? Well we put our mast in the water and then she rolled right back up again. The aha! moment: she rolled right back up again. Yes, yes, I think, she rolled right back up again. So, all she has to do is keep going so, and in ten to twelve days or so I'll be home again? Right.

Ah sure that's grand. All we have to do is shut up and sail the boat. And besides, think of the others now, all of your fellow crew, Steve up there sailing us all through, consider these others, what it means to them that you command yourself, that you work this through.

Yes, I think, if it came to it now, out here on the vast ocean, suddenly and simply welling with life and gratitude, yes I could, yes I could.

And that's it, really. I remember giving a great big comfortable stretch as I snugged myself down; I remember saying a small prayer to the Star of the Sea, for us all, then falling over into a great big black pit of sleep. And nothing after.

Diane is shaking me 'Wake up, Theo, wake up. It's time to get up, you're on in five minutes, Fed's already called you.'

'What? Oh yeah.'

Unzip bag, up and over and on my feet, so fast she startles back.

'Sorry, Di, sorry. Everything OK?'

Boots, lean against locker, one foot, hop, the other. 'You OK?'

She's just standing there in the passageway, not standing exactly, leaning back and sideways against the hanging foulies. 'God!' She says it again, 'God!'

'Bit rough up there, yeah?'

'I never saw anything like it, honestly, I never... you could hardly stand. My God, when it got bright and you could *see* what's out there! I'm exhausted, I just want to crawl in there and fall unconscious.'

If it didn't feel somehow inappropriate, I'd take her in my arms and hold her for a minute. Just let her sag there.

'You know what, Di? That is one brutal day out there, I think you should feel proud of yourself for getting through a watch in this weather.'

I don't want her to tell me she's anxious, nervous, frightened, and to be fair to her, I don't think she is. She may have had little idea of what to expect out here, but we've had rough days before now and she's coped, and she's coping with this, too. Admirable. Really. Exhausted? Why wouldn't she be, who isn't?

'You know what, Di? I'm going to open out my sleeping bag and you pull it over you like a duvet. Be toasty warm that way, help you sleep.'

'Oh that's really...' she's too tired for words, just flaps her hand, smiles a faint smile.

'Ah, get in there would you, we'll just—'

She cuts in, 'Shut up and sail the boat! I know!'

This time a real smile.

I can't say I bounded up, anyone trying bounding here this morning would skull themselves on the roof, break at least two legs and an arm coming back down (or sideways) again, but a bright, cheery, 'Morning all!' gets me some very funny looks. I want to see what's out there, and then for a brief moment, I wish it wasn't. What's out there is very cold and very wet and very mountainous, great sliding grey-backed swells, bright with foam, spindrift going by at speeds that would blind you, lances of sunlight through the murk, a ripped bed of clouds flying by up there, a cold mountainy wet cold sort of mountainy sea rolling in from behind us, with nothing at all in mind except catching up with us, rolling over us and smashing us down, down, down into cold wet overwhelming dark forever. That kind of morning.

'Tea? Why thank you, Fed. Ah, Mike, the Fuegan situation? Nothing too ominous, I trust?'

This particular engine runs for about two minutes and then I take another look out there and think, you can ease

[211]

back now, Theo, that is a bad-looking sea and she's still blowing (peer at the log) 50+, just calm down now, there's a good lad. Let's not get too carried away. So I open the valve and a little anxiety bleeds out of the system, a fair bit, actually, but not too much now, not too much.

'Watch the roll!' Steve's back, he's been down grabbing an hour it seems, now he's back 'for a look around'. He peers at the bar, 'Well at least it's not going down anymore, eh? Gonna be like this for the next twenty-four, thirty-six maybe, I've just been having a look. Not as bad as last night, though. Phew, that was a bit of a stinker. You sleep, Theo?'

All this in a breath, pivoting on his heels, right palm flat against the roof, watching, watching.

'Yeah, sat there for a bit then went out like a light.'

'Oh you missed the fun, though, didn't he, Kev?'

My mind jumps to parting shrouds, ripped sails, desperate manoeuvres in the dark… Steve has his hand up for attention, 'What happened was, Spice Boy went out for a smoke-o, right? Parked himself out there on the bench, humped over like a turtle trying to keep it dry and' – he has to stop laughing before he can finish this – 'a sodding great big wave, I mean like a monster came right up over us from behind and fell in on him like a fucking brick shit house!'

Now he's really hooting, Kevin as bad, and I have to say this doesn't really strike me as very funny when Steve, perhaps seeing some prim expression on my face says, 'No, no, mate, wait for the best bit. The fucking cockpit's full of water, right? I mean like a bloody swimming pool or something, right? And his fucking life jacket goes off! Bang! Instant inflation, all's you can see is his face sticking up out of a big yellow balloon! He looked like… a startled bloody beagle, mate, that's what he looked like!'

Simon, listening to all this, last of his watch to go below, is laughing and wriggling at the same time, trying to get the poker-playing mask back on but seeing the funny side of this, for sure – and maybe, too, happy that he can?

'Come on, Simon,' I say, checking that I have a lighter, 'double or quits?' Nobody has to tell us to put on life jackets, or to clip on.

'Think I'll join you, matter of fact,' says Steve.

'Ah, a grand fresh day entirely,' says Kevin, reaching for his jacket. 'I might as well come too.'

'Do you know,' says Justin, 'that at 06.23 this morning, when we went over, I could see clear blue water outside the hatch above my bunk? Big beam sea, remember? Blue water, through the hatch over my bunk.'

'Beam sea?' Macken asks, 'are you sure? Through the hatch? At, when was it, 06.23 was it?'

Justin is looking at him suspiciously when Kevin sticks his oar in. 'Mr Macken, why don't you tell the Admiral what happened to you at, uh, 06.23?'

'Ah feck off, I'm going down to make tea.'

'Barry's?' Justin enquires innocently. 'Ah feck you, too, and the horse you rode into town on.'

Our comrade reappears with four mugs, trying to look cross, failing miserably to repress a grin.

It's cold out here, and the deck is maintaining an average slant of 40 degrees, which means of course that, from time to time, we are standing almost on our beam ends, the mast arcing towards the water. The sun is bright behind an all-enveloping pearly haze, so that the great grey-blue, foam-bright waves that keep rolling up behind us seem possessed of some deep interior light of their own. It's a brisk 50 knots, gusting 60 sometimes, and we sit in the cockpit shelter entirely composed, at ease with and trusting in this powerful boat, confident in our captain, perhaps just a little pleased with ourselves that we know enough now to trust in both. We rock and we roll, we balance and hold our places like men for whom being here, out in this, has become second nature. We are, for the moment, very much at home.

'Deck check,' says Justin suddenly, 'come on, Mr Dorgan, buckle up!'

We clip on, then Tony clips on, stands in behind the wheel and says, 'Go ahead there, men, I'll catch ye if ye get blown back this way.'

We go slowly, still laughing, and scrutinise everything as we go. We're always meticulous, but after last night we are minute in our inspection. The broken poles haven't moved, not even a fraction, their lashings immobile after all that pounding. Good man Simon, I think. All shackles and split pins present and correct, very little sign of chafe, though Justin thinks the starboard running backstay may be starting to wear as it goes through the forward block. We meet at the bow, and we could go straight back but there's something extraordinarily exhilarating about hanging on there, wrapped tightly around the forestay, shoulder to shoulder as the bow rises and plunges at tremendous speed, maybe 5 metres from the top of the rise to the hollow when she slams down. Up here it's all air and water mixed, great curtains of spray flung out around us in all directions. 'You know what?' I yell to Justin, a foot away, 'this would make a great country and western song, "The Sixty-Five Mile an Hour Deck Check".'

Then I look behind me at a great wall of white water hanging above my head and I think, oh fuck, I'm going to get wet here, already too late to get my hood up, to stop the downfall of water sluicing inside my collar. Of course this sets the hooded Justin off hooting with laughter again, and we head back to where Macken is shaking his head, 'Ye're a mad pair of bastards, you should have seen yourselves!'

Kevin deadpans a salute, 'Well, gentlemen, anything to report up there?'

'No, sir, a dead shark, some torpedo damage but nothing we can't fix with a welding torch; otherwise all fine.'

'Tone?' Steve has popped up again, in shorts and furry boots. 'Tony, come and have a look at this.' He's bent over the log, points at an entry, 'This your handwriting, yeah?'

'It is,' says Tony, wary.

'Fuck me, first time I ever saw that,' says Steve, his face grave.

Now Tony's nervous, 'What? What?'

'Well, see here, under wave height, yeah?' We're all crowding in now. 'You have 6 metres, right?'

'I have, yes.'

'Tony mate, those waves were 12 metres, the bugger that knocked us down must have been fourteen! This is a first, mate, sailors are always exaggerating the height of waves but fuck me, this is the first time I've ever seen anyone *underestimate*! By half!'

When the hooting and jeering has died down, Tony asks, 'So we were flat yeah, knocked flat?'

'Oh yeah,' says Steve, 'top of the mast in the water, broke a leg on the windex. Here, have a look through the glasses. She's a tough old girl and no mistake.'

She is, too, and we all raise a mental glass to Skip Novak, Tony Castro and South African welders, onlie begetters of our tough little world.

'Well, what did you think of last night then, Theo?' I'm having a cigarette with Steve, watching the long roll of the swell come up and go past.

'Well, I've never been out in anything like that,' I say.

'Yep,' he says, 'scared were ya, a bit?'

'Of course I was,' I say straight out, 'be mad not to be. But, well, what can you do, eh? Sail the boat, wait and see.'

'Dead right, mate, you'd be nuts not to be scared if you didn't know what one of these was like; scared is good sometimes, least it means people are paying attention, eh?'

'Yes,' I said, 'but, in the end, you know how I got through to just ordinary everyday anxiety?'

He's taking this seriously now, not being flippant, 'No, how?'

'Well, I figured 9 tonnes of iron is a hell of a lot of righting moment, yeah? And I couldn't see any way for water to get in and swamp us, right? But really, I went off to sleep because it was obvious you knew exactly what you were doing. Not just how you sailed the boat, how you made us all feel everything was in good hands.'

I don't think he knows how to deal with this, quite. I like Steve, but I can't say we get on particularly well – there's something about me he doesn't trust, something he can't quite put his finger on, but he's too polite to say so; we both know that we have to get on until we reach Cape Town anyway, so we let things lie. Now, though, I want him to know I admire his seamanship, and I admire his skill in bringing a very mixed bunch of people along with him in tough conditions. At giving us confidence in him, in the boat, in ourselves. 'Yeah,' he says, eventually, 'well, you know yourself it could all have gone pear-shaped, eh? But thanks, mate.' Seconds later he grabs me by the arm as the starboard quarter explodes upward, 'Watch the roll!'

We bucket along through the late afternoon, on into the night, charging down on Tristan at speed, kicked and jolted every which way, a rougher and faster ride than we've seen any day up to now but, somehow, it doesn't seem to matter as much as it would have before the blow. Someone has flung out fistfuls of stars on the dark ground of night, the racing sea is etched and trimmed in long lines of silver and glinting black, and we drive on into deep space, a low fizzy bubbling in our blood. As if we've woken up a degree or two in our attunement to boat and ocean, as if we are, by some increment or another, that little bit more at home out here on planet water. Tested and passed, for the moment at any rate. Touch wood.

⚓

DAY
## 27

Wednesday, 31 May 2006

Due on today at 06.00, but I rise an hour early to write the piece for *The Irish Times* that's due. This, I reflect, will require delicate handling. On the one hand, we've had the kind of blow that everyone, myself included, would have anticipated down here in the wild ocean, and it would be a pity not to write about it. On the other hand, I usually send a safety copy of the *IT* e-mail to Paula, which means she'll be reading it in a few hours, and even though I know she'll be worrying anyway, I don't want her imagining me in imminent peril of a storm-tossed death in the icy wastes. The larger truth is sometimes best served by elision and tactful silence, I decide, so the waves can be, say, 6 metres and today, filing day, can be the calm after the storm.

The desk to which the laptop is velcroed runs out from the starboard side of the saloon, as does the bench on which we sit to write, facing the stern. The boat's at an angle of 40 degrees to the horizontal still, sometimes even more, and there's the usual twisting and bucking going on as well, so that writing anything at all is a business best outsourced to an acrobatic audio-typist monkey. In the absence of which, I type the piece letter by letter, stabbing with one finger while my left hand is hooked into the fiddle on the shelf above the desk and I hang at an extreme angle, my right foot thrown out almost horizontally to brace myself against the engine room wall. It takes me nearly an hour, by which time the rest of the comrades are awake.

Justin asks, 'What did you say about yesterday's weather?'

We refrain from calling it a storm, all too aware of the far tougher experiences of many who have gone before us in these waters.

'Well,' I say, 'I thought it best to accept Mr Macken's estimation of the wave height, and I don't think people are really that interested in tales of drama on the high seas anyway, do you?'

'Very wise,' says the Admiral judiciously, considering how to word his own e-mail home, 'very wise. No point in worrying people, eh?'

'Anyone been in the forepeak since yesterday?' I ask. The lads are checking our position on the chart and on the chart plotter, comparing one with the other. We've had the radar out to its widest range, but no sign of Tristan or its outliers yet. Nobody answers. 'I guess I'll take a look anyway, you never know.'

It's as well I did, before Steve got to see the sodden chaotic mess that greets me. There's very little water in the bilges, a bit more than usual maybe, but compared to most boats after the weather we've been having, nothing to write home about. The problem is that this water is full of crushed tomatoes, cabbage leaves, onions, and God alone knows what else. To the right of the heavy watertight door, as you enter, is where we store our fruit and vegetables in plastic crates, stacked up on metal racks. Here is where Tony comes to ferret for dinner, and today it's an absolute mess – crates upended, fruit and vegetable contents all mixed in with each other, rolling in the bilges or otherwise distributed around the forepeak. On one of the aluminium floorboards of the RIB, caged securely on the port side, a carrot has impaled itself. There's an orange bleeding to death between the hull and the long heavy propshaft of 'Little' *Pelagic*. I have no doubt but that when eventually we dig out the RIB we will find the remains of kamikaze courgettes secreted in its folds. I get down on my knees and feel around in the murky water for packets of meat – well at least that's something, they're all intact, no blood in the water. Hmm, not much meat left.

'Vegetable Armageddon in the forepeak,' I report back. 'We'd better get a bucket and sponges up there before Steve sees the mess.' It doesn't matter that the mess is nothing to do with us – in the sense that we didn't cause it – the point is it's become visible on our watch, and now it's our duty to deal with it. Which of course we do, collecting some interesting bruises in interesting places in the process – being up here while she's slamming is like being inside a concrete mixer falling down a mountain. We leave the carrot where it is, as a tourist attraction.

Then it's back to the chart table, out on deck, chart table, deck, until out of the murk ahead I see… land, is it? 'Hey, Justin, what's the bearing to Tristan now?'

He calls it back and I take a deep breath before yelling, 'Land Ho!'

I know it's corny, I tell the lads, but sure what the hell, there's a lot of empty water behind us.

'Yessir,' says Kevin, 'that's Tristan, and that' – pause, check again with the glasses – 'that there down to starboard I do believe is Inaccessible. What's the bearing, Justin? Uh huh, Inaccessible. Now gentlemen, in between those two we should expect to see twin peaks to the south, and that will be Nightingale.'

Fifteen days out of Stanley, we are closing with Tristan da Cunha. Slowly. Out there in the great wastes, time seems to pass of its own accord, though the brute press of the wind in our sails, the deep running swell coming up from behind, give a feeling of swiftness to our onward passage. Yesterday, indeed, we were flying, buoyed up and borne on by wind and wave. Nothing has changed, we're still making much the same speed, but now that there's something out there ahead to aim for we seem to hang in each trough, stall and fall back. Nevertheless, we are steadily getting closer. We smarten ourselves up, a bit, in anticipation of going ashore. Clean and tidy will do for today, we'll be gone by sundown.

The sky is clearing, a high pale blue from horizon to horizon, small white clouds for depth and perspective. The architect of things, perhaps remembering our delight back there, oh very far back there now at Cathedral Rocks, sends a rainbow to stand over Tristan, one foot in the sea towards Nightingale, the other planted on the scattering of green fields and house that make up Tristan's only settlement, Edinburgh of the Seven Seas. We draw closer; now we can see the tiny white houses, their roofs red and green, occasionally blue. The little fields are viridian, emerald, shimmering in the light, hatched with stone walls. They stand on a small bluff of level land, a couple of hundred acres at best under the towering bulk of the volcanic mountain. There's snow on St Mary's Peak, glittering like one of those glaciers in the Beagle Channel, a hint of blue there, as if sky and mountain were blending gently, one into the other.

A voice on the radio, hailing us. 'What ship?'

Steve takes the fist mike in his grip. 'Ah, good morning, Tristan. This is *Pelagic Australis*, *Pelagic Australis*, over.'

Inspector Conrad Glass, the famed Rock Hopper Copper (RHC), welcomes us. 'Swell's not too bad,' he says. 'You wouldn't have been able to land yesterday, mind, and it's not looking good tomorrow, either.'

Steve tells him we'll anchor off, and we'll need the services of a RIB to get crew in and out. The RHC says that'll be £15 a head landing fee, then, and £15 per RIB ferry journey. Our Great Leader isn't having any of that.

'We're bringing bags and official papers from Stanley,' he says, 'and there will be a delivery charge of £2,500.'

'Crikey,' exclaims Justin, speaking for the open-mouthed lot of us. There's a pause, and then RHC is back, '*Pelagic*, it'll be good to have you visit. We'll waive the landing charge, OK? When d'you want the RIBs?'

'Oh,' says OGL, 'shall we say in about an hour? Thank you very much, Tristan, see you shortly, *Pelagic Australis* out.'

Attaboy Steve, we say, delighted with his performance, not so much for saving us £15 each, we don't care about that, but for the sheer brass neck of coming up with such an outlandish delivery charge on the spot. Was there ever a crew, I ask myself, that didn't admire audacity in a skipper?

'Let's have the anchor up then, Kev.'

'Oh fuck,' mutters Kevin. 'I knew it, I just knew it.'

Macken is quick as a tern to his ear, 'Kevin, only yesterday I was thinking that fit young lads like Simon and Fed must be really feeling the lack of exercise by now...'

'Har, har,' says Kevin. 'I like your thinking, Mr Macken, sir...'

We furl the foresails, drop and stack the main, while Debs drives us parallel to the shore, keeping about 200 metres off from a short clean vertical lava cliff.

'That looks pretty recent,' Mike murmurs, and more than one person looks thoughtfully up at the baleful bulk of the volcano.

Steve, in the bow, with Kevin calling the depth to him from the cockpit, is finally satisfied with our position and gives the vigorous hand signal to drop anchor. Down rattles what sounds like an awful lot of chain and *Pelagic*, to all intents and purposes, comes to a stop.

Two guys in a yellow RIB are on their way out to us. Upright, silent, not unfriendly but some deep reticence there, a grave quality to their greeting.

'OK,' says Steve. 'I'm going to pop ashore, do the business, get everyone's passports stamped an' all that malarkey. Simon, Theo, you come with me, when we come back anyone else wants to can go ashore.'

We hand down the bag and packets we've brought from Stanley, climb down into the RIB and head for the entrance to the small harbour. It's a rough looking place, right enough, the sea walls great boulders with concrete caissons piled higgledy-piggledy on top. There's a surfer's wave runs into the harbour; the guy on the wheel holds us outside on the throttle until a surge comes up behind, then he races in on the face of it, veering off at the last second to the right. The surge crashes against the wall behind us to the left. Now we see the point of using their RIB and not ours. The harbour, like island harbours everywhere, is a confusion of rusted discarded engines, mysterious skeletons of abandoned small cranes, piles of lobster pots, skeins of net hung out to dry or to be repaired, piles of rock and gravel, great coils of steel cable lying at random, and boats in every stage of repair. Big-bellied things they are, like oversized whalers, deep in the sections and broad in the beam. There are relics of wooden boats here and there, but the boats in use or under repair are either bullet-proof heavy fibreglass or aluminium. There are a few guys of indeterminate function on the jetty, here to greet us or taking a break from work it's hard to say. Shy men, squat and strong, they look Portuguese but the accents are deep, unhurried south of England.

'Welcome to Tristan,' the guy with the hand-held radio says, and his handshake says he means it. 'Lucky you could get in,' he says, looking out past us to where *Pelagic* is riding gently up and down at anchor. 'You wouldn't have got in yesterday. Bad 'un that was, shifted that, see?' He points to a caisson, dislodged from the top of the wall. Must weigh, what, 20 tonnes? 'Night before last that was, just knocked her off, gentle like.'

Simon looks at the guy, looks at me, says, 'Riiight.'

There's a shed at the bottom of the steep ramp leading up from the harbour, painted in gay vertical candy stripes of red and white. The neatly executed lettering across the top reads: 'Welcome to Tristan da Cunha – 500th Anniversary (1506–2006)'. The RHC meets us at the top of the long steep ramp, a short distance from his small office to one side of the neat administration building. The flag resembles that of the Falklands, navy blue, the Union flag in the top left, a rather baroque coat of arms front and centre with the motto: 'Our faith is our strength.' RHC stamps our passports and Steve hands over the bundle of buff official envelopes, all marked OHMS, On Her Majesty's Service.

I feel for a moment sorry, indeed, that I'm not in blue and buff, the mildew scraped off the gold braid, cocked hat tucked crisply under me arm. Sure, I think, sure; far more likely you'd have been sent swinging from a yard arm for a Fenian reprobate. I buy a copy of his autobiography from the RHC, and Steve gets directions to the house of James and Felicity Glass. The bag we've brought in is their daughter's. We walk to the house along unpaved paths, winding through close-cropped grass, between neat, single-storey cottages and bungalows, all painted white, most with green or red or blue corrugated iron roofs, some roofed in asbestos, lichened and discoloured. The lane winds between tall, dry-stone walls, there are fuchsias and ferns, black and white cattle here and there, small knots of men taking their time over some job or other, women brisking from one house to another. I feel extraordinarily at home, and why wouldn't I? This reminds me of nothing so much as West Cork or Kerry as I remember them in those glorious summers of the 1970s – the high sun, blue sky, white clouds, tang of the sea, unhurried pace, cattle and sheep, houses and washing lines bringing colour to the vivid green of the fields. It reminds me so much of the Cork and Kerry Gaeltachts of my childhood that I salute some poor man, met rounding a corner, in Irish. Quite possibly, the first time the language has been spoken on what bills itself proudly as 'The Remotest Island' – but then you never know: the British Navy planted a garrison of marines on the island in 1816, when Napoleon was exiled to Saint Helena, to ensure that no effort to rescue him, if one came, could take on water and stores here – and who's to say that, down through the years, some soldier or seaman of Corca Dhuibnne, Tír Chonaill, Múscraí, Rinn, Conamara or Iorras didn't land in here?

The leader of that little garrison, James Glass tells us, was James Glass of Devon, his direct ancestor. Glass is still the principal surname on the island, he says.

'Will you have a beer?' his wife Felicity asks, and then laughs and goes to get glasses anyway.

Islanders, faced with sailors newly landed, know a redundant question when they utter one. These are kind people, courteous, welcoming, very much at their ease. I sit in the sun outside for a while, throwing a ball for their small brown dog, Hayley, to fetch. Two black and white sheepdogs look on from the sun-warmed wall.

'It's so warm,' Simon says to Felicity, 'when you consider there's snow on the mountain.'

'Ah is there?' she says. 'I thought there might be, from the wind; we can't see the top you know, except from out at sea.'

James volunteers some more information. The islanders don't permit immigration, largely on the grounds that there is no more space to build houses. The young people go to Cape Town or England for their education, and then they return.

'What, all of them?'

'Almost all, sure. This is their home.' Each family is permitted seven cows and two sheep, the numbers arrived at by empirical study of what the grazing will sustain; the animals are grazed collectively. Many people here work for the government, as mechanics, carpenters, etc. Yes, they still make a fair bit from issuing stamps (how well I remember learning to pronounce the name of this exotic place from the mixed packets of stamps I used to buy as a boy). Nowadays there is a tourist trade, too: some cruise ships have put Tristan on their itinerary: there's money to be made, ferrying the people back and forth to the big liners, (money to be made from landing fees, too, I think) but they never stay overnight – where would they stay? The islanders are keeping a close eye on this business: all very well to be making a few pounds, but you wouldn't want the place swamped now, would you?

'How's the fishing?' Steve asks.

'Good, good. There's a quota of course, small enough, but we get good prices, 27 dollars a kilo for lobsters and such. Nowadays we sell them mostly to Japan.'

From Felicity, before we leave, we will buy some good quality cotton shirts, with the Tristan crest on. Now *that*, I think, would give Justin swanking points when next he swaggers into the Royal Ocean Racing Club, not to mention Macken, walking modestly into Kinsale; must send them up here.

It's a small enough kindness, God knows, that Steve has done the Glass family, bringing home a bag for their daughter, but they insist on giving us a bag of potatoes, and another bag full of frozen lobster tails as we leave. I feel as if we've been visiting a well-liked uncle and aunt.

They take Falklands money here, and we buy some first-day covers, some tiny unlikely looking hand-knitted penguins with small woollen hats of banded green and white. I imagine some enterprising child, settled in for the winter, tongue sticking out of the corner of her mouth, working the awkward needles, and I am uncomfortably moved. We were like that once, I think, content with immediate horizons, dreaming of the wider world, preparing ourselves for it at our own pace, but not yet made anxious by its nagging virtual presence in the daily moment. There was time in the world then, I think, and now there seems to be no time at all. Too many worlds colliding in the daily run of things.

I'm not, I hope, being sentimental. They're far from cut off here; some of the young people are building a good website, the islanders are in and out to Cape Town, in fact they seem to own a house there for the use of anyone passing through. The RHC learned his policing in Sussex, he drives the standard UK-issue white Land Rover with chequered markings, he sells his book by mail order all over the world and he's never had to lock anyone up.

'What do you do if someone gets out of order?' I asked him earlier.

'Oh, a few people call round to him' – he doesn't, I notice, say 'or her' – 'and have a word. That always straightens things out.'

It's an unremarkable life, not exotic, and not, as far as I can tell, a life that leaves people feeling constrained. I hope they manage to keep it. I hope nobody finds oil out there in the nearby void.

There's a certain air on board when we get back. Nothing you'd go so far as to call mutinous, but we're not exactly greeted with broad smiles and 'hope you enjoyed yourselves'. They've been scrubbing ship, with particular attention to the forepeak, and there is perhaps a certain feeling we might have dallied too long ashore. Everyone piles unceremoniously into the RIB, impatient to be off. Debs 'doesn't feel like it now'. I think I might have a little read. In my bunk. With the curtain pulled over. Steve goes to talk to Debs. Simon decides to have a little read. In his bunk. With the door pulled shut.

Near sundown, everyone's back on board again, cheerful again, bantering again. We've done the prep for dinner, washed and chopped vegetables, salad, etc., all ready to go.

'C'mon then, Kevin, I'll give you a hand with the anchor.'

'My man!' he says, 'Let's go!'

'Oh, all right then,' say the other grumpy old men, 'we'll give a hand.'

'To make sure you don't do it wrong, like,' Macken adds helpfully, and my Union card is stamped 'valid' again.

Debs takes us out. 'Right then, Simon my boy, let's get some flappy white things up, eh?' She points us north, to clear the island, before we turn east by north for the open sea again, and Cape Town.

Justin's at the chart table; we're waiting for dinner to come up. 'What d'ye reckon there, Admiral?'

He snaps the dividers shut, consults his notes, straightens up. 'Seven and a half days, morning Thursday, the 8th,' he says crisply. Then, still deadpan, 'Weather permitting of course.'

We eat on deck, silent now as we watch Tristan and its outliers fade under the banner of mountaintop cloud in the sunset.

'Look at that,' Fed says, rapt; 'you know, some day I will wonder if I was there at all, you know? Seems like a dream.

⚓

DAY
# 28
Thursday, 1 June 2006

A calm, restorative day. Blue sea, a kind of deep aquamarine, long ovoids of silver shimmering across the face of the
gentle swell, wavering like jellyfish into figures of eight as
the swell dips to pass under the hull. Tristan Tactical Air
Patrol on station since early morning, seeing us off the
premises I suppose, managing the exclusion zone firmly
but with some tact.

We pass through the morning in a kind of reflective daze,
the ship clean and tidy, the course clear, Yankee and staysail
flying, one reef in the main. There's a long floating dip to our

progress, the bow eating steadily into the long toll of miles before us, in for the long haul, strong and stately.

The Port Watch Parliament has convened in the cockpit, Kev with his ever-present protein shake to hand, the Grumpy Old Men with good strong coffee. Some unspoken sartorial covenant has seen us all come up in thermal tops and leggings, shorts and sea boots. Out of nowhere, Southern Ocean Chic has reared its unlovely head.

'Tell us about the tattoo business then, Kevin.' The Admiral is in mischievous mood.

'Well, there ain't a whole lot to tell. It's a business, it's a business. I've got two parlours, y'all know they're called parlours, right? Well, got a couple guys working for me in each. One guy, now, he's what you might call an artist. Most guys in the business work from what's called flash books, right? Your standard stuff, eagles, flags, snakes and roses, lotta call these days for rosebuds, 'specially from the young women. But this guy, now, he works out his own designs, right, all kindsa strange perspectives and shit. He's good, man, real good.'

Kevin himself is a billboard for the business, all kinds of busy work up and down his arms, a four-master for God's sake on his bare forearm there as he tips yet another of his 'power shakes' to chapped lips.

The tip of Tony's nose is quivering, he's on the scent now. 'You, ah, get a lot of women then, Kev?'

'These days, sure. All kinds, too. College girls, college professors, moms, working ladies – I mean business ladies, y'understand here – young girls, older women...'

'And what do they usually go for?'

'Well, like I said, rosebuds; you know what's curious, there's been a real fashion this past few years for a little rosebud right here,' he twists where he's standing, points, 'right here above the butt? Sometimes on the butt? Some guys call it the tramp stamp but that's kind of out of line, you ask me. Yeah, and some like a butterfly on a breast, or maybe on a shoulder blade?'

He might be describing Grafton Street or Patrick Street on a sunny day, I tell him.

'Really? You mean it? Man, you got chicks getting tattoos in Ireland? Wow, I wouldna have thought...'

'Oh yeah,' says Tony, 'sure we've got electricity now, too, and cars, and women have the vote...'

'Get outta here, Macken,' Kev is hooting. 'You know what I mean. Hell, I didn't invent your tourist board and all them country, what d'ya call 'em, colleens? What was I saying before Mr Macken started taking the piss? Oh yeah. Man, I got lawyers coming in, real handsome women, man, and I think of 'em standing up there in court, dressed all proper, giving it the whole nine yards and, man, if that judge had any idea what they've got tattooed under them clothes, man, whooee!'

Now the Admiral's interest is sharpening. 'Piercings, too? You do piercings as well?'

'Funny you should ask that,' says Kev, shaking his head. 'You see them shackles? My woman gives me one every time I go off on a long trip, correction, every time I *come back from* a long trip. Cool, huh? Now this, here (gold earring, other ear), this here I earned, just like Mr Dorgan here just earned his; that right, Theo?'

'Yep,' I say, 'that's right, Kev.'

'How d'you mean?' Tony asks.

Justin explains. 'It's a tradition, when you round the Horn you're entitled to wear a gold earring in your left ear.'

'Oh, I see,' says Tony. 'You know how Theo's deaf in his other ear? I always thought that yoke was a hearing aid.'

No point in kicking him, I'd have to get off my comfortable perch between the starboard winches. 'I'd like to send you home to Kathleen with an earring, see what she'd make of you.'

'Kathleen wouldn't mind,' he mock-simpers, 'sure she's mad about me anyway, and why wouldn't she be?'

Justin shakes his head, but resumes his pursuit of piercings. 'Why do you think people do it, then, Kevin, piercing? I don't mean earrings, I mean tongue studs, navels, all the rest of the palaver?'

Kevin gives this some thought. 'Well' – is this John Wayne 'well' natural, or is he gently sending us up? – 'I suppose people want to be different, that's all. Then you got people who want to belong to the different, you following me? You getta bunch of high school kids come in, they all want their belly buttons pierced, you know? Kind of a gang thing? You gotta be real, real careful with that, man, kids coming in drunk or stoned or whatever, getting stuff done, tattoos or piercing, whatever, and then they're back with their momma and their lawyer suing ten kinds a shit outta ya. Man, we make them sign waivers, y'know?'

'And, Kevin, what would you say is the most unusual kind of piercing?'

'Oh, that's an easy one, man, course it's maybe not that unusual now that I come to think of it…'

'Yes, and that's?'

'Huh? Oh yeah, I guess clitoral piercing is the most unusual.'

'Whaaat?' The Admiral chokes on his coffee, an interesting sight in itself, made more diverting when he splutters all over his neat khaki shorts. 'Are you serious?'

'Oh yeah, man, we do one or two a week, for sure. Classy gals, too, sometimes, you know? All kinds. I don't do 'em, though, got a woman does them special. Man, I'd find that kinda disturbing, wouldn't you? I mean, that kinda work, you gotta look real close to be sure what you're doing, be kinda hard to concentrate…'

We are twenty-eight days out of Punta Arenas, at least ten days more before any of us walks in the garden gate again – well, except for Macken, who's being met in Cape Town. There's a long silence while we meditate, each in his own way, on the vista that has so unexpectedly unfolded before us. Finally, I look up from far away, meet Tony's eye, Kevin's, Justin's – and there is an explosion of laughter, the good true old-fashioned kind, all of us doubling up, whooping, tears in the eyes, heads back for air and doubling up again.

'What's so funny, eh?' Fed and Di put their heads, together, out the wheelhouse door, perplexed and intrigued by this outbreak of seeming madness.

'Yes, what are you all laughing at, tell us?'

Oh bloody hell, I think, this is too much.

'Eh, Justin? Tony and I are going to start lunch now, why don't you tell Fed and Di what we were just talking about? Kevin, you want to give us a hand?'

'Jaysus,' says Macken, pushing me down the steps into the galley, 'you're a bad bastard, poor Justin. I wonder where those two have been?'

So, Steve wants to know, 'You guys up for this Yachtmaster exam, then?'

'Absolutely,' says Tony, 'yes, yes.'

Me. I'm not sure, and Justin has reservations. I'm not sure because it's difficult to concentrate here, the wheelhouse under way is not the most ideal of classrooms, and the long-term fatigue isn't much help, either. Justin's reservations are more forthright: he wouldn't trust any qualification he earned out here, in these circumstances. Not the teaching, he says, it's not that, he just isn't sure how much of what he might seem to have learned is actually going in. This is not what Steve expected, and he's in a bit of a huff about it. 'Well, jeez, you paid for this, you know? And I mean, you know the stuff, I can see that every night. So, I don't understand your problems here, guys. To be frank.' And out with him to smoke and talk to Kev. He's taking this as a criticism of him and his teaching, gone off on the wrong tack entirely, but there's nothing we can do about this right now.

We haven't really considered or discussed the question with any seriousness. When I came across the offer of this trip on Skip Novak's website, it was the length of it that attracted me, the prospect of a long testing passage in the South Atlantic, the long reflective silences, the irresistible lure of rounding the Horn, the undertow of family history and duty.

It seemed like a good idea, in the abstract, to study for a qualification en route; I suppose I didn't think about it enough, assumed that it would be, somehow, a process of osmosis. I hadn't bargained on formal lessons, though, of course, I should have, and I certainly hadn't envisaged the conditions under which the teaching would take place. Steve knows his stuff, no two ways about that, and he can get it across, that's not the problem even though, right now, I know he thinks it is. The difficulty I have, and that Tony and Justin share, is we don't know how much of what we seem to be learning is lodging in short-term memory only.

Every day we've been at sea there have been lessons, and Steve's way of reinforcing these lessons is to pit one watch against the other, every night, in competition to see who has retained the most. It's not a bad idea in itself, and it livens up the evenings to an extent, but night after night I've been getting more irritated about these quizzes. As far as the Grumpy Old Men are concerned, the point is to learn, absorb and retain flags, Morse, collision regulations, weather, knots, navigation, pilotage, provisioning, crew-management, passage planning, maintenance and all those other good things that the excellent syllabus covers. We want to know these things because we want to be capable of skippering a boat on an offshore passage, we want to learn things we expect we will need to know. Competition's fun, in a low-key kind of way, an amusement of sorts, and it does give a focus to memorising. What's happened, though, is that our comrades on the other watch have become focused on, in some mild way obsessed with, winning the nightly competition, and this seems to us more than slightly absurd. In fact, it annoys us. Inside the time frame of the nightly game, sure we want to win; in some ways, in fact, we're probably even more competitive than they are – well, not more than Fed is perhaps. But, when it's over, it's over is how we look at it.

Take last Monday. We'd been studying colregs (collision regulations), and had lost, narrowly, on points.

'Well,' said Tony, studying the flash cards, 'I'd say, Theo, after this you'll recognise a tug with a tow of more than 50 metres alongside not under way, if you ever run into one.'

And then Di called up to Fed, 'Come on, we're all having a glass of wine to celebrate our victory!'

Victory? To his credit, Fed looks embarrassed. He cringes when she follows this with, 'We have to get cracking on lights now, and win that.'

'Ah for fuck's sake,' says Tony, softly, turning away. Kev, cleaning his sextant at the chart table, just shakes his head in sorrow.

So, we have all this in mind now, turning it all over. Steve has calmed down. 'Ah look, guys, I know what you all want here. You want to know that you really know what you've learned, right? C'mon, I know you're all serious, that you're not doing this for some piece of paper, right? Right, Tony? Look, think about it. I think you know your stuff; sure, Theo, to be honest mate, you've got some brushing up to do, no mistake, but you guys will pass, no worries. Don't think I'd pass you if I didn't think you know your stuff, if that's what's worrying you. Have a think, all right? We'll talk about it tomorrow.'

We'll think about it, sure.

I do the handover, for a change, to a puzzled-looking Fed.

'What's up, Fed?'

'It's Diane,' he says, 'she's not feeling too well, she says; no, she says "feeling unwell", yes? She's not coming up for the watch.'

Debs disappears down the passageway, comes back a minute or two later, shrugs and says, 'Well she's crook, that's what she says.'

Big Mike's concerned, 'It might be a uh, eh, female thing maybe?'

'Nah,' says Debs, who has a real gift for the terse.

'Oh,' says Mike, and not a word out of him about Fuegans.

Fed's out on deck a short while later. 'You know, Theo? I never heard of this before on a boat. Di wants to introduce the thirty-five-hour week, I think.'

'Well you know, Fed, it is becoming the EU norm now.'

He looks at me startled. 'Are you serious? Come on, man. You can't do that on a boat!'

I look at him, going for inscrutable here, guileless even, but he sees through me. 'Ah get out of here, you're joking, right? Get out of here!'

I haven't seen him smile like that since Cape Horn.

Well, I decide, not my problem; now, where am I going to sleep? Simon has figured out what I'm thinking. 'You can crash in my bunk, if you like.' A beat, and then. 'While we figure out who's going to draw up the list now.' He's eyeing the wheel speculatively. Arnie, like me, may be in for a rest.

I wake for dinner, straight from sleep, no floundering, no swimming up through murk. I lie there a while, getting the feel of the boat. Wind's gone north-west, I think; I'd guess the sea is at 1.5–2 metres and the wind… 7–10 knots? Dress and go up, check the log, the instruments: bang on.

'So, any thoughts about the exam?' Tony wants to know; it's the end of our watch, it's dark out there, nothing to light the water coursing past the port beside the desk as we check for e-mails.

'Dunno,' I say, 'still thinking about it. You know what won't help with the revision, though?'

'What?' he asks.

'Have a look at the weather,' I say, and he does.

'Uh-oh,' he says, then, 'don't like the look of that.'

⚓

Another grey, dark dawn. Fed calls me, stands there in the passageway when I flick on the reading light, his eyes hollow. He shakes his head, says, 'I'm sorry to wake you, it's not a very good day up there.' He sees I am struggling to wake, says, 'It's OK, you got ten minutes.'

I need every one of them for the laborious business of dressing, crouched in a corner of this confined space, wedging myself against the lumpy roll. Dressed, I reach for my foul-weather gear; having seen how wet Fed is in his, I know exactly what kind of day it is up there. We're getting beam seas, I lurch to the irregular thump of each wave as it bumps heavily on the hull.

I don't like the whine of the wind, either, sounds like it's come up in the past four hours. In the wheelhouse, when I trudge up, everyone is subdued. Little talk, none of the usual banter. Mike hands me a cup, shakes his head when I look at him, clearly thinking of his bunk and sleep. No sign of Steve; outside Debs and Kev are having their usual cigarette together, not talking. Di is already heading down. I grunt at Macken and the Admiral, even that takes an effort, and peer at the instruments: 50 knots. Yeah, thought it might be something like that. A lurch sends us all bumping into each other, nobody says a word. We're canted over at a big angle, I can't even be bothered guessing at what the angle is.

I lean in the doorway. Squinting out, I turn and look enquiringly at Mike. 'You know what?' he says. 'I think even the fucking Fuegans are giving it a rest today.'

I'm awake now, well, slightly more awake: this is the first time I've heard Mike swear. 'Bed, Mike,' I say. 'Morpheus time, close eyes and wait for this to pass?'

'You betcha,' he says, 'you betcha.'

I've forgotten my fleece hat. Di is already in the bunk. 'Oh, I am so tired,' she says, 'so very, very tired.' She looks it, too, her skin almost translucent, deep rings around her eyes.

'Ah you'll be fine,' I say, probably unconvincingly.

'Well,' she sighs, 'I suppose you'd better go off and sail the boat, eh?'

Simon brushes past in the passageway, we shuffle by each other with the briefest of looks exchanged. Not a word.

This is deep fatigue now. Justin is slumped at the chart table, staring at the plotter, his eyes unfocused; Tony's on the port side bench, humped down into himself, head turned to stare out ahead at the bursts of spray coming off the bow. There's a bit of Yankee out, three reefs in the main I think, it might be two, it's hard to see out through the rain sluicing down the windows. No sign of Kevin, he must have gone down again on some errand of his own. I could curl up here on the floor and sleep for a week. This isn't good; this is when bad shit happens, I sluggishly realise. A tired crew, crap weather after a glorious day yesterday, and probably the after-effects of that big blow kicking in, too. Justin's ahead of me. Even as my thoughts struggle to form, I see him straighten up, shiver, shake his head vigorously. 'Mr Macken,' he says, turning, 'what's happening with your boat while you're motorcycling through Africa?'

Oh, that's brilliant, I think, oh very neat Mr Admiral sir, very neat. Tony peers over his glasses, suspicious, sensing something is up. 'Why? What do you mean?'

My turn, 'Well, is it in the water, for instance, or up on the hard?'

Still suspicious, 'Why?'

I see Kevin standing at the foot of the passageway stairs, where Tony can't see him, not moving, waiting to hear where this is going.

Justin's turn. 'Well, Mr Dorgan and I were thinking we'd do you a favour while you're away, look after the boat.' We were? We are now, it seems.

'What do you mean, look after?' Sitting upright now.

'Well,' me next, 'I've been telling Justin how beautiful it is along the coast from Kinsale to, say, Dingle? So I was thinking, while you're away, like, that we could look after the boat for you, take it out for an airing?'

'Heh, very nice, very nice, but, eh, she's up on the hard, getting painted, you know.'

'Oh, where's that, Tone?'

'Crosshaven… fella called Mick is looking after her for me.'

'Mick is it? Sure I know Mick,' – I do not – 'one of my brothers is going out with his daughter! Ah sure, Mick would let us have the boat, Justin, no problem there.'

Wolfish, Kevin, still unseen by Tony, winks.

'Splendid!' Justin is brisk, business concluded. 'Well, that's that, then. When do you think, Theo, say last week of June?'

'Oh, that would be perfect, perfect; give us time to sort ourselves out at home before heading out again.'

'Ah, now here, lads, calm down, calm down, ye're not serious?'

Now Kevin displays his sense of timing, stomps up the steps. 'Serious about what, Tony my man?'

Justin cuts in before Tony can answer. 'Tony, very generous of him I must say, has offered Theo and myself the use of his boat until he gets home.'

'I did not! I did not! Don't mind them, Kevin, they're only ball-hopping.' But he's unsure, blinking rapidly now, peering from Justin to me and back again, trying to read the situation.

We leave him hanging there, all of us awake now. 'Deck check, Mr Dorgan?' Justin might be proposing a swift pint before dinner.

'Mm… Yes indeed, Mr Slawson, wind's only tipping 50, why not, why not – a brisk constitutional, eh?'

'Did you see his face?' We're crammed in the doorway, both trying to exit at the same time. Macken roars after us, 'Fecking chancers! I knew it! I knew it!'

Now how did he hear that? I can't hear anything except the roar of the wind, gone down to a bass register suddenly after the high howling. Getting up, I wonder? Or some local coincidence of the rumble of surf, low sky and wind speed? It sure looks wet up there. 'I'll take the low side, for a change?'

'You sure? OK.'

'I got your backs,' says Kevin, bareheaded, cold-showering himself fully awake.

I'm taking the low side because I've brought up my own harness with its double hooks. The boat harnesses, perfectly adequate in other respects, have to be unclipped for a moment when going past the shrouds, passed around and then re-clipped. It's not such a problem on the high side, but down in the lee scuppers with water, as now, roaring along the deck, with the rail in the water, it's slightly dodgy. I clip the second hook with its short tether on the far side of the shroud before unclipping the long tether and passing it around, clipping it on again. A small increment of safety, but this is a day for extra care. Green water is sluicing past, up to my knees, and it doesn't even occur to me to be concerned, why should it? I'm clipped on, the deck underfoot is solid, the guard wires are strong enough to hold me if I stumble, what's to worry about? Idiot, I tell myself, you're not out here to enjoy yourself. As usual, we pause for a moment up in the bow, enjoying the express elevator, and today we get thoroughly hosed, head to heel. It isn't bravado, the Grumpy Old Men don't do bravado, but it is certainly exhilarating, plunged in the full weight of the ocean on a rearing foredeck in a force 10.

Kevin always gets it. 'Good, huh? You guys like that, huh?'

Justin tries unconvincingly to grumble, 'Bloody wet up there, Kevin!'

Kev isn't having any. 'Get outta here, that's why you do it, man. That's why you do it.' He might be right, too.

Brother Macken has forgiven us: fruit salad and coffee for all.

We do the log, we redo our calculations regarding ETA Cape Town, we do our best to keep a heading of 085° in the conditions, but that's all there is to do on this watch, so we settle to daydreaming: one eye for the boat, the other turned inward.

My admiration for the mental and physical toughness of solo sailors has been growing by the day. I can scarcely imagine what it would be like: to be hammering across this ocean, day after day, night after night, on snatched sleep, your heart in your mouth half the time, battling boat, gear, wind and sea, and fending away that most dangerous and insidious of enemies, the fatal indifference of the body and mind fatigued beyond endurance. The solo *racing* sailors I cannot understand at all. I read the accounts, I comprehend what I'm being told, but something slips away in the flow of the narrative, some quality of credence. It isn't that I don't *believe* Goss, Autissier, MacArthur and those others: I believe them very readily, but I cannot project myself into their psyches, I cannot imagine myself possessed of their competitive spirits. I exult in their achievements, I am often deeply moved by the strange and touching ways in which human will manifests in their actions, how they plough on through all adversities with an eye on the prize, schooling and shaping body and mind to one purpose, and one purpose only: getting there first.

I feel more kinship with Moitessier, the semi-Buddhist, half-mystic Frenchman who, in with a real chance of winning the first round-the-world yacht race, the *Sunday Times* Golden Globe in 1968–1969, came round the Horn in the lead – and changed his mind. Taking thought out here in the Southern Atlantic, he put up his helm and made again for the Cape of Good Hope, for the Indian Ocean after that and on to Tahiti, when his course should have taken him north up the Atlantic highway, to England and a fleeting moment of fame. He said, 'I chose to save my soul', and I understand him, today, here, now, and for many days past. The great seduction of the deep ocean is this: that a man begins to think 'I could do this on my own, I could be out here for ever, day after day, taking the wind and the weather as it comes, and that would be world enough for me.' Wake and sail, sleep and the boat can sail itself. The sky this morning is bright maybe, or perhaps dark and cloud-driven? OK, either is fine. Take it as it comes. Hungry? Make something to eat. Tired? Sleep, set the internal alarm for as long as you can bear to be away, then wake. Wind getting up? Shorten sail. A good day today? Pole out the headsails, take the wind over the quarter or over the stern, and sail on, sail on. In a well-found boat, well handled and well provisioned, you need hardly touch the earth at all; you can stay out here in this better element, out here on planet water, where time is the time of the eternal now, memory something that lodges in the body, tomorrow no more than another day you will have to sail through.

I've copied into my journal a passage from Moitessier's *A Sea Vagabond's World* that has given me much food for thought: 'Once the coast disappears astern, a man alone before his creator can't remain apart from the natural forces around him. His body and mind, freed from earthly bondage and attachments, can find their essence and purity in the heart of those elements in nature that the ancients made into gods. Wind, Sun, and Sea, the sailor's divine Trinity.'

Nonsense, of course, I tell myself roughly, coming round from this reverie for a moment, checking the course – something's changed in our movement. The wind's gone round a bit, Arnie has fallen asleep on the job. Kevin has noticed, too, he leans forward on the high stool, punches Arnie up 5 points. We settle down again.

Nonsense, I pick up the thread. Moitessier had a wife and children, he sailed away from them when he sailed out of the race, but they didn't cease to exist because he sailed away. You have to admire the clarity of his instinct, the pure motive that drove him, but you can't approve of the selfishness of it. A man can't just sail away from responsibilities. At least, not forever. And you can't keep sailing forever, either, common sense says: you need food, repairs, new sails, diesel, water, you need to talk to other people so as not to go mad, you need money, you need… Ah but you're being too hard on him, I think then, relenting; he had the sea in him in a way you don't, and probably never will. He hoped, as he said himself when he abandoned the Golden Globe race, to save his soul by staying out at sea.

Am I muttering out loud, talking to myself? Tony has just said, apropos nothing at all, to the air in front of him rather than to any one of us, 'I often wonder what it would be like, to head off on a long solo voyage? You know? To just sail out into the great blue yonder.'

Justin chimes in. 'I was just thinking about that. Wondering what it would be like, how long I could stick it for. I must say the thought appeals, on some level. If you had a good tough boat, properly stocked up, you know, a boat that's fit for it, I wonder how long you'd stay out for before you went nuts?'

'Not me,' Kevin is decisive. 'I like sailing by myself, got myself a little Westerly, you know? Sweet boat, boy I've done a lot of work on her. I like to head out for the day, real early, just straight out, then in the evening, sun going down, head back in again. But a long trip? Solo? Not me, man.'

Well, who knows? I don't know what it is I crave, exactly, but something inside me these past years has been taken by sea-dreaming. Something inside me yearns for a long sail with my life in my hands, trusting to fortune and what I've managed to learn; to be solitary, to have deep space around me for a while, the world stripped down to the shell of the boat, the white wing of the sail, and this endless, fathomless ocean that buoys us all up a while, carries us on and then, somewhere, some when, in storm or in quiet, opens the void beneath us, lets us fall away.

Macken's up and bustling, some switch inside him has clicked open suddenly. Rubbing his hands briskly. 'I don't know about you fellas but I'd feel a lot better about being out there, solo or not, if I had a better handle on this Yachtmaster stuff. I'm going to get going on revision.'

I drag myself back to the little world of *Pelagic Australis*, reluctantly. Tony's away down to the saloon, notebook, pencils, sample chart, mug of tea (surely that tea must be cold by now? Surely that was made hours ago?) all laid out before him. 'And sure anyway,' he mutters, 'haven't I it all done before?'

It takes a few seconds for this to sink in.

'What?' Justin is quickest off the mark. 'You have what done before?

'Yachtmaster theory of course. Did it last winter.'

'You what?'

'Passed it, too.'

'You have it *already*?' I'm finally up to speed here.

'That's what I said.'

'Then why the blazes do it again?' Justin is astonished.

'Ah, for the experience, and, besides, I've probably forgotten some of it anyway. Don't tell Steve, though, all right?'

'Don't tell Steve what?' Kevin is back from a look-around on deck.

'Kevin,' I say, 'trust me; this you really don't want to know.'

'OK, if you say so. Want some tea?'

Sleep has been busy knitting up that old sleeve. Mike comes up uncalled for once, takes a quick look outside. 'Yep, they're back. Boy, some stamina, huh?'

Spice Boy comes up, freshly showered. Debs is up, shampooed, in sunny good humour, sniffing at Kevin, 'You need a shower, mate.'

It's bucketing rain now, still 50 knots, still lumpy and bumpy and bad, but something has swept through the boat, or perhaps something has been swept *off* the boat? Simon leans close to me, murmurs, 'I've stripped the bunk for you,' gesturing behind him with his eyebrows (Simon can do that sort of thing). I see Fed halfway down the passage, leaning in through the curtain, evidently talking to Di.

'You following me?'

I'm on Kevin's heels, going forward on the port side. 'Just taking the scenic road to bed, Kev.'

'Right,' he says, 'I getcha.'

He does, too, almost all the time. I think I would happily sail anywhere with Kevin Cronin.

Sometime in the late afternoon, Fed comes through with a bucket and mop. 'You really like this, don't you?' I say to him.

'Ah fuck off,' he says happily, and I fall laughing back to sleep, thinking Fed's English is improving by the day.

I might as well have stayed asleep; the next watch passes in a long dull trough of inconsequence and, at 22.00, I'm falling again into the arms of Morpheus, this time in my own bunk. I trace my fingers over Paula's smile. Seven days from home, I think, all going well. Seven days. The boat falls off a wave and I slam my face against the lee-board – touch wood, I add. Sorry.

⚓

DAY
# 30
Saturday, 3 June 2006

'Bloody hell, look at you all! Shit, watch the roll!'

Oh great, I think sourly, what we need at two o'clock in
the morning, Our Great Leader is full of the joys. I add a
new bruise to the ongoing tally, grunt at OGL and push
past, out for a cigarette and a look at this wonderful world.
He's right out after me. 'Morning, Spice Boy! Good watch,
yeah? Hiya, Debs, anything good been happening? Give's a
cig, Kev? Ta. Hey, Theo, wind's looking good, fancy a bit
of sailing, eh? Get the flappy white stuff up, do a bit of

driving, eh? Nice bit of breeze, eh? Good direction, too! What d'you think, eh, mate? What do you say, Justin?'

I know there's a gun locked away down there somewhere in his cabin. Preservation of life in the Antarctic, for the purposes of. We never go in his cabin, I haven't a clue where it might be but it's a small cabin, it wouldn't take that long to find it, surely? I grunt again, trying to keep him and his infernal briskness at bay, but it's no use. Probably under his bunk. Steve, though, methodical man, bound to keep the ammo separate. Where might that be?

Maybe just hit him over the head, torch just inside wheelhouse door, that should do it. Humane, too. Rubber covered.

Mug of coffee, down in one go. Light second cigarette. Better, much better. What was Steve saying about sailing? Sailing! 'Hey, Steve? Yeah, brilliant, let me get my gloves and hat.'

OK, OK, what've we got here? Yesterday's 4–6-metre waves have gone down considerably, can't be more than 3 metres right now, on the beam, as is the wind – 40 knots or so, I'm guessing, OK, fine. What'll he be thinking of? I'd say two reefs in main, maybe three, staysail, 50 per cent Yankee. Steve is all business now, cigarette clenched in one corner of mouth, bare headed in light drizzle, shorts and orange boots. 'OK, Justin, me and Kev'll take care of the reefs, two, maybe three, what do you think?'

I watch how he involves Justin in this. The Admiral is quick, decisive, 'Maybe three until we get the staysail and Yankee going, see what that's like, maybe let one reef out then?'

'Sounds good, mate. OK, you take charge here, then. C'mon, Kev. Clip on, mate, give's a torch there, Tony, ta.' Whoosh, he's gone bounding up the high side, Kev scrambling happily behind.

It's as simple as this. First day on watch, we figured out Justin's the better and more experienced sailor of us three, then Tony, then me. So, we're used to deferring to Justin, and he's used to taking charge. We flick through the manoeuvres one after another, practised and competent now, not needing to talk, all working smoothly together.

'Nice one, guys,' says OGL, 'Leave it at three for the minute; Justin, what do you think?'

'Wind's got up a wee bit, Skip, so, maybe, yeah. Yes, I think so.'

'Excellent, now let's have the old engine off, yeah?'

And now we're sailing. God but it feels like ages since we have been. I know that it hasn't been, not really, but still…

Big Mike hasn't gone down yet, and now he steps carefully over the high threshold of the wheelhouse door, looking for somewhere to accommodate his big frame. He perches eventually on the hard cover over the life-raft, wedged against the starboard finger, his knees folded back almost to his chest. His hood's half up, his face half-bearded, he looks tousled and sleepy and wide awake all at once. Kevin has taken the wheel, bare headed, a nimbus of drizzle and spray beading his curly hair, his moustache. He looks the perfect seadog, rangy and solid, leaning into the wheel as his arms pump this way and that, eyes forward, scrunched against the wind. Steve's folded into the shelter corner, languid, tapping a smoke out of his packet, looking aft as if he expects to find something out there. Justin and Tony are sprawled together on the starboard bench, hoods back, sweating slightly from their exertions, grinning and silent, companionable. I'm watching this from the after-deck, one hand on the gantry, the other jammed in a pocket, bent at the knees to allow for the roll, full of oxygen and spray and salt and, suddenly, pure well being. These are good people, I'm thinking, each with his sorrows and secrets, his life elsewhere, but here, now, in the dark of the early hours, bright phosphorescence lighting the near air, deep dark overhead, we are good company, we are *a* good company and I feel awkwardly, shyly, very happy indeed to be here, now, on this boat, with these guys, driving forward into the morning, somewhere out there beyond the great spray crashed up and back by the plunging bow.

Four hours of this, taking turns at the helm, making tea, making log entries, taking a break inside to work out what's left of this long voyage, how far there is to go now. There's an intimation of things ending, of a great arc coming round to a point of stillness. We sail on a slant, 35–40 degrees, starboard tack, making 085°, just north of due east. The boat is in a groove, tracking uncommonly true; with the engine off, we fit ourselves better to the wind and swell, we sail the conditions more than the course, making off a little north as the wind backs, making down again later as it veers. This way and that, onward but not to a ruler-drawn course, more in the sea and working with it, than on it and working against it. We're tired, of course, at the point now where the bone-deep fatigue is beginning to seep through, but we could stay here, we think, all night, on through the dawn and well into the day.

A good call by Steve, I figure; warranted by the conditions, sure, and for God's sake the man is a sailor above all else, but a good call, too, in terms of morale, a boost to the spirits for those who get to sail the boat, a more restful night for the watch gone down to sleep.

When they come back up, and Justin begins the handover to Fed, it's almost painful to see Fed's anguish as Simon slips past to commandeer the wheel. Mike is already up and out when his comrades come smartly up, out there on the afterdeck looking forward, as one who expects of the coming day nothing but good things. 'Isn't it wonderful, not having the noise of that *bloody* engine?' Diane says, startling me with her vehemence. 'God the noise of it was driving me crazy! Sorry, Theo, didn't mean to bark!'

'Ah, bark away, girl, sure we all have to bark now and then.'

One of the greatest pleasures in life is to stretch at your ease in a warm bunk, somewhere deep in the ocean, in a good boat making headway in a heavy sea, and consider where you are; to lie there and listen to the sound of water rushing past your ear, millimetres away on the other side of the hull; to feel the boat as a live thing in good hands, each shock and jar softened immediately by a helm who bears very slightly away to cushion the impact, feeds the wheel back again just in time to carve the bow down, under and up again, steady and sure; to know that beneath you is nothing but alien water, a lightless dark going down for, maybe, two miles or more, to guess at what lives in these dark waters, at what might even now be tracking your boat-shape from down in the deep, wondering (or uncaring of) what you are; to hear the wind in the rigging and know this is the wind that is driving you, the heavy slat of the boom as it shifts slightly and settles, the crash of wave over deck, the slosh and gurgle of it pouring off again; to hear the groans and small sounds that speak to you of a thousand things you have come to know in the boat, the creak of the gimballed cooker, say, the squeak of a wet sea boot on the wheelhouse floor, the deep whirr of the winch, the dry click, click, of the wheel; to lie there and hear and know and sense and think of these and a myriad other things – all this is sailing, the pure pleasure of sailing, and to have all these things in your head and heart as you turn over in a warm bunk, stretch, yawn and surrender to sleep, this is the best of all.

Justin wakes me for lunch. This is unusual. What's happening? Christ! An almighty thump, a slew sideways that almost knocks Justin off balance. 'Fed's up there spooned into Di, teaching her to helm.' Oh, right, that would explain it. 'Listen,' he says, 'I've decided not to do that exam, I'm going to tell Steve this afternoon. Definite.'

'Look,' I say, 'I know what you mean about doubting the value of it, I mean learning in these conditions, retaining the stuff, all that, but why not do the exam anyway, nothing to stop you discounting it afterwards in your own mind, I'll probably do the same myself?'

'I do see what you mean, but nope, my mind's made up. Thought I'd tell you. Righto then, see you in a few minutes.'

Steve isn't pleased. Didn't think he would be. He thinks Justin's refusal is a reflection on his teaching, probably. It isn't, in the sense that Steve in a classroom ashore would have Justin's full attention and confidence, but Justin just doesn't believe he's learned what he needs to have learned to think of himself as qualified, and that, for the Admiral, is that. Whatever the rights and wrongs of it all, these two are not going to see eye to eye. On this as on other things.

'I'm keeping out of this,' I tell Tony. 'A case of the irresistible force and the immovable object, I think. And I'm not getting squashed in the middle.'

'Very wise, very wise,' says the sage Mr Macken. 'I've enough to do anyway trying to figure out feckin' secondary ports.'

I, too, try revising for a while, but it was never my strong point – and I'm soon distracted. Arnie is back on duty, ticking away out there to beat the band, and while the sea's down to about 2 metres, we're rolling heavily. We feel it most in the wheelhouse, because it's so high over the water – the pendulum effect. Because it swings more, in rough seas it can give you an exaggerated sense of how violent the weather is out there – we've taken, I notice, to popping in and out, to get a better sense of what the seas are *actually* like. The transition from inside to outside is often illuminating, and I've come to realise that, haven of comfort as it is, there is one pernicious downside to the wheelhouse: it can give you a false, as well as a true, sense of security. In here, insulated from the cold, the rain and the wind, you find a certain reluctance to brave the elements coming over you. There is a danger here that you'll lose that all-important *feel* for the ship as a whole, but there's another danger, too, one that hasn't mattered much up to now: you convince yourself more easily than you should that you're keeping a good lookout, and that's dangerous. There are blind spots in the windscreens, and people have comfort spots inside where they tend to plant themselves, unless something needs doing, for much of the watch; it takes a definite effort of will to remind yourself, to force yourself, to go outside every ten minutes and take a good, slow careful look all around the horizon.

We're sailing in out of a vast empty space, steadily closing with land. We haven't seen a single ship since leaving Stanley, not one, and we're in danger of forgetting to keep an eye out.

It's raining now, a soft steady rain, flung in on top of us in gusts with curious momentary hesitations where it hardly seems to be raining at all. I go down to make some tea for us all, decide to get some biscuits while the kettle's boiling, am moving carefully, balanced against the roll, towards the seat on the port side under which the biscuits live and then my feet shoot out from under me. I fling a hand up unthinkingly, grab the fiddle at the edge of the sink and for an agonising moment my entire weight hangs on my arm, wrenching my shoulder. The pain is terrible. I wrecked this shoulder weeks ago on a winch, and now it feels as if I've pulled my arm out of its socket. This fucking, fucking floor, I roar out, bringing Steve out of his cabin. I'm sitting back against the sink cabinet now, still seeing shooting stars, pain lancing through my shoulder in small jagged bolts. 'It's OK,' I mutter, 'it's OK. Go on back.'

'It's the floor,' says Tony helpfully, revision abandoned, helping me to my feet, to a seat. He's right, it is the floor, more exactly the flooring. Everyone's taken a tumble on it, down here or up in the wheelhouse – Fed nearly skulled himself a few days ago, just where I've gone over now, hit the deck with a thud that brought ice into the pit of my stomach, hit his head so hard I thought he might have cracked his skull. The flooring is some sort of plastic, the kind with raised circular dimples, maybe an inch across. It's lethally slippery when wet, and almost all the bruises and injuries on the boat so far can be ascribed to this surface. We skate and career all over the place down here, when we move and when we try to stand still. Groin strain, muscular strain of all kinds, knee, elbow and small of back bruising are commonplace among us, and this flooring is responsible for almost all of it – I have partly lost the use of my left arm for the past two weeks after falling on the point of my elbow in the galley. All you can say for this floor is, it's easy to clean; otherwise it has nothing, in our view, to recommend it. I know that wood, the traditional material, would be top-heavy in the wheelhouse, which has the same flooring, would help to exaggerate the already consider-able pendulum effect, would likely make the boat roll more – it's an axiom of boat design to keep weight as low down as possible. Fair enough, fair enough, but would the same be true of a wooden floor down here in the galley and saloon? There has to be a better solution than this curse of God lethal stuff.

I know with cold certainty that this shoulder is going to give me hell later on, when I try to sleep. It does.

⚓

DAY
## 31

Sunday, 4 June 2006

Someone is calling me in my dream. Fed shakes me, quite roughly. 'Sorry, Theo, sorry, wake up. It's the second time I called you. I thought you were up. Wake up...' He backs away.

Squint at my watch. Just past six. Hell, I'm late. First time ever. Angry with myself. Groggy, not sure, not *absolutely* sure this isn't a dream, struggle over the lee-board, start trying to dress. Very difficult, boat lurching, trousers, socks, wedge against roll to pull on boot, wriggle heel down, toes in. Second boot, fleece, struggle to get head through, why is zip closed? OK, next? Huh? Foulies! Corridor, high trousers, sit on floor to work over boots, stand up, straps over shoulder, next – and the boat falls off a wave, I smack the whole left side of my head against the timber frame of the upper bunk. Agony, red haze, shooting lights. I buckle, fall. Simon is standing there in the passageway, looking down at me, looking stupefied. Unmoving, he looks down at me and asks, 'Are you all right?' Stands there as I drag myself painfully to my feet in a flare of unspeaking rage, grab my jacket, push him roughly aside and stagger up to the wheelhouse.

I shove through the small knot of people, don't know who's there, don't care, lurch out into the shelter, mangle the cigarette pack as I fumble for a cigarette, light up, close my eyes, take a deep, deep drag. 'Are you all right?' Are you all right! What kind of stupid fucking idiotic imbecile question? I've just smacked my head off a solid timber with enough force to almost knock myself out, and the fucker asks am I all right. Rage, cold, self-pitying, furious rage. I'm dragging so hard, the cigarette's too hot to smoke. I stumble to my feet, lean around the shelter on the lee side, toss the butt in the water, sit back heavily and fish out another smoke. A hand grips me firmly on the bicep. Kevin. 'OK, man, take it easy now. It's cool, take it easy.' He thumbs a lighter and I take a deep steadying drag. 'You OK now, OK? Sit there, I'll get you a coffee.'

In fact Justin brings the coffee. 'God, you look terrible, what's wrong?'

I tell him, he tilts my head towards the spill of light from the door, says it doesn't look too bad, more flushed than bruised, 'Can you see OK?'

I nod, not wanting to say any more, still shocked, by the impact, sure, but also, with a slight sick feeling, by that sudden explosion of cold rage. A small sure voice inside me says, breathe, just breathe, this is the low point, this is the bottom of the curve, just breathe, breathe, wait.

The guys just sit there, not speaking, not looking at me or at each other. Slowly, I come to. That's just what it feels like, as if I have been away in there somewhere and am slowly making my way back.

So, probe with splayed fingers, work jaw, doesn't feel as if anything's cracked. Eyes are OK, I see a thin band of pre-dawn light between clouds and horizon, a coppery-green washed out blue. I sit up; more accurately, perhaps, I unslump.

'Sorry, lads, sorry I was late coming up.' They wave it away, a thing of nothing. 'Yeah and, eh, sorry about the temper, too.'

'Yes,' says Justin, 'I was wondering about that.'

I tell them about Simon, standing there, looking at me in severe pain, unable to get up off the floor, him standing there, not helping, not wanting to help – and that's what prompted the rage, I realise, the not wanting to help. What it felt like, then and there, was a kind of indifferent, incurious coldness, utter disinterest. Betrayal, I think, it felt like he was betraying all the investment in each other that we have made for so long. I don't put it quite like that to Kevin and Justin, finding terse Anglo-Saxon more fit for the purpose, but even in the abbreviated explanation I'm offering them I hear a note of whining self-pity that wakes me completely. Ah for the love of Jesus, I scold myself, would you get a grip: you're bloody exhausted, but so is Simon, probably so exhausted he couldn't even process what was happening right in front of his eyes. Would you give over and get on with it!

'See that?' Justin nudges Kevin. 'He's back. That looked like an interesting conversation you were having, Mr Dorgan?'

I stand up and stretch. 'Ah sure, Simon is probably even more knackered than I am, and he was coming off watch.'

'He couldn't be more knackered than me, I can tell you that,' Tony in the doorway. 'Gentlemen, I propose scrambled eggs, toast and coffee.'

'Excellent idea, but, Tony, there's no bread.'

'Ah, that's where you're wrong. Debs made some during their watch. Eh, Theo, would you do the scrambled eggs?' There's always a catch.

The day is brightening, bit by bit. A high blue sky, few clouds, a hint of sapphire over aquamarine in the water, the deeper notes of green, and grey under that, the lustrous grey of the deep ocean. The lacy lines running in on us in serried ranks are more beaded translucent water than froth and foam.

Steve left us with Yankee and staysail full out, one reef in the main, and now the towering white sails are full and steady, the wind on the beam driving us on at 8–9 knots. Our motion is almost stately, wave length and boat length evenly matched. There have been days when anyone watching us from a distance would have pitied us, out there on the stormy vastness, the boiling water, in anything so small and pitiable and driven; today, seen from the bridge of a tanker or some great container ship, we would look something to envy, graceful and carefree, at one with the wind and the waves.

I perch at the chart table, sideways on, and leaf back through the log. My God, thirty-one days out from Punta Arenas, who'd have thought it! How far back that seems. I think of my first sight of the boat, arriving with Marko and Simon from the airport, this big, high-volume aluminium vessel, her towering mast, the no-nonsense robust look of her, the reels of line on her foredeck and under her after-deck, the solid strength of her wheelhouse – here, I thought, is a prize fighter, not a dancer, here's a boat that's built for the rough stuff. Now, looking about me, so far from our beginning, so close now to our end, I feel an upwelling of affection for this boat. How well she's looked after us, how far she has carried us. Such a motley crew, I think then, so odd in our ways, pitched in here from such very different worlds. We've managed it, though, I think; not perfectly, not so as we'd all sign up en masse to go somewhere else together, but we've held it together well enough, managed some sense of common purpose. Credit to Steve, I think, and to Kevin and Debs, they've made us into enough of a crew to have come this far without anyone getting killed. I remember a snatch of an old ballad, from 1800 or so:

'Each man, whate'er his station be,
When duty's call commands,
Should take his stand,
And lend a hand,
As the common cause demands.'

'What're you laughing at?' Macken wants to know.

'I'm just congratulating us all on not having killed each other.'

'What? Sometimes I wonder about what goes through your mind, I really do. Why would we have killed each other? Sure aren't we all one great big happy family? C'mere, I can't figure out this thing here with secondary ports...'

Simon, back up for lunch, has taken thought, and so have I. A small dance of courtesies, a lighting of cigarettes, everything's resolved.

Unwilling to go below, like a cat with wet fur I want to turn my belly to the light and air on this bright afternoon. I sit with Debs, chatting idly, and bit by bit she lets glimpses of her life show through. The years in her wooden boat, *Caribbean*, blue water gypsy, now here now there a month or two, then raising the anchor, turning out again. Her son, at home now, reared at sea. She's quietly proud of him, sees something of him, perhaps, in Simon – her daily greeting, 'How's my boy? Sleep well?' She has a small place back home in New Zealand; a garden, high fences against deer, goes down to the water's edge. Has an old boat, wooden, a beauty but tired now, not sure if the work on her would be justified?

'What about you, Theo? Got a boat?'

'No I haven't, no.'

'What would you buy, d'ye reckon?'

I give her the short version, in deference to the mood of the afternoon, desultory, laconic, studded with silences. Steel, I think, or aluminium, for strength. Too much stuff floating around in the water these days.

'Not a wooden boat, then?'

'Ah they're beautiful, but the maintenance…'

'You're right there, mate.'

'Maybe 36–40 foot,' I say. 'Cutter rig, I think, mast not too tall, well-cut staysail, furling gennie. Adaptable to all weathers. Longkeeler, for tracking, for easy motion in a sea.'

'Not like this baby,' she says, nodding. 'Christ but doesn't she slam. Good old boat, though, gets us through, don't it?'

'Have to be something I could sail singlehanded, too,' I say. 'Oversized winches, windvane.'

'Your wife doesn't sail, then?'

I tell her what Paula always says when the subject comes up. 'I don't mind sailing where, when you fall in the water, it's warm; I don't see the point in dressing up like the Michelin man to get cold and wet and frightened.'

A sunny smile from Debs. 'Sounds like a sensible woman.'

'She is,' I say, 'but she's got terrible taste in men.'

The best laugh I've got out of Debs in the whole trip. 'I can see that, mate,' she says, 'I can see that. Hey, Spice Boy, you doing dinner tonight?' And to me, in a murmur, 'Hope so, he's the only one of 'em as can cook, less you count Di's curry.'

'Come on then, Si, let's have a look-see in the forepeak. See if there's anything left to eat before we get stuck into the canned muck.'

Down in my bunk I finish Hastings and Jenkins' history of the Falklands War, one of only two books I've managed to read on this whole trip. It's a sorry book about a sorry business. If Galtieri hadn't needed some major distraction to keep the rising tide of democracy at bay, if that dreadful woman had not been so tempted by fantasies of grandeur… it was a slow, dirty and often mismanaged business, that little war, fought for a piece of low-lying, boggy and more or less worthless land. The Argentine conscripts were lied to, badly officered, poorly supplied and, in the end, left half-starved to their fates. The Brits took a pounding from an air-force they had badly underestimated, and neither side had, for far too long, the least bit of interest in a mediated resolution. I think of the anonymous para, quoted after the war, who said, 'I can see why they landed us at night; if we'd seen the bloody place by daylight we'd never have got off the ship.' Perhaps the most telling passage in this badly written book is the one where a local Falklands worthy enquires of his gallant rescuers, 'And when will you be going home, then?' Like islanders everywhere, the Falklanders of Las Malvinas want only to be left alone.

Were we really there? I wonder, tumbling into sleep, delayed a moment by the novel spectacle of reflected sunlight lancing through the cabin. I remember Howard and his talk of oil, Carolina's gift of herbs. It all seems so very long ago.

And it seems no time at all has passed before I'm woken for dinner. 'Marko! Marko just came into my mind,' says Tony. The Grumpy Old Men are in the cockpit, dinner's over, Kevin and Debs are having their companionable cigarette up in the bow, gone up to join Steve. We're enjoying the last of the sun, the cool blue twilight after. There's a fresh little breeze for Mike to play with and he's enjoying himself.

'What about Marko?' I ask him.

'Well, you know, I was just wondering how he's getting on. Hope he's all right, like.'

Justin leans over, says, 'Heard about Steve's little discovery, then?'

'Eh, no?'

'You know how he's always rattling about in the bilges, adjusting valves and whatnot? Well, this morning he came across a couple of packets of biscuits, some salamis and a bottle of some kind of hooch, Slivovitz or something like that. Some kind of stash. Blimey!'

Tony is fascinated (so am I). 'But, what's that about, eh? I mean we can eat anything that's not tied down, basically. It's not as if we were on rations?' Here's a nice puzzle to take us through the watch.

On the handover, in the quiet dark, Steve gives us all his latest projection: Cape Town early morning, four days' time. There's a long, thoughtful silence, and then Diane gets out her list, Mike stands to his Fuegan watch and, for a change, Fed beats Simon to the wheel. As I'm filing my second last piece for *The Irish Times*, Steve is rattling out a long e-mail to Skip Novak. The world is closing in on us now, with its cares and demands. Our little world is almost ready to dissolve itself, to fade and then forget. Sharp as ever, Steve looks up as I rise from the bench. 'Nearly there, mate, eh? Be sorry to see it end then, will you, Theo?'

'I will.' I'm surprised by the note of certainty. 'I will actually. I'm looking forward to being home, but I'll be sorry to see it end. You did a very good job of looking after us. Thank you.'

If he's surprised by this, then so am I, I hadn't meant to say anything of the sort – but I'm glad I did.

'Thanks, mate. I believe you mean it.'

'Yeah, I do, be a weird thing to say if I didn't, wouldn't it?'

'Ah, get outta here, get some sleep. Glad you enjoyed it, anyway.'

'So far, eh!' A parting shot from the steps.

'You're right there, mate, never know what could happen out here. Maybe I'll think of something to make you miserable.'

⚓

DAY

## 32

Monday, 5 June 2006

The forecast suggests light airs, going to south-east at 20–
25 knots. Suits us fine, though what this boat really likes, as
Kevin has drummed into us, is a good beam reach. 'Better
again,' he says, 'she loves a following wind – but what are
the chances of the wind going west?' And besides, a following wind means poling out the Yankee and gennie, and
after the last experience none of us thinks Steve is willing to
risk breaking the second pole. Anyway, if there is one thing
we have learned out here it's that this ocean is too change-

able by half. You never know where you stand with it: you go down to your bunk in a relative calm, and come up four hours later into storm force 10, and halfway through *that*, watch as the wind spins off around the clock 180 degrees or so and drops away. Or else backs off and climbs another force or two.

Whatever, we trust the weather we have for the moment so it's 60 per cent Yankee, one reef in the main and we're making a comfortable 8–9 knots. Lovely, as long as you don't count on it lasting.

We've all become pretty nifty at reading the GRIBs and the satellite photos by now, and a quick scan of available data cheers us up. As far as we can see, we're keeping ahead of a low that seems destined to dip below and behind us. Very good, very good, except, in the back of my mind, I still have that sat picture of the low stretching from 15° to 55° – an ocean that can give you a system so enormous can produce almost anything out of its hat. So, we sail what we have but with considerable reservations.

This constant mindfulness is tiring, but at the same time it's a sign and earnest of how far we have come as sailors, of how much we have learned. 'Expect the unexpected' is a cute slogan to paste in your school notebook, as I remember doing; it's another thing altogether when that radical stance towards the world becomes second nature to you. It's like a mirror image of paranoia, a positive investment in the proposition that all is mutable, that change is the only thing you can count on out here. Your last thought on the verge of sleep is a question, I wonder what it will be doing when I wake up again? Your first thought on waking is, I wonder what it's doing, and what it's going to change into?

Some things, of course, are changing for good and won't – can't – change back. One index of being out here is the sense of timelessness that the empty ocean induces in you, a sense reinforced by the brute mechanical succession of the watches. One watch blurs into the next, one day fades, reappears as another day, changed but essentially the same. Also, the mind cut free from its habitual round of chatter, the call and response of the known daily world, tends to float into a charged void, where anything may hold its attention for an indeterminate time. The tyranny of orderly known time gets chucked overboard, to be replaced by a kind of temporal anarchy or freefall, where progress is without consequence, one day follows another and that the next, as the days of our childhood do, with nothing there of the shadow cast by the future. Of course, we *know* we are en route for Cape Town, we mark $X$ on the chart to show our position at a given moment and each $X$ is closer to Cape Town than the last; we are closing the distance, and out ahead of us there is a moment when we must resume our lives as we knew them before. We know we are on this track, but I am not sure we entirely believe it. Easier to believe that today will be followed by tomorrow, that we will be out here in space, borne up and borne along, in our own small world, for ever and ever.

Except, of course, that nothing except for ever is for ever. There is a finite amount of water on board, we will soon exhaust it. The fresh meat has been gone for days, and now we are down to a small store of fresh fruit and vegetables. On our watch, this is measured by the garlic index, and we are very nearly out of garlic. This, in our view, is an imminent crisis. Of course under the seats in the saloon is enough tinned, preserved and dry food to last us for months – but we rebel against the idea of it: fresh food has proved essential for morale, and we have grown used to this luxury as if it were a right.

Then, it's getting warmer, we don't need the heater anymore, and besides it eats up diesel, and we want to conserve diesel because... because you never know. As a consequence, we are all of us eking out a small store of

someone conducting an audit or a financial review. A competent teacher will be satisfied, but a good teacher will keep an eye on that quiet fellow in the corner, made uneasy but not quite sure why. Macken is all furrowed brow, glasses on the tip of his nose or shoved back on his head in exasperation; he sits four-square to the saloon table, puzzling it out, puzzling it out – but let there be a joke up in the wheelhouse and he'll hear it, a stir on the afterdeck and he'll be up and out, willing to help, willing to be distracted. Concentrated, determined, his instinct for mischief is rarely far from the surface. Fed and Di study together, a constant low murmur as Fed plunges into something, races ahead to conclusions, Di bossily pulls him back, makes him go through the steps. The experienced sailor is handicapped by his practical knowledge, the inexperienced Di, a teacher after all, can follow the reasoning but lacks the experience to visualise its application; for a change the ultra-competitive Fed is by and large being led by Di, and neither, yet, is quite comfortable with this new dispensation. Fed was a fidget as a boy, I see it clearly, constantly looking out the window, and Di respected her teachers, could never quite get the class rebels. A sunny child, I imagine, and sometimes nervous.

And me? I don't like the idea of exams any more, don't like the idea of anyone sitting in judgement on me. I was a happy enough child, I realise this now, happy *and* often full of foreboding. Happy to be left to my own devices, roaming the fields, later the city, curled up with a book or just sitting there dreaming in the sun. School was a kind of torture, and yet, because it was given, you accepted it as the real. I'd have flashed through the set books by Christmas, and then I was bored for the rest of the year, impatient for more. I was a window gazer, too, an internal refusenik, more often that not deeply unconvinced by my teachers, wary of my classmates. There was a time when I liked exams, enjoyed pitting my wits against the ideal 100 per cent mark, seeing how close I could get to it, but study was a mystery to me, and still is. The idea that you can arrive at understanding by patiently following a sequence of steps defeated me as a child, and often defeats me still. I admire people who can do this, am in some way convinced that those who can work like this are the ones who really know things, but my mind works differently. It circles and curves around things, plunges in, stands back and then either grasps the whole as a whole, full and entire, or retreats in bafflement and confusion. I got geometry and arithmetic instantly, I could live until the sun is a cooling cinder before I would understand calculus.

So, if I'm going to do this exam, I have to swim up through layers of memory, anticipate sullen resistance, make myself sit there and read things slowly when I'd sooner be out on deck, working or dreaming, or down in the galley making lunch. I have to break the syllabus down into its component parts, tackle each section in order, test what I know and repair the gaps where I don't know… God, it sounds tedious, I think, put like that.

I have a great deal of sympathy with Justin's point of view: he says that he wouldn't be convinced by a qualification obtained in these circumstances. I have a slightly different perspective, in that I am never convinced by attested qualifications anyway. I could never take someone's word for it, that I know something – or, to put it another way, I know when I know something, and I know when I don't. So, I'll do the exam, and I'll spend more time afterwards thinking about what I get wrong than what I get right, because those will be the things I need to learn. It's a looking-glass way of seeing things, I suppose: Steve might decide, on the evidence, to pass me – OK, I can say I have Yachtmaster Theory. Conversely (perversely) the only real use that will be to me is that it will tell me what I don't know, and therefore need to learn.

Aargh! Mike slams his book down, takes himself up into the air. I sigh and reach for the navigation practice chart, Fed looks wistfully out through the nearest port at the skeins of white, green and aquamarine streaming past. Tony goes, 'Hah!', ticks something off on his list, gets up and puts on the kettle. Meanwhile, up in the wheelhouse, Justin and Kev are leaning companionably over the chart, calculating distance and time to Cape Town.

Boat time has changed. Nobody sleeps much during the day now, tired as we are. It's the sun, of course, the light, and the sense that our voyage is climbing to a full stop.

We set out from Punta Arenas to sail this boat, to go sailing as if it were something we were familiar with, and the channel answered to that sense of things, but we paid it little enough attention, in a strange way. We were lulled, in part, by the seeming familiarity of it all, despite the strong winds, despite knowing we were in alien and his-toric waters. We were, I see now, so fixated on the Horn that the beat down-channel was a provisional kind of experience, one we gave too little value to at the time. That leg hardly stretched us, we sailed the boat competently, worked, ate and slept at fixed times, all of us in it together. We were day-sailing, and all of us know how to do that. Then there was that glorious day when we rounded the great Cape, a milestone for each of us, with a different meaning for each of us, but nonetheless an experience held in common, enough to carry us through the two days to Falklands/Malvinas in a rush of well being. For a few, it was their first experience of the open ocean, and if they had some intimation of what lay ahead, that spark of enlightenment was soon banked down in the cool sop-orific airs of Stanley. Ocean time only really began when we cleared Stanley, nineteen days ago now, and ocean time is hard time – this we have learned in the long bruis-ing succession of days and nights, watch sliding into watch, the will brought down to little more than the dour desire to endure.

There are long ocean passages, I've made one myself, where the sun shines most of the time, it's reasonably warm, the wind gods are on your side, and there is time for reflection in the long solitary nights at the helm, in the long days as you drive on; leisurely days when the boat half sails itself and you can read, yarn with your mates or soak in the near-silence, the sibilance of the water going past, the low hum of the wind.

Down here in these latitudes it is very different, even allowing for the fact that it's winter. The ocean's more turbulent, for a start; the boat sails on its ear much of the time, when it isn't climbing and crashing, yawing and veering and plunging. The wind howls in the wire rigging, a high note that drops to a low roar or climbs to a high nerve-shredding keen as the wind goes up and down, and the wind itself is a live and uncaring thing. Fierce, wilful, angry at times, often brutish and savage, the wind here will punish the slightest mistake, will drive you down in an instant if that's what's written for you. But down here, it isn't the wind, it's the ocean itself that is master. You can trim to the wind, you can strike all sail *in extremis* and run, or heave to, under bare poles. You can compromise, up to a point, with the wind; you can bow down before it and beg for mercy, trust to your luck. But the sea!

Down here it runs unimpeded all round the world, a great river driven by mass and gravity, by the spin of the whole globe, an immense weight to it, monstrous beyond all imagining. If an island, properly seen, is the tip above water of a great drowned mountain, it often seems that each wave in a big sea is the tip of a mass that runs all the way down into the lightless dark; imagine some stormy day or night, running for your life before a great train of mountains, one after the other toppling over behind you, racing to catch you up; imagine those mountains are cold as nightmare, solid and fluid at the same time, ponderous, hostile, implacable – and think that they never end, you wake and you watch them, you sleep and you know they are there, coming on and on at you, bearing you up and forward or running against you and driving you off, or back, but always poised over you, waiting for that moment when luck runs out or the wind takes a caprice or one of the crew, maybe even you yourself, makes some small, irretrievable fatal error of judgement.

Day after day of this, night after night. Boat time out here is brute time, heavy and full; it wears you down, it goes by with weight in it, slowness and weight; you bring your bones and flesh and dourness of will to deal with it, you pay for your passage in bruising to body and mind.

And there comes a day when you realise you have gone over to boat time, to time on the ocean. The deep fatigue has set in, sure, but your nerves and your mind have stretched out to all parts of the boat, you remember things now, what it means when the boat falls off a wave, what it says as you lie there in your bunk about wave height, wind speed, the angle you're sailing at; you know what they're doing up there, braced to the roll, working the winches, taking in or letting out a reef; you hear a noise from the galley, the oven door banging down, and you figure Debs is making bread; you recognise Fed's footstep in the passageway and you know it's time to get up, you know in ten minutes you'll be peering at the log, squinting out through the rain (you can tell it's raining) to see what the night's doing, or the day. You have become part of the boat, or the boat has become an extension of you, it doesn't matter which, and now you're on boat time, locked into the matrix, with your blood and your pulse and your animal sense of where exactly you are. And more than this, as you realise when you step outside and the cold wind raps about your ears, the sea heaves and bears up to you as it bears you up, falls away from you as the deck falls away, you realise you have given yourself over to the eternal: the sea, its rhythms and colours, its troughs and its heights, you have given yourself to the whole weight of its insistent, fathomless presence, its full possession and mastery of the here and now.

I give myself time to allow these thoughts sort through themselves, to settle themselves down and take on weight. God knows how long I've been standing here, one arm wrapped round the gantry support, gazing sightlessly back along our wake. The sun is going down, thin bands of orange and black and green low in the west, clear sky then until, directly overhead, a mass of dark. I take a long slow look around before going in. If anyone asks me now what I'm thinking of, I'll say, 'Nothing at all.'

If they gave me command now, I think, and agreed to be bound by my decision, what would I do? I would be very hard put not to imitate Moitessier, it seems to me, not to put the helm up and put her head down to clear Good Hope, make on into the Indian Ocean.

I'll go down to my bunk for a while, I think. Justin looks up from the charts, eyebrows raised.

'Do you ever feel tempted,' I ask him 'when you're out like this, just to keep on going? I mean, just keep on going?'

He smiles, he nods, he puts a hand on my shoulder. 'Get some sleep, mate,' he says, 'you look as if you're in deep waters.'

Land time is coming, it's as if we smell it out there ahead of us. Some time in the early evening, I feel the shift, as if something inside my chest, a relay, a tumbler switch, has tilted and gone over. 'We're thirty-two days out from Punta Arenas,' I say casually to Justin – and then I hear myself say, 'Or three days out of Cape Town.' He looks at me levelly, saying nothing because there's no need to say anything, then we both rap our knuckles on the chart table frame. Double tap. Just to be sure.

Last thing tonight, we'd come back from the deck check, the boat almost level under a sky full of high stars. I stopped, something had caught my eye. 'What's that?'

Justin beside me, Kevin behind me. I point, away up to port, ahead of us, there, just below the horizon? We peer, then Kevin says, 'I see green, does anyone else see green, and maybe white, too?'

Macken, inside, switches on the radar, comes out for a look while it's warming up. Kevin has the glasses now, adjusting the focus. 'Yep, fishing boat by the lights.'

Justin has punched up the radar and there she is, up there bearing 035°, 12 miles. Trawling or fishing, Tony wonders.

'Longliner, must be,' says Kev. 'Too far out for a trawler and, besides, they go south, into the Argulhas current, inshore.'

Justin is checking his watch, marking the sighting into the log. The first vessel we've seen since that ship coming over the hill into Stanley.

⚓

DAY
# 33

Tuesday, 6 June 2006

Rolling home. Another bright day, maybe 1-metre swell, wind gone south-west, 20–25 knots so we're on a good reach, full Yankee and staysail, one reef in the main. We're keeping up a good average speed, there's nothing in the forecast or in the satellite pictures to suggest this won't hold, so we're bearing down on Cape Town with steady assurance.

We assume we're not the only ones. A few nights ago, scanning the routeing chart for diversion, tallying the number of days and the number of ways in which the winds we've been having confound its predictions, I allowed my eye travel onward at last to journey's end. Hmm, interesting. 'See here, Justin, where it shows the shipping routes?'

We count them, seven converging on Cape Town. Five in a broad fan from the north and west, one, ours, from west-south-west, the traditional sailing vessel route, and one from the south, coming round Cape Argulhas and the Cape of Good Hope. For amusement, and also from prudent sailorly instinct, I draw a line (in pencil!) intersecting our course at right angles, then make a careful list of the points of the compass from where, between this line and Cape Town, we might expect to find other vessels coming. Steve has been reading the Riot Act (abridged version) to the starboard watch about keeping an eye out at night, and we've had a few pointed reminders ourselves, too, about keeping a look-out; understandably enough, people get a bit lax about going out every ten minutes in the cold and the rain to see nothing at all, but we all know there's really no excuse for this. Now, from here on, the likelihood of seeing another ship has significantly increased. I tape the list to the chart table, for general use.

Hours later. 'Seen this?' Justin, mug of coffee in hand, is looking puzzled, staring down at a piece of paper taped next to my list. 'Any idea what this is?'

Tony peers at it. 'Looks like a version of Theo's list, but I can't make head nor tail of it, whose handwriting is it?'

Justin has a closer look, says, 'Looks like Fed to me. Now what's all that about?'

Kevin calls us. 'Gentlemen! If you would, please. I believe we'll take in a reef in the main, see if maybe then we need to take a few rolls in the Yankee.'

Like a comedy team, we step outside and simultaneously sniff, see if indeed the wind's got a bit sharper, then fall around laughing at ourselves. Kevin grimaces, throwing a sheet off the winch. 'Get back there, you!'

Tony bustles towards him, shoves him aside and takes the sheet out of his hand. 'You sit down. We'll take care of this. You guys go do the reef, I'll do the sheet here and then we'll see about that Yankee.'

Kevin tries to protest but we're not having any. Justin points an admonitory finger at him. 'Sit down there, or go stand back there. We'll look after this.'

Poor old Kev grumbles at this brusque handling, but he'd be a fool not to do what he's told, and besides we know he's chuffed, really, that we have decided to look after him.

A few days ago somebody lost a plastic rubbish bin overboard. Steve got in a bit of a temper about it, bustling and shouting, brought the boat round and tried to line us up to retrieve the damn thing. Kevin, stretched to his full length on the starboard deck, the low side, made a few attempts to lance the bin with the boat-hook, to no avail. Day before yesterday, without meaning to, he revealed that he'd cracked a rib in the process, dropped on the narrow aluminium toe-rail when the boat thumped sideways off a wave. He's been in considerable pain as a result and, since we found out, we have been ruthless about looking after him – as he has been painstaking, patient and assiduous in looking after us. We were talking about Kevin earlier this morning, and I found myself describing him as the perfect sergeant, the kind officers rely on and the men trust with their lives. You know that Kevin's the type who would never leave a man out there, wouldn't hesitate to put himself between his men and whatever threatened them, friend or foe. Empires are built on the shoulders of such men – and independence movements, too. As far as we're concerned, he has been exemplary, trusting us to know what we know, ready to teach us what we don't know, enjoying the fun of it, understanding the toll that the daily grind takes on us all. He's a complex man who thinks he's a simple man, and that drawly southern gentleman attitude has deceived more than one of our colleagues. Fed and Simon, for instance, don't get Kev at all; indeed the closest I've come to starting a row on this boat was when I overheard Simon condescending to Kevin, assuming that Kev wouldn't understand where the barbs were concealed. Mike, from behind me, put his hand on my shoulder. 'Leave it be, Theo,' he said. 'Kevin is well able for this kind of shit.' Misses very little, Mike.

He won't miss Yachtmaster classes at all, Mike, and this afternoon's exam was not his happiest experience on this boat. 'Jeez, that was a nightmare! You know what, Theo? I sat there with that paper in front of me and I asked myself what the hell I was doing all those afternoons, you know? I mean, I know I was there, but, hey, looks like the bit of me that's supposed to be paying attention was off watch, right?'

Myself, I did well on the general paper, screwed up secondary ports and forgot to factor in deviation when working out compass courses in the navigation section. Even the cunning ruse of wearing my Na Piarsaigh jersey couldn't summon up the powers, but Steve reckons Tony and I should resit some sections tomorrow so it looks like an evening of revision again when I'd sooner be doing anything else at all. Just as well there's a stubborn gene buried somewhere inside me, then. Fed, to his very evident satisfaction, gets a good pass, and so does Simon. Diane, who has suggested more than once in the past few days that she may never set foot in a boat again, doesn't.

Our last turn to cook dinner tomorrow (tonight's is a grim affair, best passed over in silence). Macken, ferret supreme, has cached the last onion, the last of the garlic; we figure on penne in a tomato sauce, with the onion and garlic, salami, olive oil, pesto and chopped sundried tomato. Why are we planning tomorrow night's dinner even while struggling to digest tonight's? Because time has speeded up, we know we're caught in a downward chute now, there's a great deal of cleaning and tidying work to be done on the boat and suddenly there's not enough time to get everything in.

Quietly, people are slipping away to their cabins, on watch and off, beginning the business of packing.

We are starting to subtract ourselves, to withdraw from this common enterprise. In the cockpit tonight, someone has wired up (or just discovered?) the outside speakers. Mike has B. B. King on the go, the hard-driving blues just about matching the speed and pitch of the boat. The watches are starting to blend into each other; Kevin's is on duty but one or two, sometimes all of the others, are abroad under the stars, so many restless spirits. And when we hand over to them, we stay up in our turn, sharing the duties casually, making tea and coffee, telling yarns. Steve comes and goes, chatty, relaxed, but there's something faraway in his expression when he's alone out on deck, up forward staring ahead, or slouched at the after rail mesmerised by the vanishing wake. I remind myself he is leaving his home now, this boat that is so much a part of him, this boat that has carried him who knows how many tens of thousands of southern ocean miles. What that must feel like, I cannot begin to guess.

Macken, when not rehearsing me in the arcana of secondary ports and tidal height calculations, is in fine form, yarning away, fielding questions about his proposed route through Africa, puffing on his pipe, feigning indifference as Justin and I, in exhaustive detail, explain to everyone just where we intend to take Tony's boat while he's off on his bike. At one point, as Mike is explaining the Beaufort scale to Diane, Tony interjects, 'They have that all wrong, there, that caption there.' Mike is showing Di a photo of what force 10 looks like. 'Know what they should put instead of "force 10"?' Tony says. '"For fuck's sake!"' He looks so thoroughly indignant that we all crack up.

It's that kind of night.

Every ten minutes, I stand to look out over the wheel-house roof, one foot on the wheel stand, the other braced on the forward winch, and take a long slow look around. Just before going down I take a last look. Ship, away up there to the north of us, white floods at her stern, green ahead of them. 'You see that, Kev, there?'

'Yep, I see that.'

I step down inside and mention it to Fed who's on watch. 'What ship, where?' He bustles out, takes a look around. 'No, man, there's nothing there. Are you sure? I can't see anything.'

Kev looks at him, crooks a finger: follow me. He switches the plotter to radar, waits until it warms up, punches the rings out to 12 miles. 'There, see that?'

'Oh, right.'

He grabs the binoculars, heads out again. 'Yes, yes I see it. You think it's the fishing boat you saw last night? Must be. Sure. I must put this in the log.'

Kev looks at me and he just shakes his head.

'I'm off down,' I say. 'Hey, Fed?'

'What?'

'Don't break my boat, OK?'

Steve, down in the saloon, looks up the steps at me and grins a wicked grin.

'Sleep tight, mate,' Fed says to me, 'we'll look after your boat.'

Nearly there, I say to myself, washing my face, glancing briefly in the mirror. For no reason I can think of, I start remembering the night we were knocked down, that conversation with myself where I talked myself up to the point of accepting, at least logically, that I might have to die. I recall, if not the details, then the flavour of that monologue, the cheerfulness I felt falling asleep. Now? Now I'm not sure I believe it at all, now I'm not at all convinced I was in any way ready to die. It seems to me (and I don't know why I'm thinking about this now) that I was playing games with my own head, that I never believed we were in real danger – but I was afraid I might lose it, that I might allow fear get a grip on me. That all I wanted or needed at the time was to go to sleep calmly, to accept the actual situation for what it actually was – that what I was doing, in fact, was curbing imagination, cutting off the cascade at its source. I'm so intrigued by this train of thought that I go back to the galley, make myself a cup of tea and head down to my cabin, oblivious to whoever I must have passed in the wheelhouse, in some sense rapt, not here… and that, I realise, is what I was like as a child, wrapped up in my own thoughts, a boy who went out of his way to avoid fights in a school that measured your worth, in part, by your willingness to fight. I have spent my life, I realise, thinking of myself as a kind of coward because as soon as any kind of avoidable danger threatened, I would be gripped not by fear of what was there in front of me, but by fear of some kind of unmanageable escalation, of things spinning out of control. A vivid memory now: reading in some book that a blow to the nose, properly delivered, can send the septum crashing up into the brain, causing death. I remember a kind of terror of brawling, ordinary schoolboy brawling, that took hold of me: I could never, I knew, hit someone in the face because I might kill them. And yet bloody noses were ten a penny in the schoolyard, on the playing field. Obviously what I imagined was more real to me than what I actually saw around me. I look around me now, let the whole long journey sink in – and I start laughing, shaking my head. Fuck me, I say to myself, inelegantly, did you have to sail around Cape Horn and across the Southern Ocean in winter to discover what everyone else knows by the age of seven?

Another sudden memory: somebody hit across the head in a game of hurling, blood everywhere, pouring down

⚓

DAY
# 34
Wednesday, 7 June 2006

Just coming awake as Fed calls me, I register that the engine is on again, sounding louder, as always, in the dark of night. Damn. 'Beautiful night up there,' Fed says. 'But not enough wind for sailing, pity, eh?'

It is, I think, dressing briskly, leaving my foul-weather jacket on the hook. Not cold enough for that, I decide, another time. And then, one foot on the step to go up, I realise there won't be another time. We're done with the cold, done with survival sailing.

'You have to admire their persistence. They're one hell of a bunch of guys.'

'Who, Mike?'

'See for yourself,' he gestures out and behind.

'They're back?'

'Sure as shooting, buddy. I guess they just never give up, huh?'

'Well, Mike,' I say, 'I guess they're in for a surprise when they see the bright lights of Cape Town, eh?'

'Yeah,' big dawning grin now. 'Hey, won't that be something? You think they drink beer? Man, I'm buying if they're drinking, that's a long paddle.'

Mike's Fuegan fugue seems to irritate his watch companions about as much as it, sometimes, amuses them. We like it, we look forward to each little riff on the handover. I *think* Simon gets it; an ironist himself, by choice or by nature I can't tell, he knows that Mike is aware some of the others have faint doubts about his sanity – 'Do you think maybe he really believes in some way there *are* Fuegans following us?' – and Mike plays along that delicate border like a virtuoso. If Mark Twain had found himself in a poker game with our Mike, he'd have known to watch the cards very carefully indeed.

I give him an elbow as I go past, get a solemn wink in return, walk outside, light up and look for the Southern Cross in the brilliant sky.

Steve's at the after rail, legs slightly bowed to accommodate the roll. He's got one hand jammed in his pocket, the other's holding a lit cigarette down by his side. The Milky Way curves in a great arc overhead; down near the horizon there's the metallic winking of a satellite and our creamy-green wake fans out behind us in a long band of turbulent light, flashing and rippling, fading out into the inky blue waters in pockets of bubbling phosphorescence. A sail cracks and fills again, and Steve takes a quick glance over his shoulder to check. I walk back to stand beside him. We don't say anything for a while, and then I say, 'It'll be hard to leave this, eh?'

'Yep,' he says. 'Ah, I'll be back, you know? This is where I feel most at home now.'

He means the sea, the sea at night, this ocean; he means South Georgia, Stanley, Puerto Williams, Punta Arenas, the channels, the night moorings in secret coves; he means Antarctica, the cold, the emptiness, he means the great southern void where he has room enough and time to feel that his life is his own. He doesn't say this, any of this, but I know enough to know this is what he means. When a man or a woman loves something as profoundly as Steve loves this great oceanic void, you either get it or you don't. A half-sentence here, a declaration there, a wry joke, a concentrated silence, a melancholy abstraction, even a sudden lost look when you surprise him simply staring at the sea: these things all speak if you have a mind to hear.

'You looking forward to going home then, Theo?'

'I am,' I say, pleased to hear it come out so decisively. 'But I'm going to miss this, too, you know?'

'Yeah, it's been a good trip, hasn't it, considering?'

That 'considering' hangs in the air, unresolvable for now.

'Yes it has,' I say, 'for all of us.'

He looks at me, looks away again. We still can't quite make each other out. 'You're pissed at Justin for not doing the exam, aren't you?'

'Well, you know, what did he have to lose, eh? He can do it again, right, if he feels he has to?'

'Yeah, well, that's Justin. He thinks you're a hell of a sailor, too, by the way.'

'Well, as long as you all enjoyed yourselves...'

'Enjoyed ourselves! Are you fucking mad? Beaten, battered and bruised, cold, wet, exhausted, bullied by a mad skipper, shouted and roared at, fed half-drowned sheep, driven into 12-metre waves, soaked, frozen and tortured – enjoyed ourselves?'

He's laughing now, he sweeps a fist back and thumps me in the chest. 'Get outta here, go make us all some coffee or something; this isn't a pleasure cruise, you know. Hang on, got a light?'

We motor-sail on into the dawn, headed by light airs. True to form, which is to say contrary to everything in the wind rose on the routeing chart, we're getting the wind of lowest probability for this place at this time of year.

'Ah, sure what would you expect?' says Tony, leaning back at his ease in the warming sun. 'Except the opposite of what it says – sure it's been like that the whole way across.'

Kevin has been formally inducted into the Grumpy Old Men, with full speaking and voting rights, so we have a full parliament in the cockpit this bright morning. 'You know what I read?' Justin asks. 'I read somewhere before coming out that you can't say you've rounded the Horn unless you did it from 50°S on the west side to 50°S on the east side, or vice versa, *and* under sail.'

'Oh that's all right, so,' says Macken comfortably, 'sure we didn't go round the Horn at all, then. We must have dreamt it.'

'What Skip says,' Kevin cuts in, 'is that on these trips we don't round the Horn, we visit it.'

We think about this for a while. Justin asks, 'What do you think then, Mr Dorgan, sitting there so quiet? So unusually quiet, if I might say so?'

'Mr Novak is undoubtedly right,' I say, thumbs in my chest straps, quarterdeck orator, 'insofar as tradition and the wish to maintain a certain mystique of the Horn is concerned. I am equally sure that inside the charmed circle of "Cape Horners" there is a series of inner circles, diminishing to the tough guy of all tough guys, the one who rounded the Horn on his back in a wetsuit using a tea towel for a sail, his prick for a mast, his frostbitten nose for a compass and his arse for a keel, out of Valparaiso bound for Buenos Aires. Listen, if I ask you to pop around the corner to see about something, is that the same thing as asking you to visit the corner? Eh?'

'You know, I guess what matters isn't what anyone else thinks.'

'Yes, Kevin?'

'Yeah, for myself now, I go home and I know I got in a boat, sailed down the Beagle Channel, right, around the Horn and on to… well, here, Cape Town, right? Man, I had Cape Horn to the south of me, to the east of me, to the north of me, and I passed it, right? And after Staten Island, that's what, 20 miles, right? After Staten Island I had it to the west of me. What does it matter what some people want to say. Hell, I don't want to be no "Cape Horner" anyway, that's not what it's about, man.'

'So, Justin,' I pick up the ball and run with it, 'what will your mates in the RORC have to say?'

Kevin wants to know, 'Hey, what's the RORC?'

'My dear fellow,' Macken stabs with his pipe, 'the Royal Ocean Racing Club, don't you know! The Admiral here happens to be on one of its committees, so a bit of respect here, if you please.'

'Oh, fuck off,' says Justin. We love getting Justin to swear, it sounds so incongruous in that clipped and polished accent. 'What will they have to say? Well, they've already told me I'm mad so I expect they'll just say I'm mad and lucky. Tell you what, Dorgan, remember you were saying that if you round the Horn you can put a foot up on the table when dining aboard one of Her Majesty's vessels?' ('Eh?' from Mr Macken). 'Well, I've just remembered something else. You're also entitled to wear the top shirt button undone when you're in formal dress.'

'Get outta here,' says Kevin, delighted as always with small absurdities. 'Hey, who'd know? I mean, how would they know it wasn't just your collar's too tight, right?'

'Good point,' says Justin. 'I expect it would only make sense if you were dining formally and there were sailors present. Hmm, have to think about that.'

'Wait a minute,' says Macken now. 'What's this about the foot up on the table?'

'Old Royal Navy tradition,' Justin explains. 'An officer or a visitor who's rounded the Horn is entitled to put a foot up on the table – at the brandy and cigars stage, I expect – be a bit daft when they're serving the soup.'

'You know what Steve told me?'

'What, Kev?'

'He said he's not going to examine me for Yachtmaster Ocean unless you guys pass the theory exam.'

'Jesus,' Macken is indignant, 'you're not serious?'

'Nah, I don't think he meant it, just trying to get me to put some pressure on you guys to work harder, I guess. Maybe to get me to put pressure on the Admiral here, to do the exam in the first place.'

Justin's bristling, but Kevin raises a soothing hand. 'You know what, Justin? I just up and told Steve that it's entirely your own business whether you do or don't and he should just chill, right?'

Good man, Kevin, I think, as Justin subsides, muttering a bit, staring away over the water. Kevin has a huge respect for Steve as a sailor, as do we all, but he sometimes lets that shade over into something like hero worship, and we sometimes feel he doesn't quite stand up for himself, for his own real skills and seamanship.

Tony is showing signs of restlessness, tapping at his pipe, fidgeting his feet, looking around him as if not quite sure what it is but something's missing. 'What's up, Tone?'

'Oh, I dunno, it's just that suddenly this is starting to feel like a holiday, you know? Sitting away here while the boat sails itself, yarning and having the crack like, I'm a bit disoriented, to tell you the truth.'

Kevin pounces, like a big cat that's been waiting for his chance. 'Mr Macken! I am glad to hear you say that! Follow me, please, I have a forepeak that needs cleaning.'

'Great! Lead the way!' says Tony, confounding us all.

'What d'you reckon to this motorbike trip, then, Theo?'

'Will he make it, do you mean? I have no doubt he will. Carry the bike on his back, that fella, if he has to.'

He can certainly teach secondary ports, the mysteries thereof. I fly through that part of the afternoon exam, do a meticulous navigation exercise, get in a small muddle finding safe water at a given time of the tide for a small keel boat but...

'Congratulations on passing your Yachtmaster Theory,' says Steve, pencil behind the ear, papers in one hand, the other extended. I confess, as I took his hand I wondered, does he mean this? If he were hard pressed, on a lee shore, the boat in trouble, would he rely on me to give him a safe course to follow? And then I think, what the hell, would *I* trust me? And because the answer is 'yes', and because I follow Justin's line, too, that I have at least learned what I still need to learn, and because the syllabus isn't everything and Steve doesn't mess about, I say thank you very much and permit myself a very small glow of satisfaction.

'Hey, guys, that was brilliant,' says Steve, mopping up the last of the sauce with the last of Kevin's bread. 'So where did you find onion and garlic, eh? Thought all the fresh stuff was gone, eh?'

We look elaborately everywhere but at Tony.

'Oh well, you know,' says Justin, 'all down to good management and planning ahead, really.'

Steve gives him a long, considering look then laughs. 'OK, Justin, point taken, point taken.' And Justin smiles back at him.

'I don't get it,' Di says. 'Did I miss the joke?'

Big Mike leans over, 'I think it's probably a British–Australian thing, honey, I'm not even sure these guys get it themselves.'

Big Mike is bopping to Bo Diddley under the stars, Simon and Debs are chatting quietly in the wheelhouse, Fed and Di are below in the saloon, doing techie things with laptops and digital cameras; Steve's on the satellite phone to Skip Novak, arranging berthing for tomorrow, customs clearance and passport control for us all, a sudden flurry of the world's business whirling around his head. I sit in opposite him, and e-mail our latest position and my news to Paula. She must be at her computer because her answer comes winging back. It's the last sentence that cracks me up: 'Jesus, if that's the theory what the hell must the practical be like?'

'Hey, Steve, is there a printer?'

'Yeah, there, already hooked up.' I isolate, caption and print her last sentence, show it to Steve as I reply and log off. 'Good one,' says he, chuckling. I tape it up in the wheelhouse, and every time I hear laughter for the next while I know that someone has just read it.

'You going to miss this, Theo?' Kevin is in reflective mood. We're sitting up under the mainmast, port side, keeping an eye out to the north for that longliner from last night.

'Yeah, I'm going to miss it. It's been tough though, eh?'

'Well, that's the southern ocean for ya.'

'Sure, I guess I was so fixated on the idea of the Horn that I didn't really factor in the slog over from Stanley.'

'Yep, that was a long haul, but you know what? Everyone came through, man. You guys, man I'm going to remember this watch of ours for a long time. It's been a pleasure, a real pleasure. Even if you are all nuts.'

'Who's nuts?' Macken wants to know, clambering towards us. 'I was just talking to Justin, he reckons about eight o'clock.'

'*About* eight o'clock?' I ask. 'You mean he didn't say two minutes to eight, eleven minutes past? *About*?'

'I know, I know,' says Tony gravely, 'that's what I thought too. I think he's slipping, you know?'

'I'm outta here,' says Kevin, 'you guys are at it again, trying to drive me as crazy as you are.'

We're meant to be off watch, but that means little now. Justin comes up to say he's booked a hotel room for us in Cape Town, a *twin* he says severely, as Macken opens his mouth to say something. Justin is happy he'll make his flight, is allowing himself, finally, to say how desperately he's been missing Nic and the boys.

'Of course Kathleen will be waiting for me when I get in,' says Tony complacently. 'It's all a matter of being organised, d'ye see?'

'Can he swim?' Justin asks me.

'Ah, leave him be,' I say, 'he'll be saddle-sore and eating dust for the next three months.'

The light is on in the cabin beneath us; through the hatch we see down to Mike's bed: a big zippered bag sits there, almost full; a neat pile of gear sits next to it, the big fella's going-ashore clothes.

'I think I'll go finish packing,' I say.

'Me too,' says Justin. 'God, but I've got an awful lot of laundry needs doing.'

⚓

DAY

## 35

Thursday, 8 June 2006

I wake and roll onto my back, completely relaxed, from
sleeping to waking in one fluid, easy moment. Through the
hatch overhead, I see pale blue sky, streaked with a smoky
orange. No sense of urgency now, no gathering-in of the
will, no onrush of duty, grim anticipation of the energy
needed to dress in a heaving boat. Thoughts come one by
one, calm, orderly. Little movement, the boat rocks gently
fore and aft, a slow, steady motion. Stillness in the air, no
gusts of salt and cold blowing up through the passageway.

A murmur of voices from the wheelhouse, a buzz from beyond in the cockpit. The low revving engine under that, a hoarse, purring growl, not the roar we're used to.

Above, a soft creak as the boom moves across my small square field of vision; someone is trimming the main, centring the great full sail. No wind, then, I think, or perhaps a slight wind dead on the nose. A muffled thump somewhere forward; the forepeak I decide, sifting through memory, the noise baffled and muted by coming back through the watertight door, then the open doors of Simon's cabin.

We're in, I think, or nearly in.

I reach a fingertip up to touch Paula's photo, pouch round my neck held in the other hand. Jujus, talismans, luck-bringers.

Time to dress, then. I kneel on the bunk, tug and pull until the lee-board comes free of its slots, hold it in one hand, pull the edge of the mattress back, slide the board under. Now I swing my feet out and down onto a level floor. Small luxuries, savour them. Towel, toothbrush, out, wash, brush teeth, brush hair. I take a long look at the face in the mirror then, something I haven't done for weeks. I'd almost forgotten the unaccustomed beard. I look like someone who has been through a lot, a faraway look in the eyes. Almost, I think, I am looking at a familiar stranger.

Socks, the last fresh pair; jeans, the surprising stiff texture of the cloth; T-shirt, my faded blue corduroy shirt, on its second ocean, still going strong. Do I need a fleece? No. An end to thermals, layers, hats, foul-weather gear. In the drawer by the bunkside, the lucky blue scarf she gave me before I set out. I knot it around my neck, pack a few odds and ends into my kitbag, shove my knife into a pocket – never without a knife on a boat, never. I strip the bed, stack sheets and pillow case in a neat pile, roll my sleeping bag into its pouch, the air crushed out of it.

I go out and up.

For once, Big Mike is looking forward, not astern. Debs, Steve, Simon, Fed – all on the afterdeck. We nod to each other in the rising light, unwilling to speak. Steve sees me tapping my pockets, hands me a cigarette, flicks his lighter. 'Ta.' Macken comes out behind me, and nods; we turn to look forward like the others.

Flat calm. We are nosing forward on level water, an oily sheen to it, sleek and lustrous and milky-green-blue. An occasional lazy white roll curls back from the bow.

Mist all around us, slowly rising. Diane is in the bow, she's wearing her hat with the furry microphones, she's speaking as if to herself. I look up, the great main is fully out, locked down amidships. There is scarcely a breath of wind. Look forward again, the fore hatch open, clipped to the Yankee forestay. That'll be Kevin and Justin, I think, getting ready the fenders and mooring lines, I should go and give them a hand. A tanker goes past, a half-mile off, slow and stately. The sea mist is rolling back, I feel the first glow of heat on my face; one after another huge tankers loom up out of the disappearing mist, some ponderously under way, many lying at anchor, their great black hulls all lined in the same direction, lying to the tide must be, there's so little wind. I look up and ahead, then, and the great enormous bulk of Table Mountain stands out suddenly, a shock, dark and massive ahead of us – and the orange sun, going yellow as it comes, rises up over Africa.

Somebody murmurs something, I don't know what. I go forward, uneasy on the level deck, only saved from staggering about by a slight roll that's developed; I call down the hatch to Kevin and Justin, 'Guys, come see.'

So here we are, then. All of us here. Still nobody says a word, some reluctance still has a hold on us. An unwillingness, even this close in, to make assumptions.

Coming up, by deep-grained force of habit, I'd glanced speedily at the plotter, the GPS, the chart, the clock, taking in at a glance all they had to tell me. I knew before setting foot on deck that we were ten miles out, had known before snatching those last few hours of sleep that this is where we would be when I woke. I still won't assent to it, not yet. After all this time, all these vicissitudes of weather, course changes and sail changes, day after day, watch after watch so full of the unexpected, I believe only in what I know to be the case. I still haven't double-checked.

You might, I tell myself severely, be dreaming this. I look around me, the whole crew on deck by now, and we're all in the same state of suspension, an unwillingness fully to believe, an unwillingness, it may be, to let it all go, all those miles and hours and days, those interminable weeks at sea.

And now, land. Land?

It falls to Simon to break the spell. Suddenly his hand dives into his jacket pocket, he pulls out a mobile, peers at the screen, goes forward, pecking at the keypad. I had forgotten he lived here for years, had only just moved to Hong Kong before embarking on this trip. Someone's expecting him. Now it's all bustle, warps and fenders coming up from the forepeak, laid out along the decks. Steve's on the radio to the harbour master, getting berthing instructions. Debs is supervising the lowering of the mainsail, seeing it's stowed neatly along the boom, flake after flake, seamanlike and tidy. Everyone's busy, quiet, thoughtful and purposeful. The cameras begin to appear: we alternate between the awesome sight before us, the white city spread out in the morning light under that huge high wall, and shots of each other, singly, in small groups forming and reforming. I go down to my bag for the tricolour I have carried across two oceans now, run it up to the port spreader with Tony's help. We stand in under the colours for a photograph taken by Justin; we're aware it's a sentimental gesture but for all that we are obscurely moved; I think for a fleeting moment of that other tricolour sinking down into the dark waters off

Cape Horn, a fistful of coins to pay the ferryman's toll knotted into one corner.

The last of the mist has rolled back now and we are facing into the harbour entrance, still awestruck by that sheer extraordinary wall of rock. A few small yachts go by, heading out for the day, their incurious crews immersed in their own little world, not interested in ours. Battered work-boats are buzzing this way and that, the work day beginning in a waterside city I never thought to see when I was young, when the walls of apartheid stood as high as Table Mountain, and we never thought we'd see them fall. Everything's normal under a sun already hot, though it has scarcely begun to climb, and we feel – what? Lost? We coast by a gas-extraction platform as big as a city block, small tugs fussing at its corners. Not lost, at a loss.

The ocean behind us is vast, cold and empty, as empty now as it was before we passed though its uncaring domains, and yet for a long while it was all the world to us. Discounting those brief dreamlike hours in Tristan da Cunha (I am prepared to be told we were never there at all), we have been twenty-three days at sea since leaving Stanley. The world we thought we knew has long since fallen away: the real for us, for so long now, has been the great ocean, our boat ploughing steadily over, across it and sometimes through it. We are so perfectly attuned now to the rise and fall of the barometer, to every following or broadside or quartering wave, to the deep and ominous power of the mid-ocean swell, to the howl of the wind in the rigging, the rise and twist and crashing fall of the very deck beneath our feet, that these oily harbour waters, that dented steel workboat with its hungover helmsman, the hammer and clamour of drills, cranes, trains and trucks, the commuter traffic on the motorway behind the oncom-ing marina, all these new things seem beyond unreal to us; mirage, a tenuous vision not to be trusted.

I close my eyes and, one more time, I call up that moment when we plunged through our own bow-wave, in under the great rainbow at Cathedral Rocks, and Fed put the helm hard down to round the Horn. That was us, I think to myself, that was us, we did that. A long, long time ago.

There's Fed now, sunny and lively as ever; Simon, animated, sensing perhaps what we've done; there's brave Diane, 700 miles pottering about in boats before she stepped in with us, now she's crossed a great ocean; Debs, beaming and chattering ten to the dozen, so glad to be in; Big Mike with his Fuegan retinue standing off to wave him farewell, his Tree of Liberty at Cape Horn still clear in my mind.

Steve stands to the wheel, spinning us expertly this way and that, fulfilling the contract he made with himself and with us all: he's brought us here, as promised; he taught us the ocean he loves. He's brought the boat home. He lines us up for the berth now, eases us in alongside, and Simon and Fed leap off with the shorelines. They bend and make us fast.

And everything stops. Like that.

Our world is falling apart, silently, in slow motion. The port watch is somehow gathered together on the afterdeck – Kevin, Tony, Justin, myself. Nobody dares to say a word. Such stalwart companions, I think, these good men. Nowhere I wouldn't go with them. We salute each other, still wordless; nothing, really, that needs to be said.

The launches come to take us ashore. Skip Novak, a man of few words, has already been and gone, relieved, I think, that we didn't break his boat. He's swept off with the ship's papers, Steve, Debs, Kev – customs to be dealt with, passports to be stamped, all the palaver and bustle of arrival.

The bar of the hospitable Royal Cape Yacht Club is already open; we sit under the white dockside awning, looking around us, looking at each other, nobody quite knowing what to say, unsure what the toast is.

A genial man comes ambling by, spots us, stops. 'You the guys just in from the Horn?' We are, we say, we are, that's us. He straightens, a smile growing on his face, he looks at us, one after the other. 'Well done,' he says, 'bloody well done. Welcome to Cape Town.'

I dig the phone out of my pocket, walk down the dock, lean against a sun-warm wall, tap in the numbers for home. I close my eyes. She answers on the second ring, joy in her voice. 'We're in,' I say. 'Cape Town. We're in. I'm coming home.'